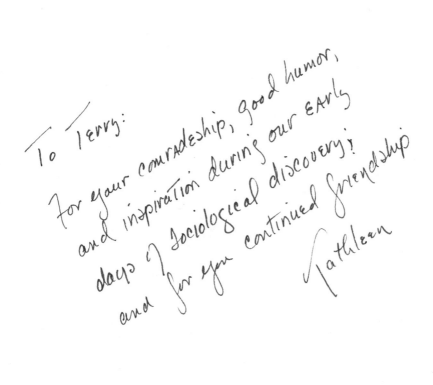

To Terry:

For your comradeship, good humor,
and inspiration during our EArly
days of Sociological discovery;
and for your continued friendship

Kathleen

The Social Origins
of Democratic Collapse

Studies in Historical Social Change

SCOTT G. McNALL AND JILL S. QUADAGNO, EDITORS

The Social Origins of Democratic Collapse

THE FIRST PORTUGUESE REPUBLIC IN THE GLOBAL ECONOMY

Kathleen C. Schwartzman

 University Press of Kansas

Published by the University Press of Kansas (Lawrence, Kansas
66045), which was organized by the Kansas Board of Regents and is
operated and funded by Emporia State University, Fort Hays State
University, Kansas State University, Pittsburg State University,
the University of Kansas, and Wichita State University

Library of Congress Cataloging-in-Publication Data

Schwartzman, Kathleen Crowley, 1948–
    The social origins of democratic collapse : the first Portuguese
  republic in the global economy / Kathleen C. Schwartzman.
        p.   cm.—(Studies in historical social change)
    Includes bibliographical references.
    ISBN 0-7006-0410-3 (alk. paper)
    1. Portugal—Politics and government—1910–1926.   2. Portugal—
Economic conditions—20th century.   3. Representative government
and representation—Portugal—History—20th century.   I. Title.
II. Series.
DP675.S39   1989   89-37218
                                                              CIP

British Library Cataloguing in Publication Data is available.

Printed in the United States of America
10 9 8 7 6 5 4 3 2 1

The paper used in this publication meets the minimum requirements of the
American National Standard for Permanence of Paper for Printed Library Materials
Z39.48-1984.

To Fernando

CONTENTS

FIGURES AND TABLES

PREFACE

On 28 May 1926, the First Portuguese Republic collapsed. This book is about that democratic collapse. Just sixteen years earlier, in 1910, support for "republicanism" had culminated in a republican revolution that ended the Portuguese monarchy and installed the First Portuguese Republic. The enthusiasm of the republicans, however, did not translate into a stable and enduring democratic regime. On the contrary, the regime was riddled with political instability and was finally terminated by a military coup.

Because Portugal exhibited extremes both as an unstable democracy and as a semiperipheral country, its study has much to offer those interested in democratic regimes, as well as those concerned about the utility of world-system analysis. The principal objective of this book is to reframe the discussion of national politics within the world-system scheme and at the same time to revitalize the world-system analysis with a discussion of national politics.

The case of the Portuguese democratic collapse also has something to offer those interested in comparative studies of authoritarian regimes and their causes. Little has been written about Portugal; thus it is conspicuously absent from a majority of comparative volumes on Western Europe. The Portuguese democratic collapse resembles other collapses such as that of the Second French Republic in 1851, the Weimar Republic (1933), and the Italian Republic (1922). However, the transformation from a democratic regime to an authoritarian one is not a singularly European phenomenon. In the 1960s and 1970s, the bureaucratic-authoritarian regimes established by the military in Argentina, Brazil, Chile, and Uruguay would remind us of those European cases. There are, of course, important ways in which these democratic collapses differ: First, mass movements spearheaded the rise of both national socialism in Germany and fascism in Italy. This was not the case in Portugal or in many of the Latin American countries. Second, the nature of the postdemocratic regimes varied. Strong executive states were directed in some cases by military juntas and in other cases, as in Portugal, by civilians. Third, some of those strong executives in Europe and Latin America began energetic programs of development, whereas others were less progressive and even reactionary. Each collapse demands its own history because each is historically unique; however, each history yields to students of political sociology one important common factor — the collapse of a democratic republic and its replacement by an authoritarian one.

Two sets of literature — which tend to remain on their respective bookshelves —

need theoretical integration: that on the European regimes between World War I and World War II and that on the Latin American bureaucratic-authoritarian regimes of the 1960s and 1970s. Although Portugal shared the subcontinent and its monarchical traditions with the rest of Europe, felt the vibrations of the turn-of-the-century world economy as did its European neighbors, and experienced World War I and the postwar crisis as a member of the European community, it had fallen far from the colonial glory of its fifteenth-century explorations and experienced economic underdevelopment and dependence of the sort typically attributed to Latin American countries. Comparing Portugal with both Europe and Latin America helps to highlight certain generic aspects of democratic collapse while downplaying the historically specific issues.

This book is a historical case study and therefore raises certain questions about the relationships between history and sociological theory and between case studies and theory. On the first, I follow Stinchcombe, who argues: "One does not apply theory to history; rather one uses history to develop theory" (1978, 1). On the relationship between case studies and theory, he writes: "The problem of eliminating false sentences by research . . . is not as problematic as the problem of having sentences interesting enough to be worth accepting or rejecting" (1978, 115).

The authors of case studies do have certain obligations. We must strive to avoid excessive use of intuition, which may render individual case studies noncomparable (Dogan and Pelassy, 1984). Stinchcombe's antidote for this is the use of general concepts: "Concepts other than epochal concepts [must] appear in these monographs." These concepts come from examination of analogies among historical instances. "The same general concepts occur in the detailed analyses of different historical sequences, sequences that had different ultimate origins and different ultimate consequences" (Stinchcombe 1978, 17).

This obligation implies the need for a framework that simultaneously attends to the theoretical problems raised by other literatures and offers a reasonable account of the Portuguese case. Although the failure of one case to fit a theoretical model could not justify the rejection of that model, the case study can reveal the relative successes and failures of various theories. More important, this case study is particularly suited to examine the specific dynamics that link placement in the world-system to the form of the state. I believe that the hypothesis-generating capacity of this case study outweighs any disadvantages of the method.

Two fundamental questions propel this inquiry, a historical one and an analytical one. They are, respectively, "What accounts for the collapse of the Portuguese Republic in 1926?" and "What are the social origins of democratic instability?" The Portuguese extremes of democratic instability and semiperipherality enrich the historical narrative but, more crucially, are the essential building blocks for the contribution to world-system theory. Such extremes render the social processes more transparent, allowing for theoretical specification, which, in turn, can inform the examination of other cases. This book is concerned with explaining the collapse of the Portuguese democratic regime; but it is equally concerned with those social conditions that place structural hindrances in the way of democratic stability.

The many historical records for this case carry an equal number of interpretations. This book purports to offer neither a complete nor a chronological sociopolitical narrative of the First Portuguese Republic. The necessary trade-off between the detail of a historical narrative and the sociological analysis has been a source of frustration for me. This frustration becomes particularly acute when comparing this work with chronologically ordered histories that highlight the important political events, with essays on the Republic that focus exclusively on the multitude of economic problems with which the Republic was beset, and with contemporary essays that decry the moral and political decay of the Republic. In comparison, this analysis may seem perhaps too parsimonious in its use of historical information. Those works capture the "apparent" forms of history — the froth and intense effervescence of daily life. The apparent forms of history are extremely attractive to journalists, contemporary commentators, and historians alike; in fact, events recorded in such a way often appear as the essence of history and even as causal factors rather than as phenomena to be explained. It is difficult with one book to do justice to both the history and the sociology of the Republic. In light of this limitation, I cite historical facts in accordance with the chosen sociological framework. Four major bodies of sociological literature are used in the construction of this analysis: world-systems, economic development, class analysis, and political sociology.

The political sociology of authoritarian regimes calls attention to institutional factors that contribute to democratic collapse, such as the nature of the parliamentary system, the difficulty of arriving at stable political coalitions, and the consequences of the democratically elected governments' inability to respond to the needs of all interest groups of society while maintaining their electoral support. Discussion of these institutional conflicts forms an integral part of my analysis, but I look elsewhere to learn about their origins. For this, I turn to class analysis. The class-analysis approach suggests *which* interest groups are to be used and offers a theoretical framework for positing a priori conflict among them. Thus the major conflicts are found between the working classes and the owners and among the various fractions of the owning classes. I trace these conflicts through political parties to political coalitions and finally to political crises.

Yet neither the institutional nor the class-analysis framework in itself can produce an explanation of why certain classes existed in the form that they did, and what precipitated the conflict among groups that had previously established some equilibrium or pact. Thus class analysis has to be located in the broader context of economic development and the state. Frank argues that "the composition and the behavior of the classes and their struggle to control and transform the state are influenced by their dependent participation in the process of capital accumulation and their role in the international division of labor" (1981,

232). I use two additional perspectives to address the questions unanswered by the institutional and class-analysis frameworks. First, the literature on economic development informs the historical narrative. Portugal experienced a certain type of economic development and underwent economic crises associated with that process of development. A profound crisis followed the collapse of the agro-export system and the sporadic attempts to promote industrial growth. These factors form the context of the analysis of class conflicts and of institutional instability. Second, the world-system literature provides the conceptual tools for focusing on Portugal's semiperipheral linkages to the world economy and the impact of its location on its economic and political development.

In this book, I argue that changes in the form of the state, far from being random, can be attributed to profound and turbulent crises that tear societies apart. The theoretical framework developed in this book is woven from two analytical threads—a conjunctural one and a structural one. Each has its own subset of questions that form the basis of the investigation. From a conjunctural perspective, I ask whether there are stages in economic development when democratic states are presented with particularly stressful challenges. I ask if there was something about Portugal's capitalist development at the turn of the century that rendered the democratic state less viable. The second set of questions asks about the contribution of certain structural factors to democratic instability. Specifically, what is the relationship between the form of the state and its location in the world-system? Are all forms of state equally likely to appear in the world's core, periphery, and semiperiphery, or are those countries called semiperipheral more hospitable to some forms of state and less so to others?

My conclusion is that Portugal, by virtue of its semiperipheral status in the world economy, possessed a highly disarticulated economy, which created the material conditions for competitive hegemonic projects advocated by respective fractions of the bourgeoisie. Because the Portuguese bourgeoisie could not unite under the umbrella of the democratic state, political instability and continual shifts in the political regime continued for sixteen years. The unstable political climate made impossible the resolution of developmental problems that had become acute toward the end of the nineteenth century. This political climate culminated in the collapse of the democratic regime and its replacement by an authoritarian one in 1926. The new regime, called the Estado Novo (New State), succeeded in consolidating an alliance between industry and agriculture, something that the economic fractions had not been able to do earlier with the tools and rules of the democratic state.

In part 1 (chapters 1 and 2), I describe the problem theoretically and empirically. The fate of democratic regimes has varied. Some have been stable and robust, others have been suffocated by foreign invaders, and still others have collapsed from internal conflict. Democratic collapses due to internal factors are perhaps the most puzzling. In chapter 1, I summarize the major theoretical approaches to the problem. Democratic collapses due to internal conflict have been attributed to personality conflicts and political party divisions or to other reified political processes. Some writers attribute democratic collapses to a litany of fiscal and economic factors: monetary circulation problems, negative balance of payments, shifting population, and the like. Although such factors appear as plausible roots of democratic instability, the precise nature of the causal connection is often ambiguous. It is unclear at what point personality conflicts or economic problems should culminate in a democratic collapse. I argue in chapter 1 that perspectives are needed that confront more forcefully the ways in which certain social arrangements constrain the democratic process. I end by reformulating the more general question of the rise of authoritarian regimes to a more restricted question of the causes of democratic instability. Here the principal question that guides the work is put forth. It combines world-system structural analysis with the economic crisis and class-conflict conjunctural analysis. In this context, the use of cabinets as the main unit of analysis is justified.

In chapter 2, I present evidence for the political crisis that preceded the collapse of the democratic regime. It demonstrates how political instability not only was the basis for the antirepublican sentiment prevalent among various segments of the Portuguese population but also was the reason given by many for supporting the regime's overthrow.

In part 2 (chapters 3, 4, and 5), I locate Portugal in the world economy both historically and structurally. I introduce the first strand of the conjunctural analysis in chapter 3. I argue that the Portuguese monarchy faced a profound political and economic crisis. The political crisis was resolved with the collapse of the monarchy, but the economic crisis (a crisis of economic development) was inherited by the Republic. In chapter 4, I introduce the structural peculiarities of the Portuguese economy that constitute the domestic counterpart, or reflection, of its semiperipheral location in the world economy. The conclusion of this chapter is that Portugal had a highly disarticulated economy. I suggest in chapter 5 the alternative directions of growth that Portugal could have followed, as presented by the economic elites of the time.

In part 3 (chapters 6, 7, and 8), I link the economic structural factors to the political arena. In chapter 6, I carry the structural analysis from the economic sphere into the political one, relating the political instabilities and political disunity to the disarticulated economy. At this point, I preview the explanation for the Portuguese case: that semiperipheral status creates structural propensities for democratic instability. My analysis is not deterministic, however, and thus the book continues beyond chapter 6.

In chapter 7, I raise the question of how such an inherently unstable political system was brought to eventual collapse by the conjunctural crisis of the postwar period. Thus I turn back to the conjunctural analysis and demonstrate the interplay between the conjunctural crisis and the structural propensities already set out. In the final chapter, chapter 8, I return to the major questions raised by this research: Is there something inherent in semiperipheral countries that renders them less hospitable to democracies in general and during times of crisis in particular? Although Portugal may show extreme characteristics of the semi-periphery, neither semiperipheral status nor democratic instability are unique to this country. Whether these two factors have been associated in other countries to the extent suggested in the Portuguese case is an empirical question worthy, in my opinion, of consideration. This question has a corollary: Was the Portuguese dictatorship more akin to recent cases of Latin American bureaucratic-authoritarian regimes than it was to European interwar authoritarian states? Clearly, the conjunctures vary by country because they all follow different paths and velocities of economic development. The challenge to democracy may lie in the way in which conjunctural crises hit structural propensities. Although Portugal shared some conjunctural crises with Europe, it also shared many relevant structural characteristics with semiperipheral Latin American countries such as Brazil and Mexico. Herein, I believe, is located one set of sociological foundations for the collapse of the Portuguese democratic regime.

ACKNOWLEDGMENTS

My rendition of the sociological pursuit is a collage constructed from pieces of Stanley Lieberson, who taught me that sociological data are not just about North American individuals but also about other nations; of Arnold Feldman, who taught me that sociological data are about economic production; and of Richard Taub, who taught me that sociological data are about historical processes.

The idea for the project was first fashioned during a seminar on political parties, democracy, and the state given by Adam Przeworski at the University of Chicago. Without his direction, I would have never been inspired to write this book. For their guidance and patience through false starts and many false finishes, I am indebted not only to Adam but also to Art Stinchcombe and Richard Taub.

I am grateful to William H. Sewell, Jr., who launched me on the voyage of revision, and to others who made helpful comments on earlier drafts: Albert Bergesen, Neil Fligstein, Thomas Hall, Michael Hechter, Doug McAdam, Scott McNall, Walter Opello, Richard Rubinson, and Philippe Schmitter.

Thanks to a grant from the American Association of University Women, I was able to travel to Portugal to begin this research. Compensating in large measure for the benign neglect of the Sociology Department at the University of Chicago during my graduate studies there, I am grateful to Pat Bova, Lou Boyle, Alice Crowley, James Darby, Joan Fox-Przeworski, Hana Fuchs, Celia and Peter Homans, Manuel Machado, Len Radinsky, and Wayne Schwartzman, who all helped to mitigate the multiple poverties of graduate-student life. Finally, for tirelessly cajoling me toward completion from the first day until the last, I thank Michael Burawoy.

ACRONYMS

ACAP	Associação Central de Agricultura Portuguesa (Central Association of Portuguese Farmers)
ACI	Associação Comércio e Indústrias (Association of Commerce and Industry)
ACL	Associação Comercial de Lisboa (Commercial Association of Lisbon)
ACLL	Associação Comercial de Lojistas de Lisboa (Commercial Association of Lisbon Retailers)
ACP	Associação Comercial do Porto (Commercial Association of Oporto)
Ag-Exp	Agro-export
AIP	Associação Industrial de Portugal (Industrial Association of Portugal)
AIp	Associação Industrial Portuense (Industrial Association of Oporto)
CC	Centro Colonial (Colonial Center)
CGTP	Confederação Geral do Trabalho Portuguesa (Portuguese General Confederation of Labor)
Dom-Ag	Domestic farm sector
ELI	Export-led industrialization or industries
GNP	Gross national product
GNR	Guarda Nacional Republicana (National Republican Guard)
ISI	Import-substitution industrialization or industries
LDCs	Less developed countries
PAR	Partido Acção Republicana (Republican Action party)
PDP	Partido Democrático de Portugal (Portuguese Democratic party)
PRE	Partido Republicano Evolucionista (Republican Evolutionist party)
PRL	Partido Republicano Liberal (Republican Liberal party)
PRP	Partido Republicano Português (Portuguese Republican party)

PRN   Partido Republicano Nacionalista (Republican Nationalist party)

PRRN   Partido Republicano de Reconstituição Nacional (Republican National Reconstitution party)

PUR   Partido União Republicana (Republican Unionist party)

SG   Sociedade de Geografia de Lisboa (Lisbon Geography Society)

TME   Transportes Marítimos do Estado (State Maritime Transportation Company)

UA   União Agricultura (Agricultural Union)

UACI   União de Agricultura, Comércio e Indústria (Union of Farming, Commerce, and Industry)

UIE   União de Interesses Económicas (Union of Economic Interests)

UON   União Operária Nacional (National Workers' Union)

PART ONE

Democratic Instability
in Theory and in Practice

CHAPTER 1

The Rise and Fall of States:
Bad Leaders or Bad Cycles?

In 1910 a republican revolution put a definitive end to the crumbling eight-century-old monarchy; sixteen years later, in 1926, the parliamentary democracy was replaced by a military dictatorship. After a brief description of events surrounding the 1926 military coup,[1] I evaluate several theoretical approaches that offer explanations of the rise of authoritarian regimes and others that offer explanations of democratic collapses. The main focus of this chapter is a critical reading of these theories, including the rescue of some elements and their incorporation into a new theoretical alternative. The main thrust of my critical reading is that political instability cannot be totally understood from within the political realm. We are forced into socioeconomic structures — indeed worldwide socioeconomic structures — for a full understanding of democratic instability.

A revolutionary military junta, which had formed in the northern city of Braga in January 1926, planned the successful coup that unfolded in May of that year. Ministers of the forty-fifth (and last) republican cabinet met with some of the military chiefs and were convinced that the military junta did not intend a military takeover but the installation of a "national" government headed by a military official. After this conference, the forty-fifth prime minister publicly announced his confidence in the marines and the army (Peres 1954, 419).

That confidence was betrayed. On the twenty-eighth of May, in Braga, General Manuel de Oliveira Gomes da Costa, a war hero, addressed the nation by radio and declared himself in open rebellion against the current political situation. He said that the nation wanted a national military government staffed with competent men who would have the salvation of the nation as their only mission (Peres 1954, 420). The uprising in the north was echoed by uprisings in Lisbon, where another military junta had already formed. A few days after the announcement of the military uprising, the democratic cabinet offered its resignation, and President Bernardino Machado, as his last official act before resigning, appointed an extraparty military prime minister who represented the Lisbon branch of the military opposition (Peres 1954, 423). After its last session, the doors of the parliament were closed, prisoners taken, the opposition deported, and the press censored.

There was light resistance in several garrisons and other failed attempts from loyal troops in the north, but the movement of the twenty-eighth of May was victorious. General António Oscar de Fragoso Carmona, who later emerged as the leader, said: "I went to Lisbon and joined the government. . . . I am a sol-

1

dier, I stand for the army . . . and that is all" (Figueiredo 1975, 58). On 6 June a large military parade was held to celebrate the victory over the Republic. That 1926 *golpe* — sometimes referred to as the overthrow of the Republic, sometimes as its collapse or fall, and still other times as its dissolution — ushered out a democratic regime and ushered in an authoritarian one. The military coup was far from ephemeral; it brought with it significant and lasting changes.

The democratic Republic and the subsequent authoritarian regime, called the Estado Novo (New State), were quite dissimilar in two fundamental ways: in state organization and in the manner in which individuals and groups were represented in the state and thus the way citizens granted legitimacy to the state.

First, the two states differed in their juridical structure. Under the Republic, power resided in the parliament, and law (or the judicial branch) regulated that power. In the Estado Novo, power was transferred from the legislative to the executive, which in turn organized the society following corporatist principles. After the military dictatorship dissolved the parliament, the military junta and its civilian successor ruled by decrees that were above any judicial review. The cabinet, which was controlled by the president, had no autonomous political power. On 25 June, the municipal governments of Lisbon and Oporto were disbanded and on 11 July, all administrative bodies of continental Portugal and the islands of Madeira and Açores were abolished.

Second, in the representation of interests the Republic differed from the Estado Novo, as it had also differed from the monarchy. Under the democratic regime, major interest groups, rather than being represented by a council to the king or by an appointed member of the Estado Novo corporatist organization, were self-organized in political parties. The Republic permitted the free, unhindered organization of most groups, which in turn gave rise to a host of organizations. In addition to political parties, there were labor unions, businessmen's organizations, and religious and intellectual groups. The republican state bureaucracy was staffed by elected or appointed members of political parties. Thus political parties were the intermediaries between the "popular will" and the state. The pluralist party system was the vehicle for representing interests, and through elections citizens also granted or denied legitimacy to the actions of officeholders.

In contrast, the Estado Novo solicited neither the "popular will" nor the legitimacy of the masses. It limited the accessibility of citizens to the state. António Salazar said that newspapers are the spiritual food of the people and, like all foods, they must be controlled (Delzell 1971, 335). Suspension of constitutional and civil rights meant, among other things, the end of the franchise, political parties, and unofficial organizations. Strikes and labor activities likewise were declared illegal. Peasant organizations were disbanded (Antunes 1978, 64), and controls were placed on firearms (Payne 1973, 664). In banishing political struggle from the land, the Estado Novo deprived workers as well as capitalists of their autonomous organizations.

In place of self-organized representative groups or political parties, the representation of interests — for owners as well as workers — was mandated from above. An official political party was created by the executive, although it did not function as a system of representation. The organization of economic interests was mandated along sectoral lines, which meant that capitalists were joined with workers. Employers' associations (*grêmios*) were given a juridical identity and represented all employers in a given industry. Pacts agreed upon by appointed representatives were binding on all laborers and capitalists.

Poulantzas, who refers to such nondemocratic states as "exceptional," says that "what is typical of the exceptional State is not so much that it violates its rules, as that it does not even lay down rules for functioning" (1974, 322). Many have argued that different state forms are more than just varying technical instruments of rule; rather, they have direct consequences for political class struggles (Gramsci 1971, 136–37; O'Donnell 1979; Poulantzas 1974, 321). State forms determine the way in which individuals are organized as political forces (as citizens equal under the law, as political parties, as members of some corporate hierarchy, or as nonentities) and determine the accessibility that different political forces will have to the state. Following Poulantzas, Jessop (1982, 230) argues that although parliamentarianism politically fragments economic groupings and produces political individuals, corporatism encourages the consolidation of opposing economic classes into functionally homogeneous, interdependent, and formally equivalent groupings. In short, the vehicles of interest representation and legitimization — the way they were integrated into the government, as well as the limits on the exercise of political power — were completely transformed under the Estado Novo.

Many different nomenclatures have been attached to the Portuguese Estado Novo. Payne, for example, in his study on fascism, writes that Portugal was not fascist, preferring to call it "conservative right" (1980, 16). He justifies this placement on two grounds: first, because the Portuguese government "based themselves upon religion more than upon any new cultural mystique" (which he identifies with fascism); second, because economic development was not a goal of the Estado Novo (1980, 19). Lipset considers it fascism of the right (1963, 130). Poulantzas does not consider it fascist because of the type of political crisis that precipitated the emergence of the exceptional state. Cassels thinks that "it is, of course, debatable whether Salazar's paternalistic dictatorship should be termed fascist at all" (in Turner 1975, 79). Woolf agrees that there was nothing specifically fascist about the Portuguese dictatorship (1968, 34); Delzell considers it a semifascistic regime (1971, 331). Although the label attached to the Estado Novo is relevant, especially if it is derived from the explanatory scheme, I will not try to resolve the conflicts surrounding the appellation of the Estado Novo. All of these authors who have analyzed the Estado Novo concur that it was a strong executive regime that completely penetrated civil society. Although in this book I do not describe the institutions and actions of the Estado Novo, I do describe the social, political, and economic conditions that brought it about.

HISTORICAL ANALYSES OF THE FIRST REPUBLIC

The turbulent period of the Republic and the transition to the Estado Novo did not pass without political commentary. Two major types of explanation are evident in the "historical analysis" of the democratic collapse. The first simply points out that Portugal is a member of a set of European interwar dictatorships. The second rests on the allegedly unique qualities of Portuguese politicians and the particular historical events.

One group of analysts invokes the philosophies that were dominant in late nineteenth- and early twentieth-century Europe. To the extent that they associate the earlier European period with liberal democracy, they associate the later one with corporatism. Maier (1975), for example, in his study of the postwar European processes, demonstrates that fundamental sociopolitical shifts were occurring in France, Germany, and Italy. Likewise Carr (1964), in a book on the period between 1919 and 1939, emphasizes the crises that all European nations had to face. Payne (1980, 3) underscores the historical uniqueness of the fascist phenomenon by suggesting that it was a direct product of the war itself, although he is quick to add that confusion has resulted from the extension of the adjective "fascism" to describe an entire period. World-system writers, such as Bergesen, argue that the interwar period was one of economic downturn and that the emergence of interventionist states could be seen in all areas of the world (Bergesen 1985). Thus, albeit with variations, this period saw many nations — industrial as well as less developed — tighten executive control over civil society. All of these works attempt to explain the democratic instability of Portugal, or any European country, by reference to the particular historical processes of the interwar period.

The second type of historical explanation — one that lies 180 degrees from the universal processes imputed above — focuses on the singular Portuguese experience. Writers in this group range from politicians and social commentators of the Republic, to functionaries of the Secretary of National Propaganda of the Estado Novo, to the post-1974 revolution writers. These writers invoke the common explanation that the idiosyncratic nature and extent of political instability was mainly responsible for the democratic breakdown. Portuguese historiography, from the time of the Republic to the 1980s, leans heavily upon the concept of political instability both for explaining the fall of the Republic and for justifying the installation of a military dictatorship. The causal chain implicit in these histories is that personality conflicts among political leaders precipitated party disputes, and party factionalization in turn produced a growing and pervasive political instability and chaos that not only provoked the republican collapse but generated the necessity for a regime that would install social order.

A famous republican politician and one-time prime minister, José Relvas, wrote in his memoirs that the Republic was lost because it was directed by idiots, anarchists, and egoists. He claimed that special responsibility in this regard was held by two equally famous politicians—Afonso Costa and Bernardino Machado (Relvas 1977, 1:14). Typical of later Estado Novo publications, the unauthored pamphlet *O Estado Novo princípios e realizações* (*The Ideals and Accomplishments of the New State*) described republican Portugal as a country of revolutions and bombs, strikes, and coup d'états, which reduced its international prestige to its lowest level. This plight, the pamphlet claims, was terminated by the Estado Novo (1940, 47). Estado Novo histories appeared as late as 1966. Cavalheiro (1966), of the Portuguese Academy of History, wrote a little pamphlet explaining the occurrence of the twenty-eighth of May. His explanation is similar to that of Relvas: The twenty-eighth of May was necessary in order to put to rest the anarchy and chaos that infected the Republic. Forty-odd years later, and writing after the 1974 revolution, Marques, a prominent modern historian, attributes the fall of the Republic to the high level of political instability. The instability, he alleges, resulted from the excessive weight of the parliament in the political life of the country. The parliament met an average of seven months annually and meddled with every aspect of governmental life, rendering the cabinets completely dependent upon parliamentary majorities (Marques 1972, 2:162). Perhaps because personality conflicts are either more visible than structural conflicts or are the essence of daily newspaper reports, they catch the eye of historians. Wheeler (1978), following this line of historiography, cites personal conflicts and ambitions as keys to the lack of cooperation and the subsequent instability. This explanation has been accepted by others, such as Opello (1985, 90).

Such analyses have a good deal of apparent plausibility, and this is undoubtedly why they hold such a salient and tenacious place both in Portuguese historiography and in the conventional wisdom on the collapse of the Republic. There is no doubt that instability existed and that it contributed to the fall of the Republic. What seems less clear is the causal role that rampant political instability plays in an explanatory model of democratic collapse.

The causal role of individuals is also ambiguous in theories that rest upon volitions and/or conspiracies of individual actors. One can cite a host of individual motives for the overthrow of the Portuguese or any other democratic regime. As will become clear in the Portuguese case, there were multiple sources of discontent with the democratic regime: The working classes were dissatisfied with the policies of the Portuguese Democratic party (PDP), other republican parties objected to the PDP monopolization of government, the nonrepublican opposition did not like any form of parliamentary democratic rule, and the bourgeoisie blamed parliamentary democracy for both the disorder in state institutions and in society. Further, some of the landed aristocracy and industrialists opposed the democratic state, preferring in its place an authoritarian state.

Still, those who desire a different type of state have many obstacles to surmount before such desires can be translated into institutions. Or, as Skocpol has written in her review of Moore, explanations for these social transformations may lie as much in class capacities as in class interests (1973, 21). And, in fact, the opposition listed above had limited success in institutionalizing its preferences within the democratic framework.

Individual actors negatively assessed the compatibility between their own perceived interests and the possibilities of achieving them within the framework of parliamentary democracy. The enumeration of oppositional sentiments to the democratic regime is crucial because it suggests that the military coup d'état occurred with the silent support, if not the active approval, of many groups. But is this why the Republic collapsed? The unstated assumption of such an approach is that we can make a causal link between individual desires and the sociopolitical transformation. Yet the demonstration of these political desires constitutes an inadequate explanation for the collapse of the democratic Republic and the establishment of an authoritarian regime. Although there were actors who conspired to bring about the emergence of the new regime and others who supported them, were their actions the principal explanatory force? I argue that the social process of democratic breakdown cannot be attributed simply to the collective or aggregated preferences of these historical actors. On this matter, Luke writes that "the collective's preference or indifference gain[s] expression only as a function of the aggregate individual choices between alternatives" (1985, 71). First, it is necessary to specify the social construction of alternatives that actors (individuals or groups) faced and the constraints upon their choices, specifying how the overthrow of the democratic regime became a more highly valued and viable alternative in 1926 than it had been in earlier years. In short, it is necessary to specify how an authoritarian regime came to be preferred over the democratic one, and why that took place when it did. To answer such questions, one must look beyond individual actors to their relationships in the social structure as a whole.

Wiarda's book *Corporatism and Development: The Portuguese Experience* (1977) is neither of these two types, although it is somewhat akin to the "historically specific" explanations of Portugal. Wiarda's interpretation of the emergence of the Estado Novo (and therefore of the demise of the Republic) is, metaphorically speaking, a nation's search for the state form that best suits it. Wiarda believes that Portugal has always been a corporatist state: "Corporatism, authoritarianism and patrimonialism may be characteristic, even permanent features of the Portuguese and Iberic-Latin systems." (1977, xi). The origin of these features lies in the Iberic-Latin development of the "Roman system of civil law, politics, and administration, in the spreading Thomistic philosophy of hierarchy and natural law, and in the emerging semifeudal pattern of land and conquest as the basis of wealth with payment in goods, services, and loyalty. . . . The Church, the military, and the advisors of the king all became a part of the same centralizing, bureaucratic, state apparatus . . . of rule from above " (Wiarda 1977, 32). This view converts the Estado Novo of Salazar into nothing more than a modern manifestation of what was at the root of Portuguese twelfth-century society—"the logical, sequential, twentieth-century extension and elaboration of an older, deeper 'natural' corporatist tradition that had long governed the structure of political institutions and behavior" (Wiarda 1977, 8).

In this natural state of corporatist social organization, we must see republican rule, Wiarda implies, as an aberration in which many Portuguese, the carriers of this long tradition of corporatism, experienced distress and moved to end the national agony of the Republic. His support for this interpretation includes statements such as "the coup was also widely popular among the civilian classes . . . elite and aristocratic elements . . . middle and lower sectors as well . . . as welcomed by virtually all political parties" (1977, 92).

A Westerner living in Portugal can easily identify the traits that Wiarda mentions and may also feel that they are permanent characteristics of Portuguese society. However, when cultural traits are posited to be permanent and universal, they become ineffective in explaining variations such as the revolution against the monarchy and the installation of the First Portuguese Republic. Further, as I argue below, assigning a political regime the status of "aberration" in the longer historical tradition of corporatism results in the nonserious treatment of its origins, its institutionalization, and its collapse. Wiarda seems to have followed this course. Because the republican form was at odds with what he considers the natural state of Portuguese society, he scarcely addresses the question of its emergence and only treats its functioning and collapse as it shows movement toward or reveals aspects of corporatism. In contrast to Wiarda, I treat the institutional form of the Republic seriously and assume that, despite universal and pervasive cultural traits, institutional state forms impose dynamics, constraints, and/or modifications on cultural traits that can be studied apart.

SOCIOLOGICAL APPROACHES TO BUILD UPON

The Portuguese democratic collapse is not a historically unique event; rather, it is part of a larger set of collapses that span two centuries and several continents. These collapses include the fall of the Second French Republic in 1851 at the hands of Louis Napoleon Bonaparte, the collapse of the Weimar Republic in Germany (1933), the extinction of the Italian Republic by the fascist movement (1922), and the numerous transformations from democratic regimes to authoritarian ones in Latin America in the 1960s and 1970s. Thus one cannot be content with a historically specific account that fails to identify the generic social process—the replacement of a democratic republic by an authoritarian one. It follows that no analysis of Portugal is complete without reference to the wealth of literature that has resulted from the rise of authoritarian regimes or the collapse of democracies.

Sociohistorical analyses of democratic formations do not herald democratic births as the progenies solely of "desires" for democracy. Rather, while not denying desires, these analyses typically have given democracies a sociological parentage. The historical roots of democracy have been found in social, economic, and cultural traits; what Lipset saw in the attributes of individuals (for example, percentage of the population employed in the industrial sector and living in urban areas, or levels of literacy), Moore found in the attributes of societies (for example, strength of the bourgeoisie) (Lipset 1963; Moore 1966). The breakdown of democracy likewise has been attributed to various sociological phenomena: what Linz and Stepan (1978) saw in the withdrawal of legitimacy and political instability, others have seen in the dissolution of a social compromise (Gramsci 1971; Przeworski 1980).

I begin with theories that treat political processes as autonomous and therefore look for purely political explanations of democratic collapse. Included are theories that note the absence of democratic values, as well as those that assess the legitimacy and efficiency of the government. I then treat those explanations that contextualize the political processes in terms of domestic economic struggles, such as the threat from the working classes, and the need for dictators as political representations of various economic projects. Finally, I deal with theories that push the explanatory realm beyond the politics and/or economy of the nation-state and look at world-system explanations. My objective is not to test each of the hypotheses with the Portuguese case but rather to explore the theoretical advantages of the wider approach.[2] In this presentation, I argue that political factors are important mediators between the larger socioeconomic realm and the form of the state, but that one truncates the social process by locating the causal factors narrowly within the political realm. I make a similar argument for the economic factors that are defined solely as processes and conflicts occurring within the nation-state.

Linz is one of the leaders in the political analysis of forms of the state. In explaining democratic breakdowns, he accords an important theoretical status to political instability, and his model formalizes the historically specific explanations mentioned above (Linz and Stepan 1978). Linz uses the nomenclature of "breakdown" because his focus is on the dynamics of the institutional disaggregation, malfunctioning, and collapse of a political system. Among the phenomena Linz notes in the breakdown process are attacks on the democratic system, systematic defamation of politicians, and political-party factionalization. This perspective captures the events involved in the progressive unraveling of democratic regimes and their final collapse and offers a guide for studying the process of democratic collapse. Although I think Linz's model is useful for tracing the precipitating causes of democratic collapse, at least two problems hinder its ex-planatory potential: It is tautological, and it reduces to social-psychological factors.

I consider Linz's explanation to be tautological in the following way. In the Portuguese case, political instability is usually taken to include cabinet insta-bility and the wave of civilian disorders, monarchist invasions, and military pronouncements. But was the historic pronouncement of 28 May 1926 really different from those that preceded it? Certainly it differed in its consequences because it announced the installation of a lasting change in the form of state, whereas the previous pronouncements had resulted either in temporary changes or none at all. Nevertheless, there were similarities between the twenty-eighth of May and some of the earlier pronouncements. The former articulated goals that had been expressed during earlier pronouncements; involved military units that had engaged in some earlier uprisings; and unfolded in much the same way as earlier military uprisings. And, finally, the forty-fifth and final cabinet crisis looked like those that had preceded it (at least in the initial judgment of the forty-fifth prime minister António Maria da Silva, who anticipated a cabinet reconstitution like the many that had previously taken place). In short, I think there is little justification for separating the earlier forty-four cabinet crises from the forty-fifth, elevating the former to the status of an explanation for the latter. Explaining the collapse of the Republic in terms of previous political instability is tautological because it is tantamount to explaining one instability by others.

Second, explanatory difficulties arise because Linz's theory rests on social-psychological processes. When the explanation is restricted to the narrow realm of political processes, actors' psychological and behavioral characteristics seem to take on inordinate importance. Lepsius (in Linz and Stepan 1978), in his anal-ysis of Germany, interprets political change as a political crisis that stems from a lack of cooperation and a reduced willingness to cooperate. In the same vol-ume, Stepan explains the collapse of the Brazilian democratic regime in 1964 with heavy reference to specific political strategies and acts, decisions and non-decisions, and the quality and style of leadership that contributed to the con-solidation of the opposition. Stepan argues that the acts of Brazilian President João Goulart undermined the democracy and contributed to the general senti-ment that the regime lacked legitimacy and the ingredients for survival. In short, Linz's model relies on socially unrooted psychological states to link politi-cal instability and systemic breakdown. The potential for psychological or insti-tutional reductionism and tautological explanations rests, I would argue, on the erroneous assumption that the political arena is the exclusive place to find ex-planations for political phenomena, or, in other words, that the political arena is autonomous.[3]

There are others who also have explained democratic instability solely with reference to the political realm but who have conceptualized its presence dif-ferently than Linz. Fraenkel, in an essay on the historical obstacles to parliamen-tary government in Germany (Eschenburg, Fraenkel et al. 1966), attributes the failure of the Weimar Republic to the absence of certain sociopolitical conditions that had been present in the society upon which the British parliamentary regime was constructed. The Weimar Republic, "hastily established on the English model" (1966, 20), was an unsuccessful transplant. Fraenkel cites conditions that favored the British parliamentary system, such as a readiness to compromise; citing Ernst Barker, "the structural flexibility of English society which prevented any deep rift from developing between the aristocracy and the middle classes" (1966, 21); and, as both men argue, controversies conducted between groups sufficiently united to agree on essentials. In contrast to the British case, Fraenkel claims, the Germans installed a parliamentary system that selectively excluded some unfamiliar attributes. For Fraenkel, the most crucial of these seems to have been the German insistence that representatives not be tied to particular interests but instead represent the common good of the nation—a failure to distinguish the idea of representation from the principle of plebiscite. This practice meant that the parliament was not the arena for either conflict or compromise of pluralistic forces.

Fraenkel concludes that Germany did not develop an organic democracy. At a minimum, such a democracy requires that the citizens have developed the capacity to compromise and that the representatives are tied to specific economic interests, not detached from a pluralistic social base, as was the case for the German parliamentary representatives (1966, 24). Fraenkel argues that political values lie at the base of political forms, and the two may not be severed.

Such political factors, be they the faulty installation of political values or the withdrawal of legitimacy, beg a fundamental question: What are the historic conditions under which representatives become dislodged from interest groups or politicians are moved to withdraw legitimacy? Was it simply a cultural given that German politicians would look after the common will whereas the British would look after specific interests? Was there always "a typical English readiness to accept compromise and temporary measures"? I argue that these cultural states are not universals; on the contrary, they emerged from the social processes that preceded their appearance. That it appeared impossible for a deep rift to develop between the middle classes and the aristocracy in Britain is a result of other social processes.

Is it reasonable, then, to confine the study of state forms to the political level? There was an institutional crisis in the Portuguese democratic state, and political instability obviously did play a crucial role in the collapse of the Republic. Further, the institutional crisis did have consequences for other social conflicts. But despite these factors, I must answer "no"—political institutions in themselves are not the sole origin of social antagonisms. These institutional crises (which the above-mentioned works unequivocally identify as important) must not be taken for the answer. Rather, they must be considered as part of the question (Poulantzas 1974, 63).

In this work, I argue that what appears as the collapse of an institutional form was the political recognition of and response to an untenable social arrangement. My analysis, while addressing the democratic collapse, also confronts why personality rivalries, party conflicts, and political instability so beset and decimated the Portuguese Republic—in short, why the very dismembering of the state occurred.[4] In summary, I do not reject the importance of the political factors identified by the above-mentioned authors. I reject the explanatory importance given to these factors. The reconciliation of our two reactions is a redefinition of their status: The works I have noted above consider political factors as part of the answer; I treat them as part of the question.

To move from the political level, from political explanations for democratic collapse, we must move behind the political instability. We can begin by asking about the role of political instability in a democratic regime. Political factors are important because in parliamentary democracies, classes as well as other actors determine or influence economic outcomes via noneconomic—namely, political—strategies. Such strategies are directed to and processed by the state apparatus. Thus to understand why such shifts among political parties occur, one must determine what underlying social forces were represented at the political level by those political parties.

In looking behind the political stage, many analysts have identified economic processes as the prime motors for political shifts. For the purpose of this discussion, I group these processes as either stage theories or conflict theories. In the first, authors conceptualize economic processes as stages and then posit an elective affinity between stages of economic development and forms of state. Such a grouping includes works ranging from Gerschenkron, to Moore, to Poulantzas. Others conceptualize economic processes in terms of class conflicts. Marx, and later reformulators of his work, identify class conflict as the motor behind major political shifts. I include elements from both groups within the theoretical framework of this book.

One stage often cited in the literature is the confrontation between preindustrial traditions and industrialization.[5] At the historic moment when incipient industrialization rears its head, it is in conflict with the preexisting social arrangement. The social origin of authoritarian regimes has been located in the reaction of traditional social arrangements to more modern industrial forces. The disturbed equilibrium among social classes precipitates a disruption in society, a disturbance that has been associated with challenges to democracy. Three outcomes of this traditional-modern confrontation can be identified: the traditional or preindustrial forces assert their power by aborting incipient industrialization; the economically progressive forces are installed but are controlled by the preindustrial political forms; and the progressive forces dominate the preindustrial ones. Different authors have seen possibilities for authoritarian regimes in all three outcomes. In such theories, the level of macroeconomic development and the unique balance of sociopolitical forces determine the final sociopolitical formation of a nation (democratic or authoritarian).

Moore's *The Social Origins of Dictatorship and Democracy* (1966) has been one of the most influential works on authoritarianism. He paints broad strokes that connect economic development and subsequent political regimes. He describes how countries, in reaction to commercial stimulus, replace agrarian structures with industrial ones. The gestures made by social and economic groups in reaction to that initial commercial impulse determine the nature of the emergent political regime. Thus democratic regimes result from a unique constellation of forces that Moore outlines as follows: a strong ascendant and independent bourgeoisie; an insignificant or defeated peasant revolutionary potential; and a market orientation on the part of the landed rural classes. Moore sees fascism, on the other hand, as a revolt of the landed elite against the peasantry (who are inadequately organized) and against the proletariat (who constitute only a small percentage of the population), in the presence of a moderate or weak bourgeoisie.

In Moore's analysis, the democratic outcome hinges on the presence of a societal group with an independent economic base that can attack obstacles to a democratic version of capitalism. A democratic outcome also hinges on the political propensities of the agrarian sector and the opportunities that exist for them to create extra-agrarian alliances. Authoritarian regimes, on the other hand, represent a victory of traditional forces over industrial ones. Although the desires of individual actors represent an important link, Moore offers a theory that connects the extant social structure to subsequent political outcomes. The political preferences of individual actors are laid upon a grid that considers how an agrarian bureaucracy, with a certain constellation of social forces, is transformed by the introduction of a commercial impulse. In this sense, Moore's work sets the requirements for a macrosocial analysis. It suggests that social actors are not merely individuals with a certain type of personality but rather are individuals who possess economic interests derived from their location in the social structure.

Organski, in another version of linking political processes to economic ones, asserts that countries which develop industrially need a strong state to fulfill certain functions such as capital accumulation. For him, fascism is one of three state forms (the other two being bourgeois democracy and Stalinism) that accomplish these functions. Historically, fascism, or "syncratic" rule, is the last victory of the landed aristocracy (1965, 155) because it is the political expression of an economic and social bargain between the agricultural and industrial elites. Such a bargain is forced upon industrialists who are too weak to take power completely from the landed aristocracy.

Gerschenkron (1962), Dahrendorf (1967), Gregor (1979), and Kurth (1979a) are a few of the advocates of the third outcome of the conflict between incipient industrialization and authoritarianism. In their models, preindustrial traditions constitute obstacles to industrialization, and thus the authoritarian regime is seen as the vehicle for overcoming these obstacles. Gerschenkron, for example, argues that late industrial development promotes, and is promoted by, authoritarian rule. He maintains that Germany, as a latecomer to the industrial world, could not afford the luxury of gradual capitalist development. Because it had to industrialize quickly and thoroughly, it needed more extensive mobilization of capital and more forceful control of popular demands than would have been feasible in a democratic state. Each of these writers contends that authoritarian regimes in Japan and Germany transformed backward agrarian societies into industrial complexes with capacities to produce capital goods such as steel and chemicals.

Kurth translates the question of "timing" into "kinds" of industrial development. In his view, textile development produced exigencies that were conducive to democratic regimes. Industrialization via steel, on the other hand, required massive infusions of capital. Historically, private domestic resources could not mobilize sufficient capital, therefore the state stepped in. According to Kurth, such developmental patterns predisposed a country toward authoritarian regimes. Analysis of Latin American bureaucratic-authoritarian regimes follows this version of economic conjunctures, with modifications made for delayed dependent states.[6] Even stronger versions of this interpretation are offered by writers such as Neumann (1944) and Schoenbaum (1966). In their works, not only did a strong state end up serving the needs of the industrial bourgeoisie, but the authoritarian state itself was the bourgeoisie's project.

Poulantzas's (1974) stage theory associates the "fascist period" with the contradictions found in the transition to monopoly capitalism. Only with fascism, he writes, did industrial-monopoly capital establish itself. Jessop's restatement of Poulantzas's argument is that a fascist regime was the only kind of state that could overcome "economic fractioning of the bourgeoisie . . . a state which displays its own internal [class] unity and institutional autonomy vis-à-vis the dominant class fractions" (1982, 155). Poulantzas argues further that this conjuncture was one in which the working classes were in a position of relative weakness. Such propositions make this theory more elaborate than other stage theories.

This body of work demonstrates the affinity between developmental stages and political forms and highlights a historic conflict between accumulation, or economic growth, and political legitimacy. These works raise the question of which sector of the economy—agrarian or industrial—will dominate the process of growth, and how that domination will affect the kind and legitimacy of government. Such works broaden the Linz analysis by asking about the developmental conditions under which legitimacy is less likely to be forthcoming, and by giving a priori indication of groups and their respective interests.

These works all argue that shifts in state are rooted in shifts in socioeconomic processes. In somewhat different language, Jessop argues that "a long-term shift in hegemony requires not only a new 'hegemonic project' but also the reorganization of the state system as a whole" (1982, 233). And, summarizing the large body of literature, Rueschemeyer and Evans argue: "Effective state intervention is now assumed to be an integral part of successful capitalist development"

(Evans et al. 1985, 44). In the historically demonstrated affinity between developmental stages and political regimes, one perforce sees the necessity of moving beyond the narrowly political realm.

A variant literature locates the affinity between the economic and political realms in class conflict and, in fact, identifies class conflict as the causal factor in the emergence of authoritarian regimes. For Marx (1969b), short lives would be endemic to democratic republics because they are nothing more than transitional forms of rule. Marx rooted this transience of democracies in at least two contradictory situations: first, that the republic was the only form of state that allowed all factions of the ruling classes to rule collectively; and, second, that the republic gave political power to citizens who did not have economic power.

With respect to the first situation, Marx writes: "The Parliamentary Republic was more than the neutral territory on which the two factions of the French Bourgeoisie . . . could dwell side by side with equality of rights. It was the unavoidable condition of their common rule, the sole form of state in which their general class interest subjected to itself at the same time both the claims of their particular factions and all the remaining classes of society" (Marx 1969b, 96).

Herein Marx found a major threat to the perpetuity of any republic. Inasmuch as societies are a combination of multiple modes of production (petty commodity, capitalist, and so on) and therefore have multiple ruling classes, the ruling bloc is an inherently contradictory unit. Whereas the prerepublican French monarchy was characterized by a political rule that excluded some factions, the French Republic was characterized by political rule that included not only a variety of republican factions but also both contenders to the throne. This situation created a contradiction within the parliamentary form of state:

> [The Republic was n]othing but the combined infamy of two monarchies . . . alliances whose first proviso is separation; struggles whose first law is indecision; wild, inane agitation in the name of tranquility . . . wearying with constant repetition of the same tensions and relaxations; antagonisms that periodically seem to work themselves up to a climax only to lose their sharpness and fall away without being able to resolve themselves (Marx 1969b, 43).

These antagonisms plant the seeds of democratic collapse. Factions are kept apart not by personal antagonisms, ideology, or royal flags but by their real material interests. Over time these antagonisms result in fractions of the bourgeoisie splitting away from their own political representatives and reappearing in direct confrontation with one another. Eventually, the ruling classes cry out for order, for a stronger government that will take them through the coming commercial crisis and suppress the rising masses. In this way, contradictions within the ruling classes can lead to democratic collapse. This process is consistent with the developmental-stage theories, but its difference lies in its specificity of the sources of democratic instability and of the power of class conflict to transform institutions. Conflicts among different bourgeois groups always exist, but Marx believes that their conflicts are heightened to irreconcilable levels by virtue of the joint rule that democracy bestows on them.

The second reason Marx predicts a short life for democratic republics was deduced from the second fundamental contradiction he sees in democratic regimes, namely, that democracy declares political equality for all in spite of their economic inequality. "The classes whose social slavery the constitution is to perpetuate, proletariat, peasants, petty bourgeoisie, it puts in possession of political power through universal suffrage. And from the classes whose old social power it sanctions, it withdraws the political guarantees of this power" (Marx 1969a, 69–70).

According to Marx, the democratic state admits hostile classes—workers and owners—into the political arena and asks them to confront each other. Further, it gives the working classes the tools for challenging the very existence of the owning classes (Marx 1969a, 67), thereby jeopardizing the domination of some classes over others. The inherent indeterminacy of any political confrontation between hostile classes, and therefore of the stability of the republic, resides in the fact that the bourgeoisie has to rule with the political participation of all classes. Inversely, through the electoral process, the economically powerless must continually reestablish their economic subordination. This contradiction, Marx argued, was bound to manifest itself in the following manner: Those who have economic power will attempt to monopolize political power, and those who have political power will try to use the franchise to increase their economic power. Marx was convinced that this would create a profound and continuous instability that would result in the collapse of democracy. Marx thought that for these reasons the bourgeoisie would relinquish its political power, trading its political expression under democracy for political suppression under a military regime. Or put another way, they would trade their right to rule for their right to make money. This literature modifies the first political literature by stressing the need to consider classes qua actors and to see the role of those classes in the historical development of national economies.

Authoritarian regimes have been described from many perspectives and attributed to many causes. However, less work has been done on the emergence of authoritarian regimes from a world-system perspective. This is not to say that historical accounts have neglected the impact of world events. To the contrary, many accounts stress the importance of extranational phenomena such as the Great Depression or World War I. Although such factors are vital, the world-system critique of such analytical approaches is precisely that the external events are considered to be exogenous.

Social structures—that is, any institutional arrangement of society—are the result not only of domestic conditions but also of the direct and indirect intervention of international actors (the military, exchanges of money, trade flows, migration, and the like). Analysis of international influences is imperative in order to fill in several lacunae left by the sociological analyses I have already mentioned. Lacunae include the sociohistorical construction of economic classes and their interests; the source of the commercial impulse; a reason why some sectors of the economy would want and are able to resist nascent industrialization (maintaining a semifeudal noncapitalist system of labor control in the countryside); and, finally, the viable alternatives for resolution of the problems of development. In other words, the world-system paradigm places the developmental stage and class-conflict theories in a broader context than other models. By recognizing Portugal's place in the world-system, for example, Moore's "farmers" are further specified as agro-export farmers and domestic farmers, and his "industrialists" as those who produce for the domestic market and those who produce for a foreign market.

What is the relationship between the form of state and world-system location? Are all forms of state, particularly democratic and authoritarian ones, equally likely to appear in core, peripheral, and semiperipheral countries? Or are semiperipheral countries, for example, more hospitable to some forms of state than to others (appendix A contains a discussion of the definitions of zones of the world-system)? Countries should be different because the attributes that qualify them as members of one particular zone of the world economy rather than another simultaneously exert pressure on the political organization, thereby resulting in a greater propensity for one form of state over another.

An association between world-system position and authoritarian regimes has been posited by Wallerstein (1974, 1979), Thomas (1984), and Szymanski (1981), among others. Although Poulantzas would most likely protest his inclusion, I think that he also has a world-system perspective.[7] The principal focus of world-system analysis on forms of state has been to explain where, why, or under what conjunctural conditions interventionist states are likely to emerge in the world-system. There are several theories of interventionist (or "exceptional," according to Poulantzas) states embedded in the world-system paradigm.

One version, which appears in *The Modern World System,* poses the structural necessity of an interventionist state in the semiperipheral areas of the world-system because of the particular system of labor control. It posits that the zones of the world economy concentrate in deliberate occupational categories. Wallerstein postulates a worldwide economic order with various modes of production and types of labor control: (1) self-employment and wage labor, (2) serfdom and tenancy, and (3) slavery. These modes were not randomly distributed throughout the world; rather, they followed certain patterns. Wallerstein asserts that the first are most likely to have been in the core (Western Europe), the second in the semiperiphery (Eastern Europe), and the last in the periphery (Africa). Why were there different modes of labor control within the world economy? Each type of control was best suited to the particular type of production within that country, and the combination was necessary to guarantee the flow of capital, which, Wallerstein maintains, allowed the world capitalist system to "take off."

In the semiperiphery, there is neither adequate central control to force peasants to stay on the land nor sufficiently powerful peasants who could indefinitely terminate their exploitation. Further, sharecropping represents a system of shared risks in that neither the landowner nor the farmer has to take all the risks.

How does Wallerstein relate this production-labor factor to the form of state? Should semiperipheral countries, with their characteristic form of labor control, be less hospitable to democratic states? "The modes of labor control greatly affect the political system (in particular the strength of the state apparatus) and the possibilities for an indigenous bourgeoisie to thrive" (Wallerstein 1974, 87). What is important in terms of the world-system paradigm is the notion that both the form of labor control and the form of state were necessary "to assure the kind of flow of surplus which enabled the capitalist system to come into existence" (1974, 87). Or "in each of these forms . . . the role of the state machinery in ensuring the coercion of unequal contract is central to the functioning of the system" (1984, 3). Thus, through an authoritarian state, the "semi-feudal" forms of labor control (tenancy or sharecropping) could be guaranteed in semiperipheral countries.

The second world-system theory of interventionist states focuses on fluidity in the world-system and locates the emergence of these states in the inherent capacity of semiperipheral countries (with a developmental dictatorship) to take advantage of a world crisis in which the core countries experience a downturn. Wallerstein (1979, 1981) argues that a crisis in the world-system — that is, a long-term disequilibrium between supply and demand that has consequences for the market — provides space for a shift in the bargaining power of various countries, principally for "a few" semiperipheral ones. This possibility derives from the fact that periodic crises force core states to release their hold on semiperipheral ones (Wallerstein 1984, 7). Thus in a worldwide crisis, some intermediate elements in the surplus extraction chain gain at the expense of those at the core of the system. The countries with distinctive internal politics and social and economic structures are best able to take advantage of this crisis. It can only be a few, however, because the worldwide crisis also means that the semiperiphery is cut off from its normal sources of income, capital, and technology transfer (Wallerstein 1984, 7). It is in semiperipheral countries, with their more or less "even mix" of core and peripheral countries, that efforts to transform the state payoff in terms of economic advantage (Wallerstein in Arrighi 1985, 35).

To take advantage of a crisis and change its worldwide position, a semiperipheral state must successfully invest the gains that the crisis bestows on it. Concretely, this means insuring and protecting the income gains, translating profits into particular imports (Wallerstein 1979, 106), and not passing on income increases to the working classes. Alternatively, if gains are to be passed on to the proletariat, it is necessary to take them from the real income of the semiproletariat (Wallerstein 1979, 107). Wallerstein suggests that one way that the impoverishment of the semiproletariat is accomplished is by depriving them of land or reducing their real income. In either case, initiating development, or transferring income from consumption to savings, is difficult within the confines of parliamentary democracy. "These shifts in advantage are reflected in the policies of states, in the degree of their nationalism and militance, and in the pattern of their international diplomatic alliances. They often result in shifts in regime where the previous regime is insufficiently flexible to respond to the changed world political situation" (Wallerstein 1979, 99). Aymard describes it as the "voluntary action of states to improve the relative position [in the world hierarchy] . . . by pursuing a policy of catching up. . . .[T]he state was unable to overcome these disparities [of uneven development within a country] . . . in fact it played on them . . . even seeking to exacerbate the disparities" (in Arrighi 1985, 40–41). In these situations, the likelihood of an exceptional state in the semiperiphery increases. At the world-system level, then, we should find crises in the core preceding the rise of authoritarian regimes in the semiperiphery.

These two versions of the emergence of interventionist states parallel the general debate about authoritarian regimes. The first theory is an extension of the arguments that authoritarian regimes are the result of the confrontation of preindustrial traditions (political backwardness, late development, incomplete national unity, and so on) with industrialization (Moore 1966; Gerschenkron 1962). The second theory extends the notion that dictatorships are necessary to make some economic leap possible. That economic leap could be to the industrial world, such as Gregor argues for Italy and Russia, or it might be to economic "deepening" with either international capital (Szymanski 1981) or domestic capital (O'Donnell 1978). In all cases, the argument is made that the mantle of military or civilian dictatorship was taken on to accomplish such quantum economic leaps.

Both world-system explanations of interventionist states are plausible deductions from the world-system theory. However, they make functionalist and instrumental assumptions about the state. They both, of necessity, make the functionalist assumption that the form of state needed is the form most likely to emerge. They also assume that the newly transformed state will act on behalf of the semiperipheral bourgeoisie. A particular problem with the first theory is its emphasis on the agricultural aspect of the semiperiphery to the exclusion of its industrial activities, thereby excluding the unique characteristic of the semiperiphery. The second theory problematically assumes that the state, via policy manipulation, is able to direct the course of future economic development. These assumptions add up to the notion that the state can pursue a policy of "catching up," which has problems: First, it anthropomorphizes the state, and second, it ignores the instability of the state produced by the admitted disparities within nations and thereby ignores the political difficulties in articulating a coherent international policy.[8]

In conclusion, several hypotheses are derivable from these theoretical perspectives: (1) authoritarian rule in Portugal was a reaction to increasingly threatening working classes; (2) it was a tool (intended or unintended) for the industrialization of Portugal; (3) it was the outcome manipulated by the large landholders in response to a heightened commercial impetus; (4) it was the functionally necessary form for a semiperipheral country to maintain a disappearing form of labor control; and (5) it was the state form that emerged from a stalemate among various sectors of Portuguese society. This work does not contain a systematic test of these hypotheses, but they appear herein nonetheless because each theory proposes concepts and corresponding relationships (reflecting some historical reality) that must be incorporated into my theoretical interpretation — either directly, to the extent that concepts or the purported relationships are utilized, or indirectly, to the extent that unanswered questions or conceptual flaws inform the new theoretical framework.

COLLAPSE OR RISE OF FORMS OF STATE

The vast literature just surveyed vacillates between two explanandums — democratic collapse and the origins of authoritarianism. The literature on the origin of authoritarian regimes, especially that which posits it as an alternative to democracy, cannot be the sole theoretical guide for the study of Portugal for one important reason: The Portuguese authoritarian regime followed upon the heels of a democratic one. Theories that isolate societal arrangements or structural factors that pose a functional necessity for an authoritarian regime are particularly problematic. To the extent that some of the theories perform well in explaining the rise of the Portuguese authoritarian regime, they are inadequate for explaining the earlier democratic one. To the extent that these theories correctly identify the structural factors that predispose a political system toward a nondemocratic solution, they err in grasping those factors that predispose it toward a democratic one. In short, the idea that the social forces were favorable for an authoritarian regime must be modified to account for the fact that a democratic regime had been established a mere sixteen years earlier. Either we view Portugal as an exception to such theories or we discount the Portuguese democracy as an unimportant aberration, a "historical blip," insignificant in the longer, more stable social formation of fifty years of authoritarian rule.[9] Thus I argue that the democratic state — pulled from one side to another, restructured over and over, and, finally, collapsing — demands equal explanatory attention as that of the emergent authoritarian regime. Therefore, we must consider separately, first, the question of the democratic collapse and, second, its replacement by an authoritarian regime.

Clearly, the analysis of the Portuguese case has to recognize both theoretical imperatives: the "ephemerality" of democracy and the social origins of authoritarianism. This suggests a focus not only on the instability of democracies and the origins of authoritarianism but also on the transition from one state to the other. The question is, What are the conditions that produce unstable democracies that, in turn, are resolved as authoritarian regimes?

In his study of state transformation, Poulantzas formalizes Marx's discussion of Bonaparte and integrates the two questions of democratic collapse and the rise of authoritarian regimes. Poulantzas argues that the transformation from one form of state to another coincides with "political crises"—conjunctures of a small number of contradictions (1976, 91). Thus although state transformations represent a general political crisis, particular state transformations correspond to particular types of crises. On crises that lead to executive dominance over parliamentary rule, Poulantzas writes: "The exceptional state comes into being in order to remedy a characteristic crisis of hegemony within the power bloc, and in this bloc's relationship with the popular masses. It corresponds to a significant shift in the balance of forces" (1976, 92).

Following Marx, he singles out two aspects: the crisis within the ruling bloc and the crisis between the dominant classes and the masses. These crises supposedly account for the emergence of a state in which the executive comes to dominate over the parliament. On the conflict within the ruling bloc, Poulantzas writes:

> For example, the characteristic predominance of the executive where the monopolies are hegemonic is a direct response to a particular incapacity to organize this hegemony, with regard to the power bloc, in the parliamentary framework. The particularly acute contradictions between various fractions of the power bloc in the monopolist stage, geared and reflected in parliament through a particular dislocation between these fractions and the parties due to the traditional "survivals" of party representation account for this organizational incapacity. Henceforth, hegemony is organized through different processes inside the executive (1973, 314).

On the crisis between the dominant classes and the masses, he writes: "The contemporary predominance of the executive corresponds effectively to the difficulties met by the monopolist fraction in organizing its political hegemony with regard to the dominated classes in parliament" (1973, 313).

This theory explains both parliamentary instability and the transition from a parliamentary democracy to a strong executive. For Poulantzas, the collapse of the Portuguese Republic could only have resulted in the executive state (Estado Novo) because underlying the democratic instability was a crisis of rule for the dominant classes in Portuguese society—they were unable to successfully exert their dominance within the parliamentary system. This approach to the question of transition makes two important points: Democratic collapse and the rise of an authoritarian regime cannot be reduced to one question; nor can they be treated as totally unrelated phenomena. Although an authoritarian regime may not always follow a democratic collapse—just as a democratic regime may not always precede an authoritarian regime—I lobby for examining the extent to which common social forces underlie the two.

The main concern in this book is the countries that experience democratic collapses. Even where a functional "need" for an authoritarian regime cannot be demonstrated, the structural challenges to democratic stability may still exist. An authoritarian regime may follow a democratic collapse, but such collapses can also be followed by civil war, military dictatorship, or even monarchical restoration. Still another alternative exists, one suggested by Rueschemeyer and Evans (Evans et al. 1985) in their discussion of the state, namely, an increased Balkanization of the state. My analysis of Portugal shows how Balkanization and collapse are related and also suggests the relationship between these two factors and increased state autonomy in the postdemocratic regime.

THEORETICAL FOCUS

The way to mitigate the unwanted instrumental and functionalist aspects of world-system theories, and still remain well within the world-system framework, is precisely by building upon some of the conceptual tools offered in these theories. My approach in this book is less functionalist and instrumentalist; I build upon many of the associations already sketched in two ways: by disentangling the question of democratic collapse from the possible subsequent rise of authoritarian regimes, thereby shifting the focus from the latter to the former; and by creating a model in which extranational factors (position in the world-system) and internal domestic ones (class struggles, domestic economic crises, and political factors) become integral parts of the theory. This theoretical offering is the inductive by-product of my analysis of the Portuguese case.

The first major departure from the other two world-system theories of authoritarian states in the semiperiphery is my emphasis on democratic instability. Rather than focusing on the functional need for an "interventionist state" derived from economic exigencies or for the "instrumentalist" actions of an interventionist state, I examine the structural constraints that the semiperipheral position poses for democratic stability. Although this may be consistent with the "need for an interventionist state" explanation, it suggests that even in the case where an interventionist state was not needed, structural challenges to democratic stability still exist. This approach does not attempt to sever the ties between economic and political processes; rather, it attempts to lessen the reliance on a functionalist or instrumental connection between the two.

Second, and perhaps most important, my theory is constructed upon a world-system view that assumes that a nation's participation in the world capitalist system influences many structural aspects of a nation's economy. It differs, however, in a number of important respects. To the extent that the world-system theories focus on global links, they slight the internal political forces (or as Brenner

[1977] charges, they slight the "institutionalized structures of class conflict"). This is undoubtedly a reaction to the plethora of explanatory approaches that have treated nations as hermetically sealed entities, ignoring the unequivocal impact that the world-system has on the shape and viability of any state. World-system theories need to go further in identifying the internal contradictions of the socioeconomic arrangement that challenge democracy. Thus my theory considers the linkages between location in the world-system and the internal socioeconomic and sociopolitical structures. It is built upon my approach to identifying zones of the world economy (appendix A) and identifies those unique political problems of the semiperiphery that stem from the particular nature of semiperipheral productive relationships. In this sense, the theory attempts to infuse the world-system theories with some concrete political structures and to root the political theories in a wider range of socioeconomic realities.

The fundamental question concerns, of course, the affinity between socioeconomic conditions and state forms.[10] In order to hypothesize that all zones of the world economy would be unequally hospitable to all forms of state, one must specify the underlying logic that unites the economic and political processes. Chase-Dunn suggests "the capitalist mode of production exhibits a single logic in which both political-military power and the appropriation of surplus value through production and sale on the world market play an integrated role. . . . Let us assume, as Marx did, that capitalism is a socioeconomic system with a deep structure, a set of underlying causal tendencies of development or developmental 'laws'" (1981, 20–21). But the assumption that an underlying logic determines both the socioeconomic structure and the form of state is an inappropriate substitute for a description of how the logic manifests itself in real societies. What restrictions does capitalist accumulation place on the installation and flourishing of any form of state? Inversely, how does the form of state, however tenuous and unstable, in turn restrict the manner in which future accumulation can take place?

The argument presented in this book is that Portugal was a typical semiperipheral country. Due to its semiperipheral status, it combined within the nation-state various uncoordinated or unintegrated forms of appropriating and accumulating capital. It was an agro-exporter, an industrial producer, and an exploiter of other peripheral countries (its African colonies). Because the semiperiphery contains multiple economies within the nation-state—many of which have more integral links with other countries than with sectors of their own economy—there are multiple economic interests represented within the democratic state.[11] With disparate and often nonreconcilable interests, these groups find reaching agreement more difficult. This problem is reflected in their continuous failure to solidify and maintain political coalitions, which results in an inordinate amount of political instability at the governmental level. Although the landed aristocracy from the first world-system theory as well as the developmental fraction from the second world-system theory were parties to such instability, the political turmoil was heightened because neither of them alone was able to fashion a national program or to assert (democratically) their preferred economic project over the others. In conclusion, it is neither the landed aristocracy nor the developmental fraction of the bourgeoisie that produces democratic instability and possibly an interventionist state. Rather, it is the existence of a disunified capitalist class, a by-product of the disarticulated semiperipheral economy, that leads to democratic collapse and opens the way to an interventionist state.

METHODOLOGY

Poulantzas asserts that we find the association of politics and economics in political practice where relations of different contradictions finally fuse (1973, 41). But where is his "political practice"? My methodological focus is the executive branch of government, particularly the cabinet. Cabinets constitute the lenses for examining the intersection between the political and the economic spheres. I justify this methodological choice as follows. In parliamentary democracies, individuals, classes, or any other political actors that want to influence political or economic processes have to do so through political strategies. Such strategies are prescribed by the rules of democracy and are processed by state institutions. Conflicts of interest, rather than being resolved by dueling, are settled within particular branches of the state. Thus many incidences of economic competition, rather than being unleashed in the marketplace, are resolved within the labyrinths of the state. For example, the competition between northern and south-central producers of sweet wines in Portugal did not appear as price wars. The northern representatives fought within parliament and the cabinets for favorable legislation and bilateral treaties granting them exclusive use of the term port wine. Thus even such seemingly apolitical events as competition between two brands of the same product were transformed into political conflicts within the state.

The state has a reciprocal effect on the economy and economic interest groups. As members of the parliament under the constitutional monarchy and then as representatives of the democratic nation, capitalists (or their representatives) gave direction to economic growth. The state was empowered to levy taxes, the cabinets to make loans, and both to decide upon expenditures and a myriad of regulations impinging on the productive practices of farmers, industrialists, and merchants. Individual actors within political institutions made the decision to close markets to foreign wheat, for example, and passed legislation to implement it. The merchants and wine producers, or their representatives, negotiated treaties that restrained industrial growth by explicitly prohibiting the manufacture of certain goods (textiles, in particular). Consequently, the implementation of a particular economic plan depended a great deal upon the political configuration of the state.

Table 1.1. Cabinet Composition

Cabinet	Number
Single party	17
Military	3
Independent	1
Coalition	21
Concentration	3
Total	45

Discovering the link between the political realm and the socioeconomic environment requires some respecification of the question of political instability.
Although at least one of the above-mentioned theorists (Linz and Stepan 1978)
suggests that political instability partly explains democratic collapse, I treat this
excessive instability in the executive branch as something that itself must be
explained—thus the first step in question respecification. In looking for the
cause of cabinet instability, I find that it derived from another factor: political
party coalition instability.

Cabinet stability, in turn, was dependent upon party politics in a crucial way.
After all, cabinet composition pivoted around parties and combinations of parties. There were several types of cabinets: single party, multiple party, military,
or independent, nonpartisan individuals.[12] Fifty-four percent of the cabinets
were of the multiple-party type (table 1.1). When several parties joined to rule
in a cabinet or in the parliament, they formed a coalition. Thus the dynamic
behind the making and unmaking of cabinets was the making and unmaking
of party coalitions. Two parties would form a coalition in order to govern, but
the moment a split arose within that coalition, the basis for the cabinet began
to erode.

This methodological choice is based upon the assumption that the cabinet
takes on additional importance as the arena of class struggle in societies in which
the various economic projects exist at parity, namely, in which one is not clearly
dominant. The greater the parity, the more immediately and directly state policies can affect the accumulation of capital and, further, the more economic
advantage a group can obtain to transform the state structure in its own behalf.
In this way, cabinet processes are conceived as the link between structural conditions and political instability. In chapter 2, I document the extent to which
cabinet instability, indeed political instability, constituted a political crisis that
precipitated the withdrawal of legitimacy on the part of any previous supporters
of the Portuguese Republic.

The second step in question respecification is to explain the nature of political
party coalition instability. In search of deeper causes, I turn to the changing balance of socioeconomic forces. Here I elaborate on the socioeconomic environ-

ment into which the Portuguese democracy was born, an environment that it in turn attempted to transform. I argue that the "geographical juxtaposition" of multiple forms of capitalist accumulation in a semiperipheral country threatens the viability of a democratic state and that Portugal's economic situation in the postwar period was precisely this.

In conclusion, the question of democratic instability/stability is much broader than that of political configuration. It involves the internal social structure of Portugal and its class struggles; Portugal's location in a world economic system; and, more generally, the role of the democratic state in capitalism. The democratic state in Portugal cannot be treated as an empirical aberration that preceded the authoritarian regime. It has to be taken seriously.

CHAPTER 2

An Unstable and Nonlegitimate Democracy

In chapter 1, I posited the need to redefine the traditionally posed question to both refine and expand the problematic. This new problematic requires the expected inquiry into the collapse of the Portuguese Republic *and* an inquiry into the instability that preceded it. I begin the latter inquiry by describing the excessive and continual reorganization of the democratic regime. However, cabinet turnover and the like is not perforce instability—it must be experienced as such. The final judgment of instability rests with the actors in the political system, and thus their perceptions are presented as data to support the claim of instability. First, I present attitudes toward instability in particular and then toward the Republic in general. Although statistics demonstrate the various aspects of instability, the subjective data alone can confirm that governmental turnover was experienced as a political crisis. The data support the interpretation that there was a political crisis, a legitimacy crisis for the government. Even though the data I present conform to several of the theories mentioned in chapter 1, I argue that they are inadequate as independent variables. I end this chapter by reaffirming the claim that political instability is more appropriately considered, along with democratic collapse, as a dependent variable, that is, something to be explained.

Portugal is often excluded from surveys of Europe, and thus its history will be unfamiliar to some readers. The following brief history concentrates on the aspects of world-system development that shaped late nineteenth- and early twentieth-century Portuguese society.[1]

PREREPUBLICAN HISTORY

Today Portugal is ranked among the poorest nations of Europe. On conventional scales of economic development (such as electrical consumption, protein intake, medical services, literacy, and gross national product), Portugal falls behind its Western and Southern European neighbors (Pintado 1964, 14–15). Yet the poverty of the nineteenth and twentieth centuries never could have been predicted from the fifteenth and sixteenth. In the late 1400s, Portugal had solved the seignorial crisis of feudalism for itself and had shown the way for the rest of Europe (Wallerstein 1974, 47–52). Wallerstein defines this crisis as the monetary impoverishment of the seignorial class due to the inability of the feudal mode of production to guarantee the ruling class a continuous source of surplus. Fourteenth century Europe had been marked by contractions in the amount of cultivated land, exhausted agrarian technology, food shortages, price increases, epidemics, population declines, wars, and general hardship. These difficulties occurred, he argues, because an optimal point had been reached in the feudal mode of production. Europe's aristocracy was headed toward ruin.

The Portuguese crisis followed a similar pattern: The revenue from real estate failed to match the profits from trade and artisanship. The black death arrived in 1348 and ravaged one-third or more of the population; at least eight plagues followed. Looking for better conditions, survivors fled to the cities, but contrary to their expectations, they found that conditions were worse there (Marques 1972, 1:109). The plagues and urban migration were followed by riots. Riots were recorded in Lisbon in 1371, 1383–1385, 1438–1441, and 1449 (Marques 1972, 1:110). Nobles, landlords, and monasteries looked in vain for labor. The king attempted to ameliorate the rural labor shortage of the landowning nobles with a series of acts between 1349 and 1401 that were intended solely to demobilize the labor force. A 1375 law, for example, bound workers to their traditional professions, preventing labor freedom (Marques 1972, 1:111). Peasant flight to the cities and subsequent rural depopulation were accompanied by a conversion of agricultural land to game reserves and pastures (Wallerstein indicates that this happened throughout much of Europe). The loss of arable land caused wheat crises that in turn produced extreme bread shortages and even famine. Fearing death from the plague, and desperately hoping to buy salvation, nobles donated their lands to the Church. Unprepared to organize large-scale production, the Church left many lands uncultivated, further contributing to food shortages.

This national crisis propelled the Portuguese into the Atlantic. Other European nations soon followed. Today it seems uncanny that a country smaller than the state of Indiana should have been so precocious. Several factors explain this (Wallerstein 1974). First, Portugal had manpower — the newly arrived migrants who had fled the countryside, nobles who were either newly marginalized or unfortunate younger sons, and merchants. Second, capital for the exploration was provided in part by the Genoese, who, for reasons owing to their own rivalry with Venice, were prepared to finance Portuguese overseas ventures.

Another factor was Portugal's geographical location, which served as an obstacle to land expansion. Its frontiers with Spain were mobile but only in the direction of Spanish expansion. Portugal's geographic location did favor, however, sea expansion. Portugal was at the mouth of oceanic currents that made for easy departure from Portuguese ports and easy arrival on the western coast of Africa. The Portuguese, in fact, had years of experience in ocean fishing, piracy, and long-distance trading (Marques 1972, 2:90). Portugal was firmly established in trade all over Western Europe. Already in 1353 the Portuguese had signed a treaty with King Edward III of England that provided safety to the merchants of both countries for fifty years.

Portuguese exports to Western Europe consisted of fruit, salt, wine, olive oil, honey, and raw materials such as wax, cork, and leather in exchange for textiles (Marques 1972, 1:92). The Portuguese also had extensive trade in the Arabian-Mediterranean world, where Portugal traded dried fish, honey, skins, wool, and some salt in exchange for spices, sugar, silk, and other luxury goods. Portugal played an intermediary role between the northern countries and southern Europe and Africa. The Portuguese market was the door through which the Arabian regions could obtain goods from the north, an exchange that was reflected in the abundance of Arabian gold and silver coins in Portugal (Marques 1972, 1:93). The Portuguese also benefited from the rich record of Arabian adventures to Atlantic Islands.

Finally, Portugal's government had the advantage of not being split by internal conflicts to the extent of other European monarchies. This political centralization facilitated the launching of the overseas enterprise (Wallerstein 1974, 51). Challenges to the king from the nobility had occurred earlier in the fifteenth century. During the somewhat weak rule of Afonso V (1438–1481), the nobility had acquired much wealth, particularly by usurping large parcels of royal land from the king (Marques 1972, 1:178), and the number of noble titles grew. The threat to the king lay in the fact that the land and titles were concentrated in the hands of no more than fifteen families. The movement to recover that patrimony was initiated by João I (1481–1495). Although not all of the land was recovered, the subsequent king, Manuel I (1495–1521), succeeded in strengthening the state by issuing subsidies and yearly allowances that made the nobility more dependent upon the crown (Marques 1972, 1:180). This dependency not only strengthened the crown; it also provided noble manpower for the growing colonial project.

From the 1450s, the Portuguese sailed and sailed. Their explorations were global and their gains were prodigious. Beginning with the capture of northern Morocco and the Atlantic Islands, they moved down the coast of Africa and came to rest in India and China. By the 1500s, Portugal had obtained nothing but victories from Arabia to Malaysia. The royalty and its institutions drew heavily on maritime expansion, and the king was proclaimed the richest monarch in all Christendom. From the mid-fifteenth century, products such as gold, spices, sugar, slaves, ivory, and dyestuffs flowed into the country.

With such a prosperous beginning, with such tremendous resources for industrialization, why did Portugal not generate self-sustained growth? The Portuguese trade was not matched by a flourishing of industrial activity. The industrial transformation of raw materials was limited to a few crude textiles and rural implements, shipbuilding, goldsmithing, and cooperage (Marques 1972, 1:95). One explanation for this puzzle can be found in Wallerstein's interpretation of why nations, and not empires, formed the base of modern capitalism (1974, 57–63).[2] He argues that the nation-state organization of feudal Europe allowed for the divorce of the polity and the economy, whereas in empires they were inseparable. The Portuguese organized their colonial possessions into an empire — a political system encompassing wide territories. When the Portuguese conquered a town, they tried to Europeanize it, converting it into a replica of what they knew at home. Colonies were organized under the king into a system of captaincies that resembled feudal Portugal. The Portuguese administrative, civil, and criminal codes as well as other pieces of European legislation were applied to Africa and Asia with few adjustments for local usages and traditions. Finances were organized in an equally centralized manner.

The Portuguese had to spend enormous resources in order to defend their vast empire. Wallerstein argues that one of the great innovations of nation-states over empires is the transfer of economic losses to political entities and of economic gains to private hands. In the Portuguese case, overseas expansion was the expansion of the crown. Trade and exploration belonged to a circumscribed number. In Brazil, the crown owned the brazilwood, slaves, spices, and drug monopolies along with a fifth of the ore and precious-stone trade. The crown used the wealth to purchase luxury goods and to erect buildings.

Whether because of the organizational shortcomings that accompanied Portugal's attempt to construct an empire, or because of the increasing strength and economic development of Britain (as Stein and Stein [1970] argue), by the 1700s Portugal had fallen irreversibly from its glorious heights. British sea superiority forced Portugal to surrender some of her trade monopolies. In other cases, the British came to be lords of lands that had belonged to the Portuguese. British tentacles also moved into the center of the Portuguese empire. Since the late thirteenth century, wine and olive oil had been exported to England (Marques 1972, 1:90). After 1650, English firms settled in Oporto, a northern Portuguese seaport, and began fostering their own wine production for export. The Methuen Treaty of 1703 inscribed in history the supremacy that England had achieved over Portugal. English wool textiles would be allowed into Portugal ("forever") without tax in exchange for the Portuguese exporting wines to England at one-third the tax paid for French wines.[3] In 1703, Portuguese imports from England were valued at around £300,000, and in 1704, one year after the treaty, they had risen to a value of £1,300,000. "So few lines [in the treaty] were necessary to ruin a country" (*A Dominação ingleza* 1883, 114). The English benefited from their penetration of the Portuguese market, from the return freight on wine moving to England on English ships, and from their access to the Brazilian gold that flowed through the Portuguese treasury (Serrão 1976, 237).

The velocity at which the stream of British textiles entered Portugal varied with the policies of those in power. An industrialization program slowed British textile imports from 57 percent in 1796 to 33 percent in 1806 (Sideri 1970, 123), but by 1819 they were up again, to 60 percent. Programs included state support of half a dozen large manufactures (Cabral 1977, 16) and the state establishment of seventy-one manufactures in the areas of textiles, paper, clothing, ceramics, glass, and sugar refining (Payne 1973, 2:407).

In 1807 Napoleon I invaded Portugal. The Portuguese royal family boarded a British vessel and fled to Brazil. The French invasion and subsequent occupation left the country politically and economically decimated. Nobles who had not fled with the royal court submitted to French domination. Those who had depended on foreign trade became destitute: Products sold for half their value, the treasury was depleted, and the price of food increased daily. With the aid of the British, the Portuguese finally expelled the invaders in 1811. Portugal paid a substantial price for the survival of its royal family and for the integrity of the nation. Politically, Portugal became a protectorate of Britain; economically, it forfeited its trade monopoly of Brazil. Portugal's king had adapted quite well to life in Brazil, and the British governing regency in Portugal showed little willingness to shift from the pre-1800 method of ruling. These two factors contributed to considerable political agitation among the rural nobility, the army, and middle-class urban intellectuals, who revolted in 1820. This revolt resulted in the departure of the British regency and the return of the king and helped give birth to a constitutional monarchy and a constitution that opened the epoch of civil wars.

Many intellectuals imagined that Portugal's solution to the economic crisis was "to produce in themselves what they are capable of" (Marques 1972, 2:1). Pursuant to this goal, they constructed legislation to remove ancient constraints on agricultural production; thus the ecclesiastical tithe and noble titles were abolished. Feudal rights such as exclusives on ovens, presses, and wine sales and payments to lords or kings disappeared. Lands belonging to religious orders and the crown were auctioned off, thereby putting much additional land into cultivation. One consequence of this legislation was to create a new class of landed bourgeoisie, which included a private company of traders and industrialists who had joined for the purchase of large meadowlands in the south (Marques 1972, 2:5). No consensus existed, however, on whether a liberal constitution and new landownership should be Portugal's fate. Civil wars, with the absolutists pitted against the liberals, raged for the next thirty years. This chapter of civil wars ended in 1851; then another, less-tumultuous period of constitutional struggles began.

From 1851 to 1910, monarchical rule was disputed in a process called *rotativismo*. Two parties shared power by rotating it every two and a half years. This power was accompanied by access to revenue, prestige, offices of the bureaucracy, and the right to manipulate the political machine. To many, the court looked like a stage for chicanery, small cliques, and personality debates and antagonisms (Marques 1972, 1:174). The king used his right from time to time to dissolve court, suspend newspapers, or issue decrees transporting political offenders to Africa (Bragança-Cunha 1911, 184).

A number of social and economic crises threatened the rule of the crown during its last century of rule. First, of course, was the effect of the janus-faced British protectorate. Although it protected the Portuguese crown from French invaders, it took the Brazilian trade monopoly from Portugal, thereby depriving many people of their major source of income. In 1890, Britain again shook the solvency of Portugal. It presented Portugal with an ultimatum—give the British the central African territory between Angola and Mozambique or lose diplomatic relations with them. The loss of this patrimony incited popular indignation in Portugal, and in the following general election, the famous African explorer, Serpa Pinto, received votes. The ministry in power at the time of this ultimatum was forced to resign. This and a subsequent treaty that gave the Delagoa Bay Railroad and the port of Lourenço Marques in Mozambique to the South African Union (Bragança-Cunha 1911, 291) cost the Portuguese monarchy legitimacy that it never recovered.

Monetary difficulties contributed heavily to the increasing problems of the monarch both at home and abroad. A first blow to the financial solvency of the Portuguese state was the cessation of remittances from Brazil following the declaration of the Brazilian Republic in 1889. The persistent trade deficit and governmental budget deficit placed Portugal in the hands of creditors. The recourse to excessive debt reflected the difficult position of the monarch, who chose debt over the alternative of taxing an already republican-prone population. Further, opposition to the royalty for acquiescing to the British claim over parts of Portuguese Africa made it more difficult for the king to negotiate loans (*TE* 16 May 1891: 624). The same governmental weakness made it difficult for the crown to balance the budget because it would have required terminating precisely those subsidies upon which monarchical support was situated.

In the foreign loan market, to which Portugal was forced to turn, it encountered additional hostility. Miguel bondholders (speculators who had bought up bonds that were originally issued in 1832 but were subsequently repudiated after the Pretender to the Throne, Dom Miguel, was expelled from Portugal) threatened to close the French markets to any new Portuguese loans if their requests for satisfactory payment were not met. Their protests caused the failure of the Portuguese Public Works loan, which had been put on the Paris market in May 1880. When the subscription opened, "large posters were carried about in the streets of Paris denouncing the Portuguese Government for repudiating its just debts" (*TE* 17 May 1890: 623). The British Foreign Office thought that the Portuguese financial position was going from bad to worse and that there were few prospects for a budget equilibrium. They estimated that the debt charge absorbed about half of Portugal's revenue (*TE* 26 July 1890: 955). In 1891 the Portuguese state used the tobacco monopoly to convert the floating debt. In exchange for a thirty-five-year working monopoly, which included a 40 percent share of the net profits, the establishment of Comptoir d'Escompte would pay the Portuguese state an annual sum and the remaining 60 percent share of the net profits (*TE* 4 April 1891: 437). To protect the success of this negotiation, the loan syndicate was forced to obtain an order from a judge in chambers suppressing the defamatory posters that the Miguel bondholders had again plastered on the walls of Paris (*TE* 25 April 1891: 533).

About one year later, another loan was announced for the Portuguese Royal Railway Company. Shortly after the bonds were issued, they were devalued, causing quite a scandal. In 1892, unable to perpetuate the system of covering recurring heavy budget deficits with temporary borrowings, and with the floating debt beginning to assume unmanageable dimensions, Portugal declared bankruptcy. This announcement reflected the exhausted faith of lenders. Disputes between Britain and Portugal also created apprehension about a complete financial breakdown. Portugal could no longer get purchasers for its bonds (*TE* 6 February 1892: 175). The bankruptcy was followed by a reduction of one-half on its interest payments on the foreign debt; the customs revenue was to be paid to the Bank of Portugal and remitted abroad weekly. When the revenue yielded a surplus, the surplus would be applied toward increasing the interest on the debt (*TE* 26 March 1892: 419). Again, in 1902, the state had to repudiate the full obligations of the debt. Half was canceled and a payment of 3 percent was restored on the balance (Bragança-Cunha 1911, 213, 286). To many, the monarchy seemed incapable of ruling and consequently was plunging the remainder of the patrimony deeper into economic ruin.

Although there was general international concern — even to the point of suggesting a foreign blockade of either Portuguese or Portuguese-African harbors — *The Economist* expressed little concern about Portugal defaulting on its bonds and even suggested that the best thing for Portugal at that juncture would be "to sell her South African territories to Great Britain, for they are just now a heavy burden upon her exchequer" (16 May 1891: 624).

Revelations about the magnitude of royal luxury and debt, the costs of supporting the royal household, and the method of paying the royal debt all contributed to the conflict between the aristocrats in the parliament and the king. Revenue was spent on lavish imports. State revenues went toward the maintenance of the royal household, court luxuries, and colonial administration. Pensions were given to wealthy and eminent citizens and continued to go to their families long after the recipient's death. Salaries were given to ambassadors who never took up their posts (*TE* 30 November 1907: 2077). One chronicler summarizes that the monarchy fell because of a general disrespect for public monies: the advancements from the public treasury, the scandal of tobacco, the corruption of the banking house Crédito Predial, and the Hinton scandal (Neves 1910, 22). Neves also notes the general disrespect for the constitutional process: The king dissolved the parliament and tried to rule with dictatorial decrees. Europeans were divided on the question of supporting the Portuguese monarchy. The House of Braganza had many allies throughout Europe, including the courts of Spain and Austria. Given these alliances, *The Economist* feared that Lord Salisbury would be urged by European royalty to give help to King Carlos of Portugal — help that would increase the king's legitimacy within Portugal (11 October 1890: 1286).

The historians' road that leads from the end of the Portuguese monarchy to the establishment of the First Republic follows a reasonably well-agreed-upon series of guideposts: the 1880 commemorations for Luís de Camões, the British ultimatum in 1890, the aborted revolt of 31 January 1891 in Oporto, the regicide in 1908, and, finally, the revolution of 5 October 1910. The Republican party, founded in the 1870s, received great impetus from events such as the British ultimatum. Following that watershed, three republicans from Oporto and four from Lisbon were elected to parliament. However, the Republican party found little favor with the monarchs and was subjected to periodic attack. Several groups joined together to successfully oppose the monarchy. They included socialists, anarchists, urban middle classes, and some ranks within the army. Opposition to the governmental mismanagement and national economic ruin attributed to the monarch did not fall along narrow class lines. Leaders of the Republican party, such as José Relvas, were drawn from the landowning classes. Relvas, a central committee member of the Republican party, objected to the corn and cattle protection laws of 1899, arguing that they did little to stimulate local enterprise. In addition, he protested the large increase in taxes on agricultural income. Although farmers' incomes had risen 22 percent between 1877 and 1908, taxes on these incomes had risen 115 percent (*TE* 3 September 1910: 463).

Everyone knew there were conspiracies against the monarchy and that opposition was widespread and growing (Neves 1910, 76). After several false starts, including premature bomb explosions that injured their own manufacturers, the revolution broke out in late afternoon on 3 October 1910. Neves reports that the movement in the streets of Lisbon that day was abnormal. Small groups gathered, loud discussions could be heard coming from the cafés, and, periodically, in the streets one could hear "Down with the Jesuits, Death to the Monks" (Neves 1910, 88). There was confusion and early attacks on the barracks of the Sixteenth Infantry, where several officers were killed (Neves 1910, 88); there was much movement and sporadic gunfire in the streets (Neves 1910, 15). The rumor spread that the revolution was about to begin, and the royal troops were readied. The downtown square of Rossio was filled with troops loyal to the last monarchy, and on the side streets, periodic exchanges broke out between the Municipal Guard and the republican forces (Neves 1910, 16). Neves tried to get a train and found that the trains as well as boat ferries out of Lisbon had been stopped (Neves 1910, 17). By 4 October, many republican flags had appeared. Still, victory for the rebels was uncertain. Although forces supposedly loyal to the king were often inactive, defections from the republican side also occurred. The revolutionary force counted about 450, including the navy, the infantry, and the artillery. On 5 October, the Portuguese monarchy ended: The king fled and the edifice collapsed.

Despite anarchist and socialist support for the revolution, the revolution was not against the Portuguese upper classes. After the rebellion, Neves observed banks, stores, and houses of monarchist politicians being guarded by civilian elements of the revolution—including anarchists. On the Avenida da Libertade, the terror of the revolution had given insomnia to the upper classes, who fully expected to be robbed of their precious possessions. Thus the protection that the revolutionaries extended to the wealthy's property during those nights won additional upper-class converts to the republican side (Neves 1910, 136). Nor was the republican revolution a nationalist revolution against foreign interests. Relvas, in a visit to London a few weeks before the revolution, spoke of the Republican party's commitment to Great Britain and to British commerce.

The first government publication, *Diário do governo*, gave amnesty to those who had supported the previous regime, decreed divorce, established freedom of the press, and announced a new era of prosperity and liberty for Portugal (Neves 1910, 142). So began the First Portuguese Republic.

THE PROGRESSIVE COLLAPSE OF DEMOCRACY

The 1926 breakdown of the Portuguese democratic regime was neither spontaneous nor sudden. The progressive disaggregation of the democracy was manifest in two phenomena—the increasing instability of the institutional structures and the increasing withdrawal of legitimacy from the regime. The actual collapse of the democratic regime punctuated a political crisis that had festered in Portuguese society since 1910.

The political history of the Republic is filled with military interventions, suspensions of the constitution, and civilian outcries. Instability was, in fact, a prevailing characteristic—it invaded the very institutions of the state and it permeated the system of political representation. In the case of the state, instability took the following form: The electorate (three times redefined) went to the polls eight times to elect eight of the nine parliaments, which in turn chose seven presidents. The presidents appointed a total of forty-five cabinets. In the case of the system of political representation, instability could be seen in the increasing factionalization and proliferation of political parties. A united Republican party gave way to three parties, later to six parties, and finally to more than nine parties, including nonrepublican ones. These two principal manifestations of political instability were punctuated with annual monarchist uprisings, civilian riots, and military pronouncements.

The constitution suffered more alterations than the constitutional assembly had forecasted. According to the 1911 constitution, the first revisions were scheduled for 1921. Before that time, the constitution had been suspended once and revised twice. In 1918, under the one-year military rule of Sidónio Pais, the parliamentary system of representation of individuals by parties was supplemented by a senate in which places were assigned to representatives of corporate interests (ten for agriculture, five for industry, four for commerce, three for public services, and so on). In addition, a presidential system replaced the parliamentary one. All of these changes were in violation of the constitution.

Table 2.1. Reasons Presidents Left Office

Reason	Number
Term expired	2[a]
Assassinated	1
Military *golpe*	2
Resigned	3

[a] Teófilio Braga completed his term, but it was only a three-month interim term.

High turnover also plagued the president's office. The average term in office, rather than the four years stipulated by the constitution, was only two years. Of the eight chiefs of state, only two served their full terms of office and left when their mandates expired. The others left office for a variety of reasons (table 2.1).

A similar instability occurred in the legislative branch. The constitution prescribed that parliaments were to have three-year terms, which would have given the Republic a total of five congresses. However, during that sixteen-year period, excluding the elections for the national constitutional assembly, there were eight legislative elections (including the 1913 supplemental election). Rather than the mandated three-year sessions, congresses averaged sessions of one year and ten months. Congresses were prevented from fulfilling their mandated time for several reasons (table 2.2).

The most spectacular turnover rate took place at the executive level. During the sixteen-year period (1910–1926), forty-five different cabinets were installed. Cabinets were not equally unstable—although the median cabinet tenure was ninety-three days, they ranged from seven days to 406 days. Nor was the historical distribution of the turnovers random. Table 2.3 (number of cabinets by year) reveals an initial period of cabinet stability broken by the war years. In the postwar period, there was a return to the stability known during the initial republican years. It was short-lived and gave way in the 1920s to a phase of rampant instability. Whether we consider the pattern in units of one year or five, the observed trend is the same—the longevity of cabinets decreased with time.

This apparent instability might not have been so serious (or noteworthy) if it had been the continual succession of a small group of republican prime ministers. Such was not the case. Of the prime ministers who headed the forty-five cabinets, twenty-two headed only one cabinet, four headed two cabinets, three headed three cabinets, and one headed six cabinets. A few of them served as presidents of the Republic, and others reappeared as ministers in various cabinets. Even thirty different prime ministers in a sixteen-year period justifies the attribution of instability. Beyond a doubt there was a high level of turnover within the state apparatus (a continuous shifting of personnel), and this turnover was often provoked, not by the rules established in the constitution for an orderly and slow substitution, but by spontaneous and external interferences.

Table 2.2. Reasons for Closing Parliament

Reason	Number
Term ended	3
Military *golpe*	4
Dissolved by president	2

Instability was also rampant within the system of political representation. What began as a united Republican party soon split into moderate and radical factions. The three lines that had been distinguishable in the 1911 constitutional assembly debates had solidified into three distinct republican parties within two years [the Portuguese Democratic party (PDP), the Republican Unionist party (PUR), and the Republican Evolutionist party (PRE)]. By 1926, seven of the thirty political parties still existed. Although the initial three parties were republican, later lists included a monarchist party, a Catholic party, and a party of businessmen. The democrats were divided into wings: Divisions existed among the conservatives, moderates, and nationalists; two prominent individuals (Cunha Leal and Alvaro de Castro) generated a whole matrix of political groups by themselves. The monarchist parties reproduced the historical divisions of constitutionalists and traditionalists. Even the Catholics were divided. Marques argues that the political factions were completely lacking in discipline (1970, 148) and perhaps because of this, the proliferation of political parties had ramifications for reduced political consensus in the parliament. Between 1911 and 1915, the parliament was able to select a president on one ballot. The third election, also in 1915, required three ballots; the last two, 1923 and 1925, required three and two ballots, respectively. And, as might be expected, the electoral votes for congress became more disperse with the proliferation of parties. In the early legislative elections between 1911 and 1915, when the average number of parties was 3.5, republican or republican-splinter parties received almost 100 percent of the vote. In the 1915 legislative elections, six parties split the vote, and a Catholic party joined the Republican and Socialist parties. From 1918, the number of parties grew, and by 1921 nine parties shared the electoral vote.

The high turnover rate and proliferation of parties had social meaning at two levels. First, they were perceived and treated as political instability by the actors and commentators of the time. Situations do exist in which political instability could be said to be apparent but not real. But the Portuguese case is not one of them. The bourgeoisie protested against the disorder of the Republic, which it saw in the streets, in the government, and in the system of representation. These subjective expressions of the Portuguese middle class justify my conclusion that the observed disorder and governmental rotations, at unexpected moments and for unexpected causes, was real political instability. Second, the political instability was part of a larger sociopolitical crisis, namely, the dismembering of the state apparatus. Poulantzas, in his discussion of the rise of fascism, describes

Table 2.3. Number of Cabinets per Year, 1910–1926

Year	Number	Year	Number	Year	Number
1910	1	1916	1	1922	3
1911	2	1917	2	1923	2
1912	1	1918	2	1924	2
1913	1	1919	4	1925	4
1914	3	1920	7	1926	1
1915	4	1921	6		

this dismemberment as a dislocation between formal and real power. Phenomena evident in this dismembering are the instability of the government; the deterioration of the judicial system; the duplication of political parties by parallel power networks that ranged from pressure groups to private militia; and a parliamentary crisis resulting from the crisis of party representation (Poulantzas 1974, 334). What Portugal faced was not a crisis of individual governments but a generalized political crisis. The bourgeoisie's withdrawal of legitimacy from the Republic and its support for the military coup were most certainly rooted in its condemnation of the instability that plagued the state, because that instability as well as worker unrest interfered with business.

GOVERNMENTAL TURNOVER AS POLITICAL INSTABILITY

Historical situations do occur in which governmental turnover does not mean instability. *Rotativismo* is one situation in which political instability, even at apparently high levels, does not constitute a political crisis. For both British theorists and some Portuguese political practitioners, *rotativismo* was the serial sharing of power between two parties or blocs—first one party would hold power and then the other. The system required two distinct but not diametrically opposed parties. It also required some degree of internal party unity and discipline. In spite of high turnover rates, *rotativismo* produced political stability. The Portuguese constitutional monarchy operated with this system from 1851 until 1906 (Pereira 1915, 694–96; Serrão 1976, 292). For *rotativismo*, what appeared as instability—constant shifts in power—was in fact stability. The rotations of personnel within the state apparatus filtered down to those connected to the respective parties at the local level but had little impact on the daily lives of the nation's majority. In short, one could conclude that Portuguese *rotativismo* was merely turnover, not political crisis. Portuguese *rotativismo* came to an end in 1906, according to Pereira, for two reasons. First, the two parties became less distinguishable, thereby violating one of the preconditions of the system. And, second, the parties were forced to continually dissolve and reconstitute the parliament in order to maintain themselves in power.

A second hypothetical situation might be found in societies in which the economic and political structures are clearly autonomous. When crucial issues are determined exclusively within nonpolitical spheres, events in the parallel political structure may be less relevant to the socioeconomic sphere. This description applies to some corporatist states. Elements that are traditionally relegated to the political arena (political parties, elections, politicians) in no way impinge upon important decisions made about the economy. Even if cabinets were turned out of office monthly, economic policies would suffer no perturbations. Schmitter (1978), for example, has shown that during the Salazar regime, more elections were held in Portugal than in any other European country. However, the locus of decision making was within the corporate structure of the state and not within the frequently elected parliamentary body.

A third situation in which political chaos does not support an inference of political instability is suggested by V. O. Key (1949). In the United States, where politics is divided horizontally among the federal, state, and local levels, Key discovers circumstances under which state-level politics became superfluous. He suggests that because of particular policy commitments at the national level, freedom for policy decisions did not exist at the state level. This is Key's explanation for the rise of what he considers circuslike politics with clownlike politicians in the southern United States. Politics, particularly Democratic party politics, did not matter within these states, which, once again, supports the conclusion that high turnover is not perforce synonymous with political instability.

To support the claim that political turnover in the First Portuguese Republic was real political instability, one must demonstrate that governmental turnover influenced governmental policy; that it was perceived by members of society as instability; and, finally, that it mattered to them. In a similar fashion, one must demonstrate that political party fragmentation was part of the general political crisis. Although the state apparatus and the system of representation are separate entities, they were sometimes described interchangeably by writers whose testimonies are presented below. Even so, these perceptions offer a valuable demonstration, because political instability can only be the makings of a political crisis when it is experienced as such. Thus the withdrawal of legitimacy from the state apparatus and from the accompanying system of representation, not political turnover per se, precipitated the collapse of the Portuguese democratic system.

That governmental turnover constituted political instability first became evident in cabinet shifts because they often resulted in policy changes. What was decreed or constructed by one cabinet was nullified or dismantled by a successor: Women and peasants were given the franchise, only to have it later withdrawn. In 1911 a cabinet decreed the separation of church and state and the expulsion of religious orders; Sidónio Pais revoked that law with his decree of 22 February 1918 (Vieira 1926, 404) and permitted the return of religious personnel with amnesty. Taxes levied by one cabinet were annulled by another; the exchange rate was set by one cabinet and reset by another; and so on.

Second, these turnovers were experienced as instability. Published complaints of organized interest groups constitute the principal evidence for this. Although the evidence is illustrative and therefore does not lend itself to measuring attitude shifts over time, it does reveal the extent to which these groups took notice of governmental instability and attributed certain inconveniences to it. Already in 1915, the Commercial Association of Lisbon (ACL) complained that each incident of instability prejudiced the economy (ACL 1915, 354). It reiterated the theme in 1919: "Due to governmental instability, there have only been inefficient measures regarding the financial equilibrium" (ACL 1919, 30). And, "because of the instability of the government, 1919 was an absolutely unproductive year as far as the national interests were concerned" (ACL 1919, 28). In its 1920/21 report, ACL wrote that a conscious policy of economic renovation could not take place with a rapid succession of governments and the pulverization of political forces. The way it saw national interests jeopardized was noted in its 1923 report: "Efforts of the 1923 directorate of the commercial association of Lisbon were next to null because of the major indifference evidenced in official spheres to complaints from this economic interest group. Due to ministerial instability, the association lost much time in conferences with ministers and when it would return to see the results of the studies promised, it would find a new cabinet in the place" (ACL 1923, 25).

The Industrial Association of Oporto (AIp), one year later, echoed this reaction: "Powers lack continuity of action indispensable to a persistent and lasting work, one ministry following upon the heels of another" (AIp 1924, 314). In a conference sponsored by the Lisbon Geography Society during its Week of Angola, Lima attributed the multiple colonial problems to the constant turnover of colonial administrators that accompanied the cabinet turnovers (1925, 9). Even the British Chamber of Commerce in Portugal complained in 1923 that trade suffered from shifts in government (BCCP 1924, 86).

There was a continuous sounding of these complaints during the last ten years of the Republic, suggesting that the concern was not epiphenomenal. Economic association reports reveal the extent to which the associations found instability undesirable. Business leaders complained that "business as usual" was jeopardized because "business as usual" required policies that could never have resulted from such short-lived cabinets. If real remuneration for export products vacillated wildly from week to week or from month to month because of governmental turnover and subsequent manipulation of the exchange rates, producers would hesitate to produce, being uncertain what profit, if any, could be made. Or if the interest rate on loans was highly unstable, borrowers would hesitate to borrow for investment.

In conclusion, turnover did impinge on daily business life. Political instability left conditions of production unpredictable, thereby jeopardizing production itself. Because of turnovers, proposals presented by the major economic associations got lost; consequently, they had to be continuously resubmitted and restudied, only to be lost again in the interstices between one cabinet and the next. Inability to predict the future economic environment and to secure favorable policy decisions were obstacles to long-term investment and planning and thus to capital accumulation.

Economic association editorialists attributed the disruptions to two aspects of the political system: the system of representation, that is, political parties; and the governmental system, that is, the (democratic) state apparatus. Economic interest groups complained about the hiatus between party politics and the interests of the nation. AIp asserted that the government was in the hands of subordinates of party organizations who worked only in the interest of the predominant political factions (AIp 1926, 585). Some politicians themselves attributed national instability to political parties and personality rivalries. Relvas (1977) attributed the destruction of liberty to personality intrigues among prominent leaders such as Afonso Costa and Bernardino Machado. Machado, a famous politician and commentator, wrote in 1922 and 1923 that parties were mere erratic products, always ephemeral; that they produced political combinations that were permutations of chiefs with their publics; and that they had lost contact with their own popular commissions—in short, they had become parties without publics (Almeida 1974, 156, 193). The multiplication of parties and the political divisions and regroupings were due, in the opinion of Nogueira (1977, 1:263), to the superimposition of personal and political party games upon the enormous problems of the country.

For some, criticism of the inconvenience or potential danger of party politics masked a more fundamental objection: not to the manner in which the system functioned but to the system itself. Not everyone was convinced that a system of popular representation produced the best policies. A few business leaders said it plainly—the solution to the political crisis was the dismantling of the 'system of representation in which political parties mediated between popular will and the government. AIp thought that popular suffrage only put stupid men in office (AIp 1915, 164) and that those put into office represented only the masses, not the "conservative classes" (its name for capitalists) (AIp 1915, 2). Having a parliament responsive to an electorate meant that the parliament passed laws that were prejudicial to national interests (AIp 1915, 161) and that the government in general made too many decisions without consulting economic groups (ACL 1918, 67). Throughout the Republic the ACAP worried that elections disrupted the nation and encouraged groups like the Bolsheviks and the Masons (1922, 63). The division of power between legislative and executive was considered inefficient because the branches acted as adversaries, with neither capable of doing useful work (Baptista [1916], 28). "For fourteen years there has been a divorce between the state and the producing classes which an angry and chaotic legislature has made worse" (AIp 1924, 813–14). One of the more articulate republican politicians, a member of the parliamentary opposition who had led one cabinet and had been minister of finance in another, judged the parliamentary system incapable of resolving problems in times of crisis. Although he thought it an adequate machine in normal periods, under periods of perturbation it lacked the adaptive capacity to produce legislation commensurate with the social and political changes of the nation (Leal [1926], 145).

The Central Association of Portuguese Farmers (ACAP) complained about unsupportive philosophy and hostile legislation and then went a step beyond criticism of politicians or policies by objecting to democracy itself. Nuno de Gusmão was one intellectual who linked the forms of state with tight labor control in the countryside; his thoughts were often reported in the *Boletim* of the ACAP. In a conference in 1920, he laid the salvation of the nation on the shoulders of syndicalism and cooperativism, and the demise of the nation on constitutionalism, with its antiscientific and antinatural emphasis on individuals (ACAP 1920, 297). Editors of the *Boletim* wrote that if they were not successful in getting representatives of agriculture into the parliament, they should push for constitutionally permitted parliamentary dissolution (ACAP 1920, 202). In 1924 the agricultural association supported the increasingly popular position that "producers" in Portugal must choose only deputies who were unequivocal representatives of their interests and not parasites of political parties (ACAP 1924, 308, 315). In a general assembly that year, one associate who advocated working within the parties of the democratic regime was booed (ACAP 1924, 306). Clearly, strong antidemocratic sentiment existed among the landholders represented by ACAP.

These complaints sound like precursors to the request for corporatist representation, which is exactly what they were. The language of opposition had not always been so blunt. This discourse was initiated as early as 1915 by AIp, which suggested corporate modifications rather than abandonment of the democratic system: "Individuals acting individually remain divorced from public powers and incapable of being represented to their advantage. To avoid this danger individuals must act as associations, *grêmios*, and under cover of law transmit to the state their complaints on public questions. Association of classes . . . [is] the social organization through which the state recognizes individuals" (AIp 1915, 66).

The Lisbon commercial association and the retailers association, along with the federation of farm unions in central Portugal, agreed on the need to have their own representatives in the senate (ACL 1920–1921, 121). The appointment of ministers on the basis of corporate representation and technical expertise was demanded with equal persistence. Writers for these interest group journals wanted technically competent ministers who were politically neutral but understood the needs of the sector to which they were to administer (AIp 1924, 316; ACL 1924, 49). Their proposal, like others, forecasted a parliamentary body composed of representatives of economic classes rather than of representatives of individual citizens (ACAP 1924, 318). In fact, after the 1918 corporatist experiment of Sidónio Pais, a protocorporatist parliament was always on the associations' agendas.

These quotations, which are sampled from a larger body of similar ones, reveal the extent to which individuals and groups were critical of governmental instability and the democratic regime that generated it. To those critics cited, the political and economic difficulties faced by the nation were directly attributable to political instability endemic to the democratic regime. For many actors, this concern with instability was transformed into a withdrawal of legitimacy from the Portuguese state.

WITHDRAWAL OF LEGITIMACY BECOMES A POLITICAL CRISIS

Political instability was soon transformed into a major political crisis as those affected by the instability moved to withdraw legitimacy from the democratic state. Stability versus instability, chaos versus order, were the rhetorical arms of the military. As the Republic aged, political instability was matched more and more with military threats to end it by ending the Republic itself. In 1926 the military acted on its threats when it staged a coup that brought down the democratic regime for good. Yet it would be wrong to exaggerate the role of the army or to reduce it to an army of occupation that imposed itself upon an unwilling society. Major republican actors were unloyal (disloyal opposition, in Linz's terms) to that political form, both because of the political instability and because of the policies of various republican governments. In many cases, the democratic state became the scapegoat for the particular policies promulgated by the Democratic party. Support for the coup d'état could be found in the last sighs of parliamentary democracy. Some historical accounts go so far as to claim that the coup was welcomed by a majority of the Portuguese: by the capitalists, the petty bourgeoisie, the workers, the anarchists, and, most enthusiastically, the non-democratic opposition (Marques 1976, 2:174; Wiarda 1977).

Political actors had their respective motives for withdrawing legitimacy from the parliamentary regime and granting it to the military coup. Actors had concrete, albeit quite different, objections to the democratic rule that followed the 1910 revolution. Antidemocratic sentiment was found among different segments of the Portuguese population—the workers, landowners, and capitalists. The withdrawal of legitimacy on the part of these various actors shows the extent to which the regime experienced a generalized political crisis. Several important actors' justifications for their withdrawal of legitimacy are discussed below.

Unions and working-class organizations opposed cabinets that repressed workers; a few groups, after opposing multiple cabinets, consented to the military overthrow because they hoped it would terminate the abuses of the Democratic party. Democratic party cabinets had from time to time closed union halls and forcibly placed striking workers on the front of moving trains during a railroad strike to save the still-in-service trains from violent sabotage by strikers. The postal and telegraph employees remained bitter toward the democrats for their treatment of state employees, who went through a seventy-day strike without pay.

Their bitterness toward the Democratic party made them willing participants in the 1926 military coup to the point of sending bogus telegrams announcing nonexistent adherences to the coup while detouring telegrams describing republican support addressed to the last democratic prime minister. This confusion contributed to the swift success of the uncontested coup (Paxeco 1937, 219).

Workers' animosity toward the Democratic party was not a surprise given the monopoly of power that the party held during the Republic. Of the final fifteen cabinets (the thirty-first through the forty-fifth), the democrats had exclusive rule in six, participated in seven, and were excluded from only two. In short, because the democrats were in power most of the time, they (and with them the Republic) became the targets of union hostility. For some workers, the overthrow of the democratic Republic was the way to overthrow the Democratic party. Those less supportive of the coup were slow to express opposition. The Portuguese General Confederation of Labor (CGTP) did not join the opposition and did not take a position regarding the coup for five days, at which time it declared a general strike. Defections from the coup followed (Costa 1979, 141). Although the working classes had been the beneficiaries of social welfare legislation, they were still dissatisfied, and this led to a divorce between the trade union movement and the government (Figueiredo 1975, 4). In no way does this imply that the twenty-eighth of May was a revolution. It was not a social movement organized or led by the working classes; although some working-class elements were present, their participation was one of support.

Support for the Republic among middle-class sectors was also on the decline: "The middle tradesman, the middle and upper civil servant—including the army and navy officer—the rural and urban owners, all those who in 1910 had been the pillars of the Republic, were now full of complaints against it. They complained about the fall in their real salaries . . . about the small margin of profit in their business, about the tax increase, about the rise of labor unions and the labor movement" (Marques 1972, 2:140).

The landed aristocracy was, perhaps, the greatest reservoir of antirepublican sentiment. Its control of the rural labor force became problematic because of changes on two fronts: general economic growth, particularly the rise of industry, and political transformations under the democratic regime. Because of these intrusions into their economic organization, the landholders placed considerable blame on the democratic regime.

Under *enfiteuse* (a system of rural labor control inherited from earlier centuries), land was ceded in perpetuity in exchange for periodic payments in kind or in monetary equivalents. The liberal regime of the 1830s had freed both land and labor. Still, remnants of the former system persisted until the time of the republican revolution when they were finally abolished. Although formally free, the landless peasants of the nineteenth century had few employment alternatives and continued to be tied to the land by necessity. Those who had received plots in the allocation of common lands soon joined the landless because of their inability to pay taxes, purchase equipment, or produce on land of inferior quality. Further, the division of the commons eliminated land that had been used for livestock grazing, forcing the poor to relinquish their meager livestock for lack of grazing land (Cutileiro 1971, 22). Land reform again received attention in the late 1800s as Portugal began to lose its share of the international produce market; however, the replacement of the diminished foreign market by the colonial one relieved the pressure for land reform (Pereira 1979, 29) and allowed the agrarian system to remain intact.

Although seasonal unemployment means seasonal misery in the periphery (or in a preindustrial semiperiphery), it means labor flight to the nonagricultural sectors in the semiperiphery. The growth of industry created new options for the peasant, which in turn created a wage push that harmed landowners. Predictably, agriculture increasingly lost labor to the industrial sector. As employment alternatives grew for rural workers, it became necessary to devise ways to keep workers in the area during off-seasons. In the 1880s and 1890s, municipal public works were created to absorb seasonally unemployed workers. Conversely, these programs were suspended during harvest seasons. In the counties of the southeast wheat belt, outmigration could be seen in population declines during the first decade of the republican era (1910–1920) (Cutileiro 1971, 6). Also ACAP complained that World War I had influenced the agricultural economy by disproportionately raising rural wages over food prices (three to one), which represented a drain on agricultural producers (ACAP 1924, 120). The practice of mounting public works during the off-season continued throughout the reign of the Republic. In 1916 public works, including superfluous ones, were again undertaken to alleviate the effects of the economic crisis (Cutileiro 1971, 77), with one important difference. Under the monarchy, the state assisted the municipalities with the expenses of public works; under the Republic, attempts were made to transfer more of the burden to individual landowners by having them support an allotted number of unemployed (based on their estate wealth). In 1910 and 1912, such legislated allocations were unpopular; by 1916 they were unenforceable (Cutileiro 1971, 79).

In order to retain farm labor in the face of industrial competition, farmers needed these projects during the nonharvest seasons; they fought (through their democratic representatives) against wage increases and income transfers to industrial workers. They also lobbied to reestablish some of the more archaic forms of labor control. For these farmers, the unfortunate factor was the proximity of other economic activities that used wage labor and paid higher wages. In conclusion, both political and economic factors eroded the agrarian system of labor control and gave these large landholders reason for opposition to the democratic regime.

Farmers also suffered price declines and market losses at the hands of industrialists, who always preferred the cheaper foreign wheat for urban workers. As bread prices rose, so did the volatility of the urban working classes, and the industrialists had to pay the price to quiet them. Cheaper foreign wheat after 1880 put farmers on the defensive and they had to continually argue for wheat protectionist legislation.

The bourgeois revolution—begun in the nineteenth century and culminating in the 1910 republican revolution—terminated the Portuguese monarchy and many of the traditional forms that accompanied it. Concretely, under the umbrella of the democratic regime, numerous political attacks were launched against the landed aristocracy. The republican regime, and particularly the Democratic party, disturbed the preexisting power balance in the countryside in four major areas: Rural laborers were granted the right to organize as a class; provisions were created for rent contracts rather than more restrictive arrangements such as share-cropping; the transfer of income and labor out of agriculture was encouraged; and land reform designed to redistribute private and public lands to the land-less, thereby robbing farmers of their rural labor supply, was instituted.

Under the Republic, citizens were given the right to form class-based organizations. Rural workers in the southeast, like other workers around the country, took advantage of this opportunity. During the three months that followed the revolution, there were eighty strikes throughout Portugal (Ventura 1977, 20), and landowners were forced to grant wage concessions. The first congress of rural workers was held in Evora on 25–26 April 1912. Rural unions continued to multiply throughout that year and 1913. The right to organize had begun what looked like a shift in the balance of power away from landlords toward the peasants.

In 1911 changes were made in the tenancy laws, giving some protection to peasant renters and sharecroppers (Payne 1973, 560). The 24 May 1911 decree explicitly mentions *enfiteuse* as an obstacle to the alienation and division of property, contrary to economic development, and prejudicial to agricultural development. In 1916 a change in the tax structure was proposed that would favor long-term rents over other forms of contracting rural labor. This move was vigorously opposed by the farmers' association (ACAP 1916, 174). However, it seemed to have little permanent success on this issue; in 1922 ACAP was still protesting the "liberalism" of land legislation (1922, 63).

In response to the wheat crisis of the early 1920s, the government proposed land reforms. The landowners countered with their own proposals, the restoration of the *enfiteuse* being among them. Nuno de Gusmão, in a conference organized by the landowners, asked, "What good is land which has been freed?" (ACAP 1922, 64). For the landowners, legislation abolishing entailments (*vinculos*) was a mortal blow to the rural aristocracy. Renting, the owners argued, led to the exhaustion of land because renters only cared to maximize their short-term gains and were never motivated to reinvest. Not only did owners think that renting was counterproductive, they also found it politically pernicious. "Renting, (helped by a spectacular pro-paganda effort) had given rise to two bolshevik farm unions" (ACAP 1922, 66). Farmers preferred the traditional forms of labor control, and they opposed the Democratic party, which tampered with those forms.

Such legislation would have achieved what the peasantry itself had not been able to do—break the omnipotent power of the landed aristocracy. Consequently, the landed aristocracy fought back with whatever tools were available to it. The Democratic party's attempts to implement land reform were met by military coups. The 1917/18 interim military dictatorship of Sidónio Pais (with support from both individual landholders and the political party representing landowners, PUR) followed upon the heels of a Democratic party proposal for land reform (the project of Lima Basto). Between then and the end of the democratic regime, there was much talk, even on the part of "conservative republicans," of expropriating land (ACAP 1920, 2). The proposed land reforms of the Democratic party (authorship: Ezequiel de Campos) in 1925 preceded the successful military coup that terminated democratic rule.

Although republican legislators did fashion these attacks on the landholding classes, one cannot conclude that the republicans were encouraging a peasant revolution. At the time that these republicans were attempting to alter the nature of agricultural landholdings, they were also using force of law against the peasantry when it seemed appropriate. The National Republican Guard (GNR) was sent out against striking rural workers in Evora in 1913 (Ventura 1977, 28), and the cavalry was sent out by democratic Prime Minister Afonso Costa against rural workers in Elvas, where some thirty were imprisoned (Ventura 1976). Due to repression and co-optation of rural leaders into the different republican parties, peasant organizations and activities declined after their 1913 peak.

Among the nonrural upper classes, little doubt exists that the bourgeoisie abdicated to the military dictatorship—some of them even courted, advocated, and subsidized the 1926 coup. ACL was the first association to voice its collaboration with the "patriotic goals" of the army (1926, 38). ACL wrote that, given daily aggravations, disorder, and the necessity of some administrative change, it was not surprising to see a national movement like the twenty-eighth of May or to see the army take it upon itself to renovate public administration. In a similar fashion, AIp recorded in its journal, O trabalho nacional, that the May 28 intervention of the army was received warmly and that the association was absolutely confident in the ability of the military to steer the national destiny (1927, 813). AIp spoke for other economic associations of Oporto (commerce, industry, wine producers—eleven in all) when it saluted the new president, expressing satisfaction with his success in establishing tranquillity (1927, 814). Many capitalists had feared the working classes and the progressive dismemberment of the state apparatus.

The democratic Republic brought freedom to organize, vote, and strike, and the working classes of Portugal utilized all of these. Throughout the Republic, the workers struck, protested, and rioted for a larger share of the national income. Workers' militancy was high soon after the declaration of the Republic. Between 1910 and 1914, 257 strikes were recorded. A general strike was called in 1912 (Oliveira 1974, 256), which led to a state of emergency: Lisbon was placed

under military rule for one month; thousands were arrested; and union headquarters were closed. The working classes took a new place in the national political scene in 1917 with the founding of CGTP (Medeiros 1978, 10). In some circumstances, they were successful; in others, they actually lost their political
power (for example, they lost their franchise, strikes were prohibited, and they
were denied the right to organize).

Although the Industrial Association of Portugal (AIP) lauded class associations that existed for the purpose of studying and developing their respective
branch of the economy or facilitating credit and machine purchases, it decried
"pure syndicalism" as revolutionary and rotten. According to AIp, bombings
were the only result of the Portuguese imitation of French law on class associations (1917/18, 106). Farmers to merchants feared the working classes, and the
1917 October Russian revolution raised their anxiety level even more. In the
House of Representatives, Deputy Cunha Leal declared, "The hour is grave for
the bourgeois state—it will win or go to the morgue" (Portugal, *Diário* 30 April
1920, 22). The speaker was criticizing Prime Minister Pereira of the twenty-
second cabinet for his lenient treatment of the railway strikers. Such condescen-
sion, the speaker claimed, is responsible more and more for the ruin of industry.

In its 1920/21 report, ACL complained about the atmosphere of terror caused
by increased strikes and bombings (124) and again, in the 1924 report, about
a new bomb wave (36). The major economic associations remonstrated against
the intense level of civil unrest. In March 1922 and again in November 1925,
the headquarters of AIP was the target of bomb attacks. The association attributed responsibility to the working classes, which, it said, were infiltrated by riff-
raff. ACL wrote that "the productive forces of today live in a regime of terror.
The attempted assassination two days ago against the industrialist Correia da
Silva is only another manifestation. A group of trouble makers exists in Lisbon
and the continuation of such a situation is impossible. It is not possible to direct
any company under such circumstances" (ACL 1924, 39).

ACL blamed government negligence for the assaults upon commercial establishments, even accusing the government of intentionally ignoring advance
warnings about such uprisings. The association called for the reorganization
of the police force to guarantee public security by cleaning the city of bums
and rabble-rousers (ACL 1924, 39). Even though the crimes were allegedly committed by members of international associations, ACL charged that the government often absolved the criminals when they were apprehended (1924, 37). Finally, the farmers' association asked in 1924, Why in organized societies, where
the exclusive function of the state is to repress troublemakers, do such people
continue to exist? The public powers have a responsibility to restore order without hesitation, using painful measures if necessary (ACAP 1924, 182). This
imperative to order was equally apparent to industrialists of the north: "Industry does not have a party . . . nor does it occupy itself with points of doctrinal
views, of administration, or forms of government. What it desires is order, ad-

ministrative regularity, economic growth, an active life and hard work" (AIp 1917/18, 51).

Civil unrest, strikes, bombings, assaults on commercial establishments, assassinations, and so on interfered with the work of production, and so economic interest groups pleaded with the government to enforce order. An editorial in the AIp journal laid out what it thought were the functions of the state: "The maintenance of public order must be the first obligation of the state" (1917/18, 117). Disorder, in the view of ACL, required intelligent action by the state and it was not forthcoming (1917, 94). "The productive forces can only be profitable when they can exercise their profession in liberty and order" (ACL 1919, 84).

In 1927, after the military had taken power, AIp justified the political change on these same grounds: "Without order, neither work, the development of wealth, nor general well-being to which all classes are entitled is possible" (1927, 816). These elements were summed up in A crise nacional (1926), in which the author, Anselmo Vieira, listed the faults of the Republic. Yet neither criticism of the democratic regime nor desires for an alternative one are sufficient conditions for democratic collapse. Complaints about democratic instability and preferences for nondemocratic regimes do not in themselves constitute political crises and do not explain the collapse of regimes. A selected reading that focuses generally on these complaints and preferences will encourage those supportive of Moore's argument that the relative strength of the agrarian, landowning classes accounted for the ultimate political outcome of fascism; whereas another selected reading of the complaints and preferences of emergent industrialists will encourage those supportive of theories of "strong states" for economic growth. But how can they both be true? Although complaints and preferences are important elements in any analysis of the Portuguese case, they leave unanswered the question of how such preferences were translated into a transformation of the state and why it happened when it did. Thus complaints and preferences may be necessary factors, but they are not sufficient. On the other hand, an analysis of the generalized withdrawal of legitimacy brings us closer to explaining the collapse of the Portuguese democratic state. Democratic institutions rest upon the organized legitimacy of society, and to the extent that legitimacy is withdrawn, rule by consent becomes impossible.

CONCLUSION

This chapter employs elements from three of the models described in chapter 1: historiography, instability, and individual volitions. All three have been offered as explanations for democratic collapse. Historians of the First Republic (Marques 1976; Wheeler 1978) have attributed the collapse of the Portuguese democratic regime to individuals and their influence on the course of history. Testimonies indicate a heightened sense of personality conflict and its consequence for political party factionalization and general unpheaval. Numerous works reflect on personalities and interpersonality conflict. In this light, Wheeler (1978) gives us interesting detail in his discussion of the interim dictator, Sidónio Pais (1917–1918)—"probably an unstable personality" (154). Later he describes the conflict between the outspoken politician Leal, ("vitriolic and slanderous") and Norton de Matos, high commissioner of Angola (1978, 219). This kind of portrait could easily be embellished with accounts of the key individuals in the monarchist invasions, coup attempts, and civilian uprisings. Such accounts enrich our visual images of the period, but their intent seems to be to overwhelm more than persuade the reader of the veracity of the argument. Confronted with an impressive list of personality-party conflicts, the reader is hard pressed to deny the linkage. Yet such explanatory models are heavily ex post facto and ad hoc. No one has suggested a threshold at which personality conflict would bring down a democratic regime. Rather than offering the history of political parties and personalities as the explanation for the collapse of the Portuguese democratic regime, I want to explain why it was that party factions appeared so frequently, and why personality conflicts were so intense that they *appeared* to be the major force accounting for social change.[4] The second factor—the instability of political institutions—also has been offered as the explanation for the Republic's collapse (Linz 1978).

Rather than explain the collapse in terms of the withdrawal of legitimacy and political instability, I want to explain why there was too much instability in the first place. And, finally, much current work would turn to the desires and preferences of individuals as the major construct of social processes. I have suggested that many such preferences preexisted the collapse, and preferences for social change do not perforce mean social change. Rather than offering them as the explanation for the democratic collapse, I want to explain why preferences for a different political regime came about, and how some preferences were translated into collective action at one time rather than at another.

These elements (personalities, parties, political preferences, and the Republic's loss of legitimacy) all constitute important pieces of the analysis: They are actually precipitating conditions. They were all visible and appeared prior to the final democratic collapse. Perhaps it was their visibility and temporality that gained them such a notable and tenacious place in accounts and explanations of the collapse. Still, instability, political crises, and withdrawal of legitimacy do not constitute a closed causal system. To the contrary, they need to be explained to the same extent as the democratic collapse. All of them must be demoted from the status of "explanation" and relabeled as phenomena "to be explained." The question is not just, Why did the democratic regime collapse? It is also, Why was the regime so beset with institutional instability and personality and party conflicts?

Perhaps the collapse of a juridical form of state (formal democracy) was the political recognition of the untenability of the socioeconomic pact. In other

PART TWO

The Socioeconomic Structure
of Democratic Instability

Location in the world-system is consequential for a country in two fundamental ways: structurally and conjuncturally. First, the world-system impinges through the internalization or "domesticization" of global structural arrangements. Second, it impinges in the particular way in which societies receive and absorb crises or shifts unleashed at the world-system level. In the following section, the dual world economy influence on Portugal is delineated.

Chapter 3 begins with a discussion of the impact of turn-of-the-century world transformations on Portuguese society. Portugal was an agricultural country that participated in the world market as an agro-exporter and a trader. However, late nineteenth-century transformations in the world economy had precipitated a crisis in Portugal of such magnitude that it undermined both the traditional economy and the political keeper of that project, the monarchy.

Chapter 4 examines the structural consequences of position in the world-system, presenting evidence for the claim that, at the turn of the century, Portugal was a semiperipheral country. Its semiperipheral place in the world-system was translated internally into a disarticulated economy. This economy — an economy of multiple sectors with little interaction among them — was the material base for multiple bourgeois interests.

Chapter 5 presents the alternatives offered by various sectors of Portuguese society to extract the country from its economic crisis and to launch it on a growth trajectory.

A conceptual apparatus is needed to connect these economic processes and structures (semiperipherality, economic crisis, disarticulated economy, and alternative economic projects) with political processes and structures. In all cases, the economic processes outlined in the following chapters had political counterparts. The misery of the falling terms of trade of the nineteenth century was transported into the political realm and became the political crisis out of which republicanism was born. Although the monarchy (albeit not the monarch) received the death sentence, the economic crisis that the world economy had bestowed upon Portugal did not. It was transferred to the hands of republicans. The debate among alternative economic trajectories was likewise transported into the political arena of the democratic state.

As is clear from this brief description, the conceptual apparatus relies heavily on the world-system framework. It also relies on the work of Gramsci. Gramsci was concerned with explaining the relations between the economic base and political and ideological superstructure, particularly as it related to the modalities of class domination (Jessop 1982, 147). For Gramsci, the two ways in which dominant classes could maintain their power in society were through force and through consent. Both mechanisms of domination require appropriate institutional apparatuses — the coercive apparatus of the state implements force while the societal-wide construction of consent maintains hegemonic control. His work dealt with the interplay and consequences of these two mechanisms of control.

The notion of hegemony provides a useful tool in analyzing Portuguese societal processes and the dynamics among them. Gramsci's epistemology was not deterministic: Political practice is not directly reducible to fundamental economic relations. Economic effects, and they certainly exist, are mediated by political forces and ideological practices (Jessop 1982, 145). This means that economic crises may weaken states but will not always result in great historical events or regime changes. Gramsci was concerned with the conditions under which such a linkage could take place. The notion of hegemony plays an important role, but it is an abstract concept and so throughout this book, I have used the term projects as its operationalization.

Projects are at one and the same time visions of how society should be organized economically, how that organization will promote general economic development, and what material basis will permit other groups to be integrated into the project. They are "forces which have the universalistic goals of problem solving for society at large" (Gramsci 1971, 168). Concretely, projects are blueprints for the socioeconomic organization — the policies necessary to install that organization. Each project is proposed by a dominant group or a group contending for that position. The economic project is the material basis of a hegemonic ideology, one that is of crucial importance when we talk about maintaining dominance through consent.

When dominance is maintained hegemonically (through consent), it implies a compromise between the dominant and dominated. Thus dominance must offer material satisfaction, not only for the dominant group but also for supporting or dependent groups. In addition, given that it is hegemonic and not installed by force, it must contain an accepted ideology that claims hegemony, that is, proclaiming its own economic interests as the general interest of the nation (the "capitalists appear as bearers of universal interests"—Przeworski 1980, 27). It is the basis for the symbiotic relationship among the classes in a broad sense. Compromise is constructed in the economic, political, and ideological realms, which means that a project contains an economic initiative, a political initiative, and an ideological initiative.

This dominance acquires the label of hegemonic to the extent that the interests of the dominant group are presented or "coordinated concretely with the general interests of the subordinate groups, and the life of the State is conceived of as a continuous process of formation and superseding of unstable equilibria

. . . between the interests of the fundamental group and those of the subordinate groups " (Gramsci 1971, 182).

Projects are the work horses that connect the economic and political. In this light, the chapters in part 2 can be redescribed. Chapter 3 describes nineteenth-century economic organization — the agro-export project; its corresponding bourgeoisie, which maintained dominance of that project through politics and ideology; and the project's decline. However, the presence or absence of such projects, and the viability of some over others, had much to do with Portugal's location in the world-system. At this point, the analysis informed by Gramsci's framework can be reinserted in that informed by world-system analysis. Because Portugal had a semiperipheral economy (chapter 4), certain projects — alternatives to the declining agro-export project — were more viable than others. Both the semiperipherality and the viability of alternative projects were influenced by the world economy at the turn of the century. It was a world economy in which major economic powers fought wars for world supremacy both in markets and on battlefields.

In chapter 5, I present the various candidates for the new hegemonic project that would integrate Portugal into this world that was being constructed by other nations. The development of a national economy and of a nation-state cannot be viewed in isolation; rather, it must be understood in terms of the overall development of the world-system — not only the location of an individual country but also changes in the system as a whole.

To preview my concluding position, I argue that neither economic development nor political organization are totally reducible to location in the world-system. Neither the economic nor the political turns that Portugal took in the beginning of the twentieth century could have been read directly from a knowledge of its nineteenth-century economy. Thus we are back at Gramsci's problem of mediation by political and ideological forces. In part 3 of this book, I take the just-elaborated structural and conjunctural analysis of the economy and show how it was mediated by political forces.

CHAPTER 3

The Death of a Project

This chapter describes the traditional economic project: How it managed to maintain its dominance historically, and why and how that dominance began to unravel. In the face of shifting relations in the world economy, Portugal faced a crisis of development. The old economic project could no longer guarantee the livelihood of those tied to it, and the depletion of the project brought with it an economic and political crisis. Both contributed to the 1910 collapse of Portugal's monarchical rule.

THE DOMINANCE OF EXPORTERS AND EMPORIUMS

Portugal was a trading nation; therein lay its past glory. For centuries, commerce had been the most clearly articulated ideology and hegemonically entrenched project in Portuguese society. The hegemonic claim rested on the grounds that Portugal had the prerequisites for organizing the economy in this fashion and that this economic arrangement benefited all members of society. The hegemonic ideology was built upon a sound base, namely, Portugal's geographic position: "Portugal, which was of indisputable value in economic history, accomplished this historic maritime, commercial and colonial function, in large part because of its exceptional geographic position" (Gomes 1919, 3).

Because of its optimal location on the trade circuits, Portugal prospered in the mid-fifteenth century. The Portuguese economy was tantamount to a revolving door into which entered merchandise—first from the Arabian world, then from India, and finally from the colonies—only to exit again to other European nations. Portugal was like a vast fair where everything was bought and sold. In this immense marketplace, magnates, soldiers, sailors, and citizens all fraternized and disputed in the battle for the immense Indian riches that seemed to be inexhaustible (Vieira 1926, 23). Bullion was so abundant that merchants, ladened down with sacks of gold and silver to pay for already received merchandise, were sometimes turned away by Lisbon customs officers, who could not keep up with the accounting (Vieira 1926, 26). Wealth was spent frantically, and everywhere was an ostentation that Oliveira Martins called "Babylonian" (Vieira 1926, 24). Nobles wore their wealth in expensive clothing and jewels; monarchs built extravagant churches. When one monarch was advised that the price of constructing the bell tower on the Convent of Mafra was exorbitant, he ordered a second to be built (ACL 1916, 301). Rivers of gold flowed first from Indian spices and then from Brazilian gold mines.

These trade activities were integrated with the agricultural sector of the economy both through the individuals involved and through the marketplace. The king was first of all — before, during, and after any commercial venture — a landowner. Land was the source of wealth for overseas expeditions. To the extent that commercial profits were not eaten, worn, or "leafed" onto churches, they were invested in land. As the greatest landlord in Portugal, the king was the embodiment of the linkage between commerce and agriculture. Following his example, nobles did not hesitate (when they were allowed) to try their luck in transportation and commerce. Unlike in Italy where the bourgeoisie rose to nobility, in Portugal the aristocracy exercised trade as a means of enriching its households (Marques 1972, 1:181).

Fluidity between merchant capital and rural landed capital increased with the liberal revolution of the mid-1800s. One of the consequences of that liberal revolution was the break-up of royal and clerical lands and their sale to the bourgeoisie. This created the conditions for the entrance of immobile rural capital into the circuits of commerce (Castro 1971, 59–60) and of commercial capital into land.

Toward the end of the nineteenth century, the colonial products (spices, gold, slaves, and so on) that had formed the basis of trading activities were supplemented with domestic agricultural products. Rather than trade following agricultural surpluses, the reverse was the case; with the security of an external market, certain kinds of domestic agriculture flourished. From 1847 to 1890, agriculture was the most dynamic sector in the Portuguese economy, producing wine, fruit, cattle, and cork, along with minerals for export (Pereira 1979, 20). The heightened commercialization of these foodstuffs and raw materials led to the intensification of their production. For example, as the price of wine rose, farmers, where they could, converted their fields to grapes. The intensification of agricultural production was particularly evident in areas near seaports and railroad lines where the exit of produce was guaranteed. The trade project existed symbiotically with an agro-export one.

The importance of the agro-export and trade project can be described quantitatively beginning in the third quarter of the nineteenth century. Judging from the trade profile, little transformation in the export character took place from 1874 to 1935 (table 3.1). From 1875 to 1935, Portugal tenaciously retained its export character. The combined exports of live animals, raw materials (of animal, vegetable, and mineral origin), and foodstuffs (including beverages) comprised more than 95 percent of exports in 1874; these same exports dropped to 85 percent by 1900 and still hovered above that point in 1935. The dominant export was, of course, wine. Both in terms of its weight in the total exported value (averaging 34 percent between 1910 and 1926) and in terms of the actual volume of export (index = 100 in 1875, and 186 in 1929), wine retained an unequivocal importance. More than half of the exports were made up of wine

Table 3.1. Exports for Major Customs Categories, Selected Years from
          1874 to 1935 (in percentages)

Year	Live Animals	Raw Materials	Threads and Textiles	Foodstuffs and Beverages	Machinery and Utensils	Diverse Manufactures
1874	5	42	2	49 (40)	0	2
1885	6	30	1	61 (57)	0	2
1892	3	19	2	71 (55)	1	5
1903	14	20	6	53 (33)	1	7
1915	2	23	7	60 (31)	1	7
1925	0	22	6	66 (36)	1	5
1935	1	30	8	52 (24)	1	8

Note: Percentages in parentheses for wine exports only.
Source: Calculated from Portugal, Ministério das Finanças, *Comércio e navegação* (Lisbon: Imprensa Nacional, 1872–1920).

(and a majority of that from Oporto), fruits, raw cork, wool, and salt. Two-thirds of the colonial products obtained by Portugal were again reexported. Finished cork stoppers were the only "industrial product" that Portugal exported in any quantity, whereas industrial and finished goods counted heavily among its imports.

With this emphasis on agro-exporting, Portugal did not produce consumer goods; it imported them. Portugal, being a trader par excellence, developed a virtual dependency on other countries for its necessities, industrial as well as agricultural. Its enormous mercantile expansion, originating in its maritime discoveries, rendered it dependent on European markets. Precisely because it had the currency to do so, Portugal bought most of what it needed; it produced little. Portugal remained a trading country with little industrial development. In the seventeenth century, it exported cotton yet had not one cloth factory. The pattern of imports poignantly reveals Portugal's dependent nature. It imported not only finished goods and capital goods, but it also had to import foodstuffs due to an inefficient and nonproductive agricultural system (table 3.2).

The natural proclivities of seaside or grape production are not in themselves so deterministic that a certain kind of socioeconomic order had to develop. Bukharin argues that it is quite possible for natural resources to be dead capital (1967, 20). Such natural proclivities constitute only the first step in understanding social organization. The dominance of trade and agro-exports was maintained politically. What began with a natural proclivity resulting from maritime position and experience was renewed by the sheer force of first the king, second Britain, and last the market. What may have appeared as economic advantage (gold to purchase cheaper foreign goods) was solidified by the more awesome rule of the monarchs and their Anglo-Portuguese treaties.

Table 3.2. Imports for Major Customs Categories, Selected Years from
1874 to 1935 (in percentages)

Year	Live Animals	Raw Materials	Threads and Textiles	Foodstuffs and Beverages	Machinery and Utensils	Diverse Manufactures
1874	3	43	22	23	0	9
1885	3	42	16	28	0	11
1892	1	40	12	35	6	7
1903	6	45	12	23	6	8
1915	0	50	9	29	5	7
1925	1	34	12	33	12	9
1935	1	46	5	15	22	11

Source: Calculated from Portugal, Ministério das Finanças, Comércio e navegação (Lisbon: Imprensa Nacional, 1872–1920).

Until the 1820s, the king was the principal organizer of commercial activities. For example, he gathered the capital necessary for maritime explorations. And, inversely, the king received more income from trading activities than he received in feudal dues.

Financially, the Crown depended neither on nobles nor on land, but on the nutritious sea and the merchant bourgeoisie which it supported in times of depression by its policy of industrialization and chartering privileged companies. On the other hand, through its own commercial activities, the state competed with private business . . . thus preventing the flowering of Portuguese capitalism (Godinho 1971, 12).

In 1515 overseas trade represented 68 percent of the Portuguese crown's resources; in 1607, 45 percent; and in the 1700s, trade with Brazil produced most of the crown's revenues (Marques 1972, 1:278). In 1506 the king declared all imports, sales of spices, silk, and shellac, exports of gold, silver, copper, and coral, together with all trade between Goa and other places, to be official royal monopolies. Only the crown could equip and send ships to the Indian Ocean. In Brazil, the crown owned the brazilwood, slaves, spices, and drug monopolies, along with a fifth part of all ores and precious stones. By depriving settlers of the major and easier source of profits, the crown practically compelled them to develop agriculture and create alternative sources of revenue. This undoubtedly inhibited the rise of an autonomous merchant class but encouraged the rise of the sugar industry. This pattern of royal monopoly was followed in Angola with the slave trade.

The Methuen Treaty, signed by Portugal and England in 1703, inscribed in international law the supremacy that England had achieved over Portugal in their bilateral trade relationship. Portugal would export its wines to England at one-third the tariff rate paid by France for its wines. In exchange, the Portuguese monarchy agreed to import English wool cloth "forever" without any duties.[1] The English benefited from penetrating the Portuguese market — in the return freight on wine moving to England and in their access to the Brazilian gold that flowed through the Portuguese treasury (Serrão 1976, 237).

When the monarchy lost some of its absolute powers in 1820, and the state became divorced from the king, several other changes occurred. Separate budgets meant that the benefits accruing to the state from commercial activity had to be extracted in a different manner. Although the state was no longer a merchant, it skimmed off a share of commercial profits by making Lisbon a compulsory harbor for colonial trade destined to European nations (Marques 1972, 1:261). Despite the formal separation of the royalty and the state, political rule was still in the hands of an oligarchy made up of the landowning classes. The ties of agro-exports and trade to landowners served to guarantee the perpetuation of an economic system even as it bore less and less fruit for society as a whole. In conclusion, the economic arrangement was rooted unequivocally in natural proclivities (maritime activity and an agricultural product amenable to export) but was reproduced and reinforced by a certain sociopolitical configuration.

SOCIOECONOMIC CONSEQUENCES OF
THE AGRO-EXPORT PROJECT

Throughout the nineteenth century, the development of agriculture and commerce was based upon European markets. These export activities contributed to the growth of the domestic market and rises in the level of consumption (Pereira 1979, 76). The wealth generated by agricultural and merchant activities contributed not only to the well-being of several sectors but also, as we have seen, to the solvency of the state.

Yet from the beginning of the project, visions were short. Monarchs preferred to gain large profits on small quantities of merchandise rather than modest profits from more established long-term commercial ventures. This myopic vision[2] of commercial activities was accompanied, according to Vieira, by the impulse to establish Portuguese colonies in all discovered territories (1926, 23). To do so required expenditures — for the construction of forts and for the maintenance of administrative posts and armies. This constituted a tremendous drain on the Portuguese treasury, contributing to the decline of Portugal from a world empire to a semiperipheral state.

Agricultural and commercial development characterized the economy until 1890 (Pereira 1979, 76). Some scholars maintain that this social arrangement was clearly favorable to the growth of a national market and that the prosperity of the social strata linked to the commercial and agricultural activities allowed for expanded consumption. On the other hand, economic growth was constrained because the fortunes of the agro-export and trade system were tied to the fates of the world market. Inasmuch as commercial agriculture flourished precisely because of international trading, the welfare of agriculture paralleled the welfare of trade. This commercial penetration of the countryside in the eighteenth and nineteenth centuries led to the substitution of grapes for cereals. "It is exactly this process which is seen in Portugal during the nineteenth century; a rapid extension of the capitalist sector of agriculture, frequently characterized by substitution of cereal cultivation by more profitable ones" (Pereira 1972, 494).

When trade wavered, agricultural income suffered. The agricultural crisis in northern Portugal followed upon the heels of the decline of exports to Brazil after 1815 (Ruíz 1980, 780).[3] The subsequent discovery of markets in Africa resurrected some of that agriculture, notably wine. The prohibition of indigenous production of alcoholic beverages in the African colonies and an increase in the white European population helped to augment that market. A temporary solution having been found, debates about agricultural reform, initiated in the mid-nineteenth century, were tabled. Still the new market, according to Pereira, was unable to restore agricultural production to its earlier levels, and it did little for fruits, vegetables, or livestock. The agro-export project continued to be vulnerable to world market forces.

Another consequence of producing agriculture for export was unbalanced agricultural production resulting in shortages for domestic consumption. At the turn of the century, Portugal was still a predominantly agricultural country: Seventy percent of the population lived in aggregates of less than 2,000; 60 percent of the actively engaged population worked in agriculture; and 80 percent of the merchandise exported from Portugal was animal, vegetable, or derivatives thereof. Yet, in spite of its overwhelmingly agricultural character, Portugal had to import foodstuffs. In 1909 Portugal produced 75 percent of the consumed wheat; the balance had to be imported. The situation was similar with other cereals, such as corn, rye, and rice. The import-export accounts recorded agricultural deficits, as did the whole group of prime materials of agricultural origin. Portugal registered deficits in woods, coal, raw cork, oils, plants, and seeds. Livestock also followed this pattern. Portugal—agricultural in the utilization of its land, agricultural in the occupation of its population, agricultural in the nature of its exports, and agricultural in the receipts of the state—had to import wheat, corn, rice, and sugar. And, in a country with 700,000 kilometers of coastline and 50,000 fishermen, it was necessary to pay foreigners for 38 tons of cod (Alp 1925, 1:395).

The perpetuation of the agro-export and trade project also resulted in the underdevelopment of industry. This effect had already been observed in the sixteenth century. Vieira somewhat sarcastically notes that industry had made progress in every part of the world blessed with colonies except Portugal. The Portuguese failed to grasp that they had an almost unlimited market in the recently discovered continents. Only they, he claims, failed to realize that it would be necessary to dress millions of humans, providing them with manufactured objects that had previously been unknown to them but would soon seem indispensable. Spain had experienced a doubling of factories in Barcelona and Seville (1926, 27). This modest progress was soon nullified, however, by the wide and persistent price differential between peninsular manufactures and manufactures from the rest of Western Europe, a differential that was due, ironically, to the influx of colonial metals. The textile industry collapsed under the pressure of cheaper woolens and silks from northern Italy, France, Holland, and England (Stein and Stein 1970, 15, 16). In Portugal, on the other hand, the introduction of the agro-export and trade project had underdeveloped its industry, first through the political force of the Methuen Treaty and then, by the end of the nineteenth century, through the force of the market. Trade brought foreign competition that damaged domestic industries, from artisan to heavy industry. The hatmaking industry was an example of an artisan industry that was continually under assault from foreign products. In 1890 the newspaper *O protesto operário* published a commentary claiming that the Portuguese hat industry was a dead industry (in Monica 1979, 870). This was its assessment of the impact of bilateral trade treaties with France and Germany that allowed foreign hats to enter the Portuguese market for less than the price of domestic hats. This market invasion was aggravated by the fact that the majority of materials for the domestic hat industry (silk elastic, ribbons, buttons, and so on) were imported and subject to a tax that forced their total cost above the finished foreign hat, even when the foreign item paid an import tax. In the 1880s, German wool hats invaded the Portuguese market. Despite their poorer quality and "half-finished" nature, they sold because they were cheaper than the domestic version. The Portuguese hat industry could not compete with the more modern industries of foreign countries (which for the most part meant machine production with female labor and cheaper raw materials). Finally, there were always new styles of hats appearing on the market that Portugal did not make. In 1882 Portuguese hat producers protested a commercial treaty with France that benefited Portuguese wine producers at the expense of other industries including the hat market. In the late 1880s, hat manufacturers again protested the German intrusion into their market. Some relief arrived with the 1892 protectionist legislation that followed upon the heels of the 1890/91 economic crisis. However, its benefits were eroded over time by interests tied to international commerce (Monica 1979, 875).

The destructive tendencies of trade operated in heavy industry as well. Portugal lacked a cast iron industry, thus all iron consumed in Portugal was cast or forged abroad. Foreign metals went into rails and bridge parts. In addition, large buildings incorporated foreign iron structures, foreign financing, foreign technology, and foreign materials (Monica 1981, 1236). Even ships and equipment purchased by the Portuguese government for the national marine were ordered from abroad.

The presence of foreign capital in the economy resulted in further hesitance to use domestically produced materials. Thus the foreign-owned gas company requested exemption from the 1885 import taxes on iron tubing, claiming that domestic producers could not meet deadlines. Domestic producers charged that the gas company withheld designs and specifications until it was too late to produce the required tubes, thereby necessitating imports (Monica 1981, 1239). The gas company won its requested import tax exemption. Foreign producers often won public bids—not only by promising short-term turnaround but also by bidding lower prices. The import tax structure perpetuated the problem. Although the tax was low (3–4 percent) on imported finished machinery, the domestic industry had to pay a higher tax (7 percent) on imported raw materials and therefore could not produce competitively priced machinery for the domestic market.

In 1909 the association of metallurgical workers complained that their industry had become dormant. In 1919 an editorialist complained that the metallurgy industry produced only rudimentary apparatuses; in 1921 a plea was presented at the congress of metallurgists for the development of a steel industry in Portugal, arguing that it was the base of industrial progress (Monica 1981, 1233). Then and later, advocates pointed out that hydroelectric energy was available and could save Portugal from the necessity of importing British coal. The socioeconomic effects of this historic underdevelopment of industry were long lasting. In 1933 the newspaper O metalúrgico complained of the weakness of the industry. In short, continuous trade of industrialized and finished items led to the destruction of Portuguese industries producing their counterparts.

The balance of the economic system was bankruptcy. From the sixteenth century on, Portugal registered negative commercial balances and even bankruptcies. As early as the sixteenth century, the king was forced to consolidate the external debt with large loans (at exorbitant interest rates) and with the sale of taxation rights. In the midst of the gold and spice influx, in the midst of those days of "too much gold," King Sebastão declared bankruptcy in 1568. And again, in 1903 as the monarchy was about to collapse, King Carlos declared bankruptcy. Portugal, the grand emporium, turning over an enormous volume of both merchandise and gold, sent that gold to pay off foreign debts.

When not driven to bankruptcy, the country maintained a negative balance of payments. From 1810 the commercial balance was persistently negative— Portugal imported more merchandise than it exported. Numerous trade indices recorded the heavy role of imports: the first index (table 3.3) shows that from 1880 to 1935 the value of imports always exceeded exports—the index never reaches 100. This foreign trade profile is an operationalization of what Gomes calls a "defective economic organization" (1919, 63).

Whereas once the agro-export and trade project had brought wealth to the

Table 3.3. Balance of Foreign Trade (value of
exports divided by imports times 100)

1880	76	1910	51
1885	69	1915	44
1890	49	1920	32
1895	68	1925	35
1900	52	1930	39
1905	48	1935	40

Source: Calculated from Portugal, Ministério das Finanças,
Comércio e navegação (Lisbon: Imprensa Nacional,
1872–1920).

empire, or at least to those politically dominant in the empire, by the end of
the nineteenth century, it brought debts to the state and poverty to the majority
of its citizens. How did this come about?

DECLINE OF THE AGRO-EXPORT AND TRADE PROJECT

The decline of the economy built upon the marriage of agro-exports and international commerce was not really sudden; rather, it resulted from a slow but
steady erosion of several pillars that had supported it. Erosion resulted from the
changing nature of economic exchanges in the world economy and from changes
in the world polity.

One area of erosion was found in international exchanges. To the extent that
Portugal did not accompany the rapid rhythm of development of the more
developed world, particularly of its main trading partners, the vitality of the
wine and merchant system was challenged. The price indices for imports and
exports moved at different velocities after 1895 (when they were each scored as
100). By 1910 imports had risen to 131, whereas exports had risen to only 110
(Castro 1973, 259). This nonparallel level of economic development can also be
seen in declining terms of trade between Portugal and its major trading partner.
Two terms-of-trade indices are presented below, one for general trade with Britain and one for the wine/textile exchanges. The unequal exchange between
Portugal and Britain is most striking in the wine/textile terms of trade that
historically represented the main merchandise flows between the two countries
(table 3.4). It is even more amazing in light of what was happening to Britain
at the time. According to Amin, the terms of trade were favorable for raw-
material exporters from 1800 to 1880; around 1880, the terms of trade turned
favorable to Britain (Amin 1976, 163). This benefit to raw-material producers
was not reflected in the Portuguese-British terms-of-trade indices; to the contrary, they fell during this period. Portugal remained in an unfavorable exchange
with Britain no matter what Britain's position was in the world economy.

Table 3.4. Portuguese Terms of Trade with Britain (1854 = 100)

Years	Wine/Textiles[a]	Wine as % of Total Exports for First Year	Textiles as % of Total Imports for First Year	General
1855–64	114.5	—	—	96.3
1865–74	58.9	—	—	95.4
1875–84	98.0	40[b]	22	104.7
1885–94	108.5	57	16	99.5
1895–1904	127.7	42	12[c]	99.2
1905–13	88.6	36	12[d]	67.0
1914–23	66.7	36	09	67.7
1924–33	25.5	33	11	75.8
1934–38	38.9	32	06	79.7

[a]Index given for first year in each grouping.
[b]Percentage of total exports for 1874.
[c]Percentage of total imports for 1892.
[d]Percentage of total imports for 1903.

Source: S. Sideri, Trade and Power (Rotterdam, Neth.: Rotterdam University Press, 1970), 258, 312.

The wine/textile terms of trade from the 1870s suggest that the principal agro-export provided less and less of the revenue needed to cover the value of the textile imports. Because the wine/textile terms-of-trade index is highly selective, it misstates the overall secular decline of the trade project. First, the wine/textile ratio underestimates the precarious state of the agro-export and trade project because it is based upon textiles, which actually experienced a reduction in price. One of the results of early industrialization was to lower the price of finished products such as textiles. In the long run, however, the price shift is in the other direction. The fruits of technological progress in industry are transferred to the producers (the workers) of manufactured goods, whereas the fruits of technological progress in agriculture are transferred to the consumers of food and raw materials (Singer 1950, 478).

Second, the increasing price gap that existed between wine and textiles was even truer for capital goods, and the latter represented an increasing portion of the imports. In 1910 textiles, although representing a major proportion of the imports from Britain, represented only 10 percent of the total import bill. Some of this drop is due to the fact that Portuguese textile production was on the rise. More significant, however, was the fact that machinery and other finished products that had much higher unit costs had been added to the import bill. The prices of these goods reflected the cost increases in manufacturing inputs in Britain. The terms of trade turned against Portugal toward the end of the 1800s and began a deterioration that was to appear irreversible, at least until 1933.

This deterioration in the exchange is suggestive of the more general trend: unequal economic development between Portugal and its trading partners. Not only did the trend portend long-run economic difficulties but, in the short run, it also eroded the base of the agro-export/merchant system. The legitimacy of such a system derived from sufficiently high levels of agro-export income that allowed the imports of necessary goods ranging from food and clothing to machinery. To the extent that what was sold abroad increasingly offered diminished returns, the Portuguese would have to restrict their consumption or find alternative sources of income to cover the import bill. Decreasing returns on agro-export products led to attempts to save the agro-export project. Attempts to secure more markets often placed producers in a downward spiral: An increase in wine production resulted in overproduction and a depression in prices, thereby aggravating the problem even further. Feverish replanting, for example, followed the 1887 phylloxera outbreak and led to overproduction and a fall in prices in the first decade of the twentieth century. On the other hand, treaties to secure wine markets carried with them reciprocal trade obligations that only furthered the penetration of foreign manufactured goods into the Portuguese market. For example, in a 1908 treaty with Germany, Portugal received the concession of placing more wine in the German market with tariffs equal to Italian wines, and Portugal's monopoly along with the terms Port and Madeira were recognized. In exchange, preferential treatment was accorded to German goods, which subsequently flooded the Portuguese market, putting new pressure on the balance of payments (Sideri 1970, 160).

The nonparallel rates of economic development were also obvious in the realms of technology and quality control. Although these are not factors to which I would assign great weight in the decline of the agro-export and trade system, they did have an impact on Portugal's share of the foreign market. The Commercial Association of Oporto (ACP) registered British complaints of receiving port wine of an inferior alcohol count (less than 7.5 degrees or 15 percent proof) (ACP 1924, 29:16). Britain was also an important market for fruits, and the Lisbon commercial association had complaints on file about these products. Grapes were exported in wooden cartons that, the complaints alleged, often had an undesirable flavor of resin and sawdust. In addition, the grape season was extremely short — only from the end of August to the beginning of September. The Spanish, in contrast, exported their grapes in cork containers and had an export season that extended from September until the next July. Based upon other complaints, the commercial association besieged respective producers to provide cleaner bottles for wine and to reduce the excessive acidity and unpleasant odors in olive oil. From the perspective of the commercial association, such inadequate quality control and lack of technological innovation would lead to a Spanish conquest of the Portuguese market, a reasonably correct assessment.

Table 3.5. Weight and Nationality of Merchant Fleet Entering
Portuguese Ports, Selected Years from 1886 to 1926
(percentage of total ship capacity, in tons)

Year	Portuguese	German	British
1886	24	11	45
1890	22	14	45
1895	21	16	45
1900	16	16	50
1905	13	27	47
1910	9	27	44
1915	13	—	52
1926	13	18	34

Note: The percentage of tonnage that these three countries had in cargo when
leaving Portuguese ports was very similar.
Source: Calculated from Portugal, Ministério das Finanças, Comércio e navegação (Lisbon: Imprensa Nacional, 1872–1920).

A final factor that both reflected and contributed to the erosion of the trading
system was the condition of the merchant marine. This factor is likewise a derivative of the unequal rates of economic growth. In spite of its glorious maritime
history, the floating stock of the merchant marine was diminished, and Portugal
became increasingly dependent on foreign flag ships for its trade activities. By
1910 the Portuguese fleet only handled a small portion of the commercial cargo
(table 3.5). Although the color of the flag mattered little, the prices, routes,
frequency of sailings, and, of course, shipping profits mattered a great deal.
With foreign flags, control of these factors was removed from the hands of exporters, leaving the Portuguese shipper little leverage. Sailing under foreign
flags meant additional costs were added onto the export products, making them
either less competitive at the point of destination or less lucrative to the shippers
and producers.

Foreign flag ships could not always be counted upon to pursue the routes that
were most profitable for the agro-export sector, especially those connecting Brazil and Africa with the northern Portuguese port of Oporto. Many obstacles were
encountered in persuading foreign lines to service these destinations. In 1921,
for example, a foreign cargo line justified its higher prices at Portuguese ports
in terms of the additional expenses at Oporto, where the water on the bar was
low, preventing cargo ships from being fully loaded in ports.

This reduction in sea power was not an abrupt loss of the twentieth century.
The Portuguese had long been surpassed by Spain, Holland, and then Britain.
With the loss of sea power had gone some of the monopoly on commercial in-
terests. The treaties of 1654 and 1661 with England and the 1661 one with

Holland gave both of these countries freedom to trade with the Portuguese empire (Marques 1972, 1:276). This meant some partitioning of Brazilian wealth with the Dutch and of some portions of African wealth with the English. The pathetic state of Portuguese sea transportation was highlighted in 1921 as the Portuguese president prepared to make a trip to Brazil. The Portuguese boat scheduled to carry the president developed mechanical problems and could not be repaired. No other suitable Portuguese boat could be found, and the trip had to be made, most humiliatingly, in a British boat loaned for the occasion. The weakness of Portuguese shipping in Portuguese trade is stunning, given the vital role of shipping in the trade project. Portugal was virtually out of the transportation business.

The growing gap between Portugal and the core countries of Britain and Germany because of unequal economic development upset a balance of economic forces that had existed for some time. However, the solidification of Portugal's position was not just a result of these market forces. Political events, domestic and worldwide, also contributed to the collapse of the agro-export and trade system.

The greatest political blow to this economic system was the loss of Brazil. In 1822 Brazil declared its independence from Portugal and the colonial empire. Although other countries had already penetrated the Brazilian market, the formal declaration of independence led to even greater competition for the Brazilian market. Independence resulted in the stagnation of the Portuguese textile industry (Castro 1971, 217) and helped the British textile industry. The commercial activities of the seventeenth and eighteenth centuries had depended heavily on Portuguese merchants who had emigrated to Brazil. Commerce had a traditional character—purchases were made from merchandise that had already arrived in Brazilian ports. Independence changed the nature of commerce. After independence, other nations moved in: the British with the London-Brazilian bank; the Germans with banks and navigation lines. Portuguese merchants, blinded by the advantages that had befallen them by the historic rights of a colonial empire and of a people with common blood, barely noticed these changes. Such neglect led to the eventual loss of the commercial monopoly. With neither banks nor boats, Portugal had to count on good will and patriotism for business (ACL 1919, 302). Of course, the Brazilian market continued to be lucrative for the Portuguese because the Brazilian market managed to absorb Portuguese production of the early 1800s and more. Still, the loss of Brazil was a significant factor in the economic destiny of Portugal.

Another significant political event that further eroded the agro-export and trade system was World War I. There were two clear consequences of the war for the agro-export and trade system: the loss of markets and the loss of merchant control of the commercial system. With commercial traffic essentially banned from the high seas, Portugal was less successful in reaching its overseas markets and in importing the consumer items, raw materials, and energy that it needed for its industrial production. For example, the export of Portuguese table wines dropped from 851,000 hectoliters in 1911 to 537,330 hectoliters in 1914. Brazil typically imported more than half of Portugal's exported table wines. The war-related shipping difficulties were made even more acute by Portugal's dependency on foreign shipping. As the British shifted their transport facilities into the war effort, they withdrew them from commercial runs. Even German boats, seized by the Portuguese in the Lisbon harbor under the pretext of fortifying the Portuguese merchant fleet, were turned over by the Portuguese government to a private British navigation company, preventing a possible restoration of the agro-export project. Due to the war, Britain drastically reduced its imports, depriving Portugal of its market for meat, wine, fruits, and vegetables. At the same time, Britain guarded its own resources parsimoniously and significantly reduced its exports of coal and prime materials (AIp 1917–1918, 18). Many Lisbon houses lost their trade altogether and had to close their doors (*JCC* 9 September 1914).

Portugal responded as did other countries: It restricted its own exports through hundreds of pieces of legislation. Because of worldwide shortages of foodstuffs and the impossibility of importing them, the government took a number of steps to limit or prohibit exports. In some cases, amounts were limited; in other cases (such as cacao), exports were subject to a heavy export surtax; in still other cases (such as livestock and fuels), exports were simply forbidden. Portugal's inability to place its traditional products in the market—either because of foreign prohibitions or export taxes—sometimes resulted in the loss of those markets. This was particularly grave for agricultural products, which were produced solely for the foreign market (ACL 1915, 37). The stockpiling of products not legally eligible for export resulted either in spoilage (as in the case of onions) or in devaluation (as in the case of wool).

During the war, the government intervened to perform functions that had been within the realm of commerce. For example, it regulated the domestic distribution of scarce imported prime materials (fertilizer, tin sheets for canning, cotton, and so on). In the case of coal, the government, completely bypassing merchants, imported the material and turned it directly over to industrial users. Restricted access to foreign currency (another difficulty associated with the war) permitted only limited liquidation of debts, particularly where it involved countries participating in the war. Although a few astute merchants unequivocally made great fortunes on the scarcities attendant to war, the trade system as a whole suffered the loss of activities and prestige.

In the world polity, other factors equally beyond the control of the Portuguese came to threaten the returns that the agro-export system brought to Portugal. Beyond terms of trade and the devaluation of agricultural products was a real but unpredictable political threat to wine. Prohibition sentiments swept parts of northern Europe after the war, and Portugal had to battle against a rash of foreign legislation aimed at keeping out Portuguese wines or at keeping their alcoholic content below an indicated degree. These laws represented a particular threat to the port wine industry. By limiting the alcoholic content of port wine to 30 proof when it was normally around 42 proof (as happened in Belgium in 1919), these countries opened the market to imitations that could capture the Port wine market.[4] Although the Portuguese foreign ministers in these particular countries pleaded the case of Portugal, in other countries they tried to bargain tax exemptions on foreign products in Portugal for the continued sale of Portuguese wines. Thus Portugal had to suffer the vicissitudes of its dependence on the political whims of other countries.

AGRO-EXPORTS AND ECONOMIC GROWTH:
SUMMARY AND REFLECTION

We have seen the decline of the Portuguese economy and the influence of both conjunctural and structural world-system forces. With regard to the conjunctural influence, changes in the world-system at large put Portugal in a precarious position. These changes were of a technological, military, and political nature that affected all countries including Portugal. The structural influence resides in the fact that Portugal, by virtue of its semiperipheral status, internalized these changes in a particular way. In other words, the decline and crisis were a result of combined conjunctural and structural world-system influences.

In this chapter, I have argued that because of shifts in both the domestic and world economies, the project of trade and agro-exports suffered progressive deterioration. The reproduction of the trade and agro-export economic system failed in the face of unequal development. And because little of the wealth that had accumulated in commercial activities had been invested in industry, Portugal became increasingly dependent on more developed countries in the world economy—even to the point of losing shipping, the principal factor necessary to perpetuate the agro-export and trade project.

Was this decline the inevitable outcome of the agro-export and trade system? Could not that system have promoted domestic development? Comparative advantage theory argues that a country can accumulate wealth even with an emphasis on raw materials. When Ricardo first wrote about comparative advantage, he used the exchange between Portuguese wine and British textiles to support his case. Yet it appears that after many years of earning foreign exchange with agricultural exports, the Portuguese had not translated these earnings into economic growth and diversification. The inability of export earnings to propel the economy forward and, worse, to maintain the standard of living reflected the declining hegemony of the economic project that had organized the economy for centuries. The gap between Portugal and the core seemed to be increasing. Other countries of the world economy developed while Portugal stood still.

Although the propensity to truck, barter, and exchange may be part of human nature (Smith 1957, 2:12), nations have shown radically different propensities on the question of whether or not to trade. And even individual nations over time have wavered in their propensity to trade. The relationship between international trade and economic development has occupied social theorists and state makers since the time of mercantilism. Mercantilists thought that only a certain kind of trade was beneficial to national economic development, namely, that which increased their wealth and power. This meant particularly the export of labor-intensive finished goods and the minimization of imports. Ricardo's conviction lay in the opposite direction, however—economic development was realized through international trade, no matter what the merchandise (cotton shirts, copper, or calculators). Each country had some comparative advantage that could only be realized as wealth through international trade. These two positions do not simply represent two different understandings of the relationship between capital accumulation and trade; they also represent different periods in economic thought. The world economy that gave birth to mercantilism was not the economy that gave birth to comparative advantage.

Equally important in understanding the relationship between trade and accumulation is a nation's location in the world economy. Classical theories of economic growth have argued that progressive integration into the world economy will promote the economic development of that country, and colonies were thought to be no exception. Such theories even include those of Marx and Lenin, who argued that integration into the capitalist world eventually would bring economic growth even to those first "victimized" by imperialism (Szymanski 1981, 25–27).

However, after several decades, study of the economic development of colonies and neocolonial nations has demonstrated unequivocally that integration into the world economy does not produce ipso facto economic development. The "development of underdevelopment" thesis argues precisely the opposite. Within this perspective, debate continues over the degree of and manner in which resources and wealth are transferred out of the colony or neocolonial country and back into the dominant countries (Szymanski 1981, 25–27) and, consequently, the degree and form of underdevelopment (Mahler 1980).

Clearly, on top of the historical moment, the relationship between trade and development must be further specified by location in the world economy. Being a core country or a country with colonies provides a nation with the conditions to translate world integration into economic differentiation. Being a colony or a peripheral country means just the inverse, namely, integration diminishes economic differentiation (Chase-Dunn 1975, 721). These questions are trade-specific versions of the more general issue advanced by both modernization and dependency theorists, who posit the final stages of modernity and underdevelopment respectively. However, both groups of theorists hesitate to specify the effects of trade on the semiperiphery. If the relationship between trade and development in the periphery is the opposite of that demonstrated in the core, what is the effect of increased world economic integration through trade on the economic development of the semiperiphery?

To answer this question, several assumptions need to be made. The first is that the diversity of the trade profile is a reflection of the diversity of the economy. It is, of course, possible that the foreign trade profile does not reflect the total range of economic production; however, even the production of nonexported items would have provoked increases in machinery and raw-material imports and thus be reflected indirectly in both of these measures. On the whole, the trade profile should shadow the economic diversity of a nation, revealing the merchandise available for export as well as necessary goods that are imported.

This diversity is described in terms of the degree of dispersion of traded merchandise among the major customs categories. In addition, economic diversity is conceptualized as the balance between finished-goods processing and raw-material extraction, a balance that is estimated with a trade composition index (TCI). The TCI measures the balance, or mix, between ideal "core" activities, such as importing raw materials and exporting finished goods, and ideal "peripheral" activities, such as exporting raw materials and importing finished goods.[5] The level of processing measured in Galtung's TCI (1971) "requires an operational distinction between 'processed goods' and 'primary products' . . . although it is acknowledged that these categories [primary products] include certain semiprocessed goods, particularly foodstuffs" (Mahler 1980, 171).

Centuries of integration into the world economy through trade did not lead to an inevitable economic differentiation. As we have seen, it worked to the contrary. Several processes become apparent from the trade data. First, Portugal was moving away from a total trade dependence on Britain. In the period 1855 to 1864, textiles made up 50 percent of British exports to Portugal, and wine made up 50 percent of Portuguese exports to Britain. From the nineteenth century into the twentieth century, Portugal became more integrated into the world economy. Integration into the world economy is measured in two ways: the number of trade partners that absorbed 75 percent of Portuguese trade, and the percentage of exports destined to the two principal trade partners. From 1872 to 1935, Portugal increased the number of countries to which it sent products. There was modest increase in the number of countries receiving wine: Although only two countries imported 88 percent of the wine in 1872, nine countries imported 75 percent in 1919. This count excludes the colonies, which as a block consumed 21 percent of the exported wine. The number of countries receiving 75 percent of all trade also increased slightly over the decades, from three in 1874 to seven in 1935 (table 3.6). The percentage of exports going to the two most important trade partners reflects the most substantial change, from 71 percent of the total exports in 1874 to 37 percent of the exports in 1935. These measures indicate that Portugal enlarged its circle of trading partners toward the end of the nineteenth century and was less dependent on Britain than it had been at the time of the famous Methuen Treaty (1703).

Table 3.6. Number of Trading Partners and Percentage
of Merchandise Received by Top Traders,
Selected Years from 1874 to 1935

Year	Number[a]	Percentage[b]
1874	3	71
1885	3	60
1892	3	63
1903	4	44
1915	4	47
1925	7	41
1935	7	37

[a]Countries receiving 75 percent of exported merchandise.
[b]Exported merchandise going to top two traders. From
1874 through 1929 Britain was the number one receiver of
Portuguese exports (except in 1916, 1917, and 1922 when
France occupied that place). The number two position was
shared during those years by Brazil, France, Germany, and
the Portuguese colonies.

Source: Calculated from Portugal, Ministério das Finanças,
Comércio e navegação (Lisbon: Imprensa Nacional,
1872–1920).

What is the relationship between increased integration into the world economy and growth; or, more modestly, between the network of trading partners
and the TCI?[6] There is a negative association suggested in the development
literature — the rise in the percentage of exports absorbed by fewer trading partners is associated with the drop in the TCI.

This interpretation can be confirmed by looking at the association of the TCI
and the product concentration of exports. Again, the literature on underdevelopment would predict a negative relationship — that is, an increased concentration
of exports in one product should be associated with a low TCI score. The Portuguese trade data show an equally negative relationship between the TCI and
product concentration. As expected, a positive relationship exists between partner concentration and product concentration.

Although the TCI data throw a shadow on any claim of economic diversification, they likewise put a shadow on any claim of a progressive specialization in
agro-exports. There is no clear secular trend in either direction. Portugal was not
moving toward increased diversification, as the comparative advantage or growth
literature might suggest; nor was it moving toward increased agro-export special-

ization, as the dependency literature suggests. This raises two questions: First, why did not the success at agro-exporting propel the economy into a greater specialization of that activity? Although the volume of wine exports was rising,[7] the monetary value of wine exports was decreasing.

The second question is, Why did not the revenues from agriculture promote industrial development? Commercial data summaries reflect some subtle yet significant changes. The value of imported threads and textiles decreased slightly, particularly after the protectionist legislation of the 1880s, while their export value rose. Although the agro-exports were directed to the core and to Brazil, the textile exports were overwhelmingly directed to the African colonies. In 1899, for example, 92 percent of textile exports went to the colonies (Mendes 1979, 40).

Reconsidering the trade profile, it appears that stagnation is not quite the correct characterization of the long-term effects of the agro-export and trade project. Many measures, although suggesting that Portugal solidified its semi-peripheral position, obscure the exact processes involved. Portugal during this period shows the fortification of two contradictory trends: a maintenance of its agro-export role, and a growth in its finished-goods exporting role. This peculiar trade profile may account for the lack of strong association between product concentration and the TCI. Thus the answer to the question of the impact of agro-exports with trading on economic growth is somewhat complicated but, I would say, relies heavily on the notion of the semiperiphery, that is, a country's location in the world economy.

The Republican party appeared as an important political force in 1890. It coalesced the discontent against the agro-export and trade project and directed it against the monarchy. The decline of the project was felt by the industrialists and by the working classes. The complaints of nineteenth-century industrialists focused heavily on inadequate tariff protection for their products, which had been sacrificed in exchange for favorable placement of Portuguese wines. When the government attempted to combat the unfavorable terms of trade with protectionist legislation, the consequence was price increases for urban consumers. Even though salaries within the textile industry, for example, increased by 22 percent between 1881 and 1910, during this same period the price index of consumption rose 25 percent and that of foodstuffs rose 37 percent. These factors contributed to the growing popularity of the Republican party, which blamed the monarchy for the declining economy.

The rise of republican opposition was tied to the failure of the old economic project. Republican opposition was aimed at annihilating the sociopolitical institution tied to the exhausted economic project. With the 1910 revolution, republicans achieved their political goal. Although one might have thought that the end of the crisis was in the hands of the republican politicians, the economic crisis was not sentenced to death — the Republic itself was. The political transformation was inadequate for the task of ameliorating the domestic manifestations of semiperipheral status. The agro-export and trade project lingered, and its progressive deterioration continued. Portugal still needed a new economic project. The domestic manifestations and the need for a new economic project are taken up, respectively, in chapters 4 and 5.

CHAPTER 4

Portugal: A Disarticulated Economy

The end-of-the-century crisis that Portugal experienced, and the way in which it experienced it, owed much to Portugal's place in the world economy. Portugal was falling further and further behind the core economies—its position in the world economy changed by virtue of movement external to Portugal itself. Those changes, the resultant economic and political crises, as well as the appearance of alternatives to the deteriorated agro-export and trade project, owed much to Portugal's place in the world economy. Portugal was a semiperipheral nation. In this chapter, I detail the structural characteristics of a semiperipheral country and how it is integrated into a world-system. By looking at the economy from the inside, it is possible to see how it internalizes or domesticates that semiperipheral position. Here I use the notion of the disarticulated economy to describe the domestic ramifications of semiperipheral integration into the world-system. In short, location in the world economy is operationalized in a concrete way. (Additional definitions and conceptualizations are summarized in appendix A.)

THE WORLD ECONOMY FROM A WORLD-SYSTEM PERSPECTIVE

Chirot (1977) examines two closely related types of social change: changes within societies that affect the international balance of power, and the ramifications of these changes for individual societies. Analysis of the decline of the agro-export project in Portugal is the second kind of change that Chirot has in mind. He argues, however, that the two are inseparable in a causal circle. Thus I want to sketch a bit of the first while introducing world-system terminology.

Since the 1500s, a major portion of the world has had contact with the modernizing, industrializing, and politically dominant Western world. By 1900 Western penetration and influence were complete, leaving in their wake a "veritable world division of labor" (Chirot 1977, 8). In the world hierarchy, certain countries were the international upper class, dominating the world; others were the international lower class, providing cheap labor and raw materials. The industrialized leaders would not have been able to make the progress they did without the economic resources that they extracted from the poorer countries. Conversely, the poorer countries would have been a bit less poor if they had been left alone by these world economic leaders. What happens in the less developed countries (LDCs), therefore, is of much concern to the more developed ones. "The twentieth century's advanced societies had, and continue to have a direct interest in turning less advanced societies in certain directions and not in others" (Chirot 1977, 9). What is a world-system?

A world-system consists of a set of interconnected societies. The state of being of each of these societies depends to some extent on its relative position in the world system, which has strong, middling, and weak members. The world-system of 1900 was a capitalist system. In the late twentieth century there is a capitalist world-system and some competitors who challenge its hegemony (Chirot 1977, 13).

By the 1900s, the core consisted of four societies: Britain, the United States, Germany, and, to a lesser extent, France. Chirot places Portugal in the periphery (1977, 24), a judgment clearly contested in this book.

Chirot estimates that in 1900, with one-eighth of the world population, the four core countries already produced three-fourths of the world's manufactured goods (1977, 24), which suggests a pressing need for markets beyond the four nation-states. Because these core societies were more developed and richer, they needed capital markets. In 1913 the investments of these four countries amounted to 85 percent of capital invested abroad. Much of this investment was in communications, minerals, and commercial houses (Chirot 1977, 31).

What relevance does this have for Portugal? To the extent that it was a member of these international exchanges, it suffered as did all noncore countries. To the extent that it exported raw materials to Britain, it developed the lopsided or deformed economy typical of other noncore countries, specializing as the core countries diversified. In the 1900s, the world-system was constituted by peripheral countries that were primarily monocultural exporters. In 1913 74 percent of Nigeria's exports were palm products; cotton made up 80 percent of Egypt's exports; and 61 percent of the value of Brazil's exports was in coffee (Chirot 1977, 35). Some peripheral countries became so dependent on the world market that the conversion to agriculture for export resulted in food deficiencies at home. Portugal too engaged in the ironic exchange of exporting wine and importing wheat. Great Britain, on the other hand, sent manufactured textile goods (27 percent of exports) as well as machinery and metals. Germany and France also exported manufactured goods. Because exporting enclaves in LDCs give the highest return on capital, they magnetize the economy, drawing investment from other areas. This market mechanism produces an overall imbalance. To the extent that there is foreign capital invested in these exporting enclaves, a second, nonmarket factor produces an overall imbalance in the economy. When the price of the main export product declines, the economy suffers and, worse, the deformation is intensified. Chirot cites the case of falling coffee prices, to which the Brazilian producers responded by increasing their production (1977, 38).

In 1870 the French, Germans, and British began their race to divide up unclaimed or weakly claimed parts of the world (Chirot 1977, 49). This development meant that as larger states built armies and navies, weaker semiperipheral states like Portugal battled to resist being reduced to peripheral-state status. In numerous cases, Portugal abdicated to the demands of Britain (for example, the 1890 ultimatum) to avoid a full confrontation, which it certainly would have lost. In other cases, such as Portugal's somewhat improbable participation on the European front during World War I, it took action hoping to demonstrate its fitness as a world leader. But, most important, the competition among the "real" leaders of the core manifested itself in attempts to secure special privileges in Portuguese markets, to get special concessions in passing goods through Angola into the German colonies, and for the exclusive cargo business of African exports. By one estimate, foreign investment by core powers increased 50 percent from 1900 to 1913 (Chirot 1977, 51). Every concession granted to these core competitors was won at the expense of Portuguese industrial development.

Lenin's theory of imperialism still remains a major part of the conventional wisdom for explaining why this world transformation came about (Chirot 1977, 49). Concentration of ownership had heightened by 1900. Classes allied with financial institutions had great political influence in their respective countries. They anticipated raw material shortages and an insufficient domestic demand for the capital surplus. The outcome was an intense scramble at the end of the nineteenth century for raw materials, markets, and profits.

THE ESSENCE OF SEMIPERIPHERALITY

Portugal exemplifies the essence of semiperipherality and further serves to help clarify the definition. Various theoretical and empirical usages of the term semiperiphery are reviewed in appendix A. Here I want to give a vivid account of what semiperipherality actually means from the global perspective, and what it concretely means to have an economy with a certain commodity mix. The origin of the disarticulation lies in the semiperipheral status of Portugal in the world economy: It was, at one and the same time, dependent upon Britain in a quasi-colonial fashion and dominant over an empire that included nine colonies.

Portugal at the beginning of the twentieth century was still in possession of a substantial colonial empire. Although no longer the glorious empire of the sixteenth century, it still held nine colonies, including the two great African territories of Angola and Mozambique.[1] That Portugal's colonial empire was continuously coveted by Britain and Germany, which conspired jointly and individually to obtain control of these Portuguese possessions, suggests its significance. The African colonies were substantially untouched, unpacified, and undeveloped until 1890. Concrete threats of appropriation by foreign powers finally persuaded the Portuguese to begin serious colonial development.

Table 4.1. Portuguese Metro-Colonial Trade, 1910 (in percentages)

Movement	Total	Metro-Colonial
Imports from colonies	3.8	9.4
Exports to colonies	17.6	22.6
Reexports: Colonies to foreign countries	89.4	56.5
Reexports: Foreign countries to colonies	89.4	11.3
All metro-colonial activity	21.4	100.0

Source: Calculated from Portugal, Ministério das Finanças, Comércio e nave-gação (Lisbon: Imprensa Nacional, 1872–1920).

The colonial relationship is inscribed in the commercial statistics. In 1910 the movement of merchandise back and forth between the metropole and the colonies accounted for 21 percent of Portuguese international trade (table 4.1). Colonial possessions conjure up notions of an abundance of riches for the metropole, yet only 4 percent of Portugal's imports for consumption originated in the colonies. Colonial possessions also suggest unlimited markets for metropolitan goods. In this, Portugal fared better—18 percent of Portugal's exports were destined for its colonies. The remaining commercial activity—reexporting—consisted of transferring colonial goods to foreign countries and vice versa. The 1910 reexport activity was predominantly shipping colonial goods to foreign countries. Portugal was an importing country, but the imports did not reflect high colonial participation.

This trade was not evenly divided among all categories of merchandise (table 4.2). For some merchandise, these commercial exchanges were paramount. Sugar and coffee ranked high among the imports, whereas threads, fabrics, table and port wines, agricultural and industrial instruments, plus some manufactured goods disproportionately found their way to the colonies. Some products could even be called colonial products: 93 percent of exported shoes, 99.86 percent of exported tinted or stamped cotton textiles, and 93 percent of exported tobacco were sent to the colonies.

Regarding reexport activities, the ratio of merchandise reexported from the colonies to merchandise reexported to the colonies ranged from one and a half times in 1885 to six and a half times in 1903. For the most part, this ratio hovered around three. Several items stood out among the reexported merchandise. The principal products reexported from the colonies were rubber and cacao, whereas the principal foreign items reexported to the colonies were cotton fabrics, industrial and agricultural machinery, and diverse manufactured goods. In summary, Portugal exploited its colonies in selective ways. It was an importing

Table 4.2. Portuguese Colonial Trade by Customs Categories, 1910
(as percentages of total)

Category	Imports from Colonies	Exports to Colonies	Colonial to Foreign Reexports	Foreign to Colonial Reexports
Live animals	0	1.5	0	0
Raw materials	3.0	3.1	83.4	0
Threads and textiles	0	86.0	0	93.1
Foodstuffs and beverages	11.8	12.1	89.3	0
Machinery and utensils	0	59.8	0	49.4
Diverse manufactures	.1	41.6	0	63.0

Source: Calculated from Portugal, Ministério das Finanças, *Comércio e navegação* (Lisbon: Imprensa Nacional, 1872–1920).

country, but it was not importing from its colonies. Even though the colonies offered unlimited market prospects for some manufactured items, 72 percent of Portugal's exports did not go to them. Portugal's dominant commercial activity with its colonies was reexporting.

Thus one orientation of the Portuguese economy was that it was a metropole with administrative and financial institutions befitting a colonial empire. Capitalists produced goods for colonial consumption; bankers loaned money for colonial investment; merchants traded between the colonies and the rest of the world; a merchant marine transported those exchanges; and a state apparatus administered it all.

Yet Portugal had another orientation: The country resembled a colony. The relationship first established between Portugal and England in the fourteenth century was multifaceted. Through a series of pacts, treaties, and alliances continuously renewed, albeit with varying degrees of Portuguese enthusiasm, Portugal and Britain had mutually bound themselves politically, militarily, and economically. That this "mutual binding" had always been asymmetrical is no surprise. In 1910 Portuguese/British dependency was visible in the nature of the trade relationships between the two countries, in British involvement in the external debt, in British capital penetration of Portuguese companies, and even in British penetration of the colonies.

Twenty-five percent of Portuguese trade activity was with Britain, which was by far the most active trading partner, followed (after the colonies) by Germany (13 percent). The British-Portuguese commercial exchanges summarize the relationship (table 4.3). British predominance among Portuguese imports was evident in fibers and textiles, industrial equipment, raw materials for industry, and

Table 4.3. Portuguese-British Trade, 1910 (in percentages)

	Trade in Each Category[a]	Total Trade
Imports	28.69	61.2
Exports	22.37	24.5
Reexports to colonies	85.56	7.5
Reexports from colonies	12.27	4.1
Total	24.96	97.3[b]

[a]Categories are live animals, raw materials, threads and textiles, foodstuffs and beverages, machinery and utensils, and diverse manufactures.
[b]Excludes transfers at sea.

Source: Calculated from Portugal, Ministério das Finanças, Comércio e navegação (Lisbon: Imprensa Nacional, 1872–1920).

manufactured goods. These British items also constituted 85.5 percent of the merchandise that Portugal reexported to its colonies.

Commercial statistics record that sophisticated industrial machinery and raw materials for industrialization, together with already manufactured goods, were being exchanged for food products (see table 4.4). Britain bought about two-thirds of Portugal's exported wine and about three-fourths of the figs, almonds, and carob beans (BCCP 1925, 12). Although the 1910 import-export trade ratio for Portuguese trade was 1.51, it was 9.94 for trade with Britain, reflecting the disproportionate size of the import bill compared with the export earnings. In former, more "glorious" centuries when there were both colonies and gold, trade deficits were covered with gold. In 1910 gold was still being transferred—100 percent of Portugal's exported gold bullion and 35.9 percent of its gold currency went to Britain.

In practice the British, according to one Portuguese journal (JCC 12 April 1911), always saw the convenience of having Portugal develop its agricultural production, to which Britain would give a privileged position in its markets but for which it also expected protection for its own textile products. Portugal was to be a British orchard.

Portuguese dependence also existed in the area of sea transportation. The British merchant fleet handled more tonnage in Portuguese ports than any other fleet, including the Portuguese (table 3.5). In still other areas, British influence was detectable. With a chronic balance of trade deficit but without a steady flow of income to balance it, Portugal was forced to import capital. At the time of World War I, Portugal was already indebted to Britain, but Britain continued to loan money for cereals and guns as Portugal, the unprepared member of the alliance, prepared to throw itself into the European battlefront.

British involvement was also notable in Portuguese industries. For example,

Table 4.4. Portuguese-British Trade by Customs Categories, 1910 (as percentages of total)

Category	Imports from Britain	Exports to Britain	Britain to Colonies Reexports	Colonies to Britain Reexports
Live animals	.5	.2	—	—
Raw materials	29.7	29.8	100.0	15.37
Threads and textiles	48.0	1.3	38.94	—
Foodstuffs and beverages	23.5	26.7	30.4	3.4
Machinery and utensils	38.9	4.9	67.13	6.0
Diverse manufactures	18.7	25.4	43.39	.9

Source: Calculated from Portugal, Ministério das Finanças, *Comércio e navegação* (Lisbon: Imprensa Nacional, 1872–1920).

the major telephone company was called Anglo-Portuguese; its name was Portuguese and its capital was British. British capital also financed the Lisbon tramway (Castro 1971, 132). The principal product of the export sector — port wine — had been in British hands for several generations. Infrastructure investments that related to the export sector were heavy. It is estimated that one-half of railway construction was built with British capital. The inflow of foreign capital went beyond the continent to the colonies. Lacking its own capital, Portugal had little choice but to throw open its empire to foreign enterprise (Kiernan 1974, 274). Much of Mozambique was under British control; more than half of the capital invested in these territories was British and had been raised in London (Sideri 1970, 60).

Domination by Britain, therefore, was Portugal's second orientation. Core countries' domination is not due simply to the fact that the peripheral economy produces only raw materials but rather to the fact that it is only a producer of those products (Amin 1976, 246). Herein lies Portugal's semidependent status — it was principally a producer and exporter of agricultural products. Although Portugal produced somewhere around half of the world's cork, it only worked about 5 percent of that material (Cabreira 1914). In peripheral economies, Amin writes, there is a predominance of agrarian capitalism, a development of an urban merchant bourgeoisie, and an incomplete industrialization as well as an incomplete proletarianization. So it might have seemed with Portugal.

The contradictory nature of these two dimensions captures the essence of the semiperiphery. It comprises countries that are simultaneously core and periphery, that are both dominating countries and dominated ones. But this description relates to their linkages with the world economy. Semiperipherality has a particular imprint inside the economy.

THE DOMESTIC MANIFESTATION OF SEMIPERIPHERALITY

One must begin by questioning whether the domestic economy of a semiperipheral state is really a "national" economy. It is not as frivolous a question as it might seem. Theories of economic growth account for the development of national economies. Whether the motor of development is seen as modern man, science, or technology (Apter 1965; Rostow 1960; Harrison 1985), development is attributed to national economies. That is, the existence of a national economy is taken for granted, and national signifies an integrated economy within a nation-state. It is the medium in which development is assumed to occur. Rostow's analysis is exemplary in this regard. The discussion of pretake-off as well as take-off is predicated upon the existence of an integrated national economy. In the earliest stages of growth, banks and other institutions for mobilizing capital appear and "all this activity proceeds at a limited pace within an economy" (Rostow 1960, 7). In describing the take-off period, Rostow again describes changes that occur within a national economy.

> During the take-off new industries expand rapidly, yielding profits a large portion of which are reinvested in new plant; and these new industries, in turn, stimulate, through their rapidly expanding requirement for factory workers, the services to support them, and for other manufactured goods, a further expansion in urban areas and in other modern industrial plants. . . . The new class of entrepreneurs expands; and it directs the enlarging flows of investment in the private sector. . . . New techniques spread in agriculture as well as industry, as agriculture is commercialized, and increasing numbers of farmers are prepared to accept new methods and the deep changes they bring to ways of life (1960, 7).

And, finally, in the drive to maturity "the now regularly growing economy drives to expand modern technology over the whole front of its economic activity" (Rostow 1960, 9). Aside from his theory's wonderfully utopian quality, Rostow, like many development theorists, took for granted the existence of a coherent national economy so that movement in one sector automatically spread to, or influenced, movement in other sectors. As recently as 1983, a similar conceptualization was offered in a survey of the economic growth literature. Reynolds assumed explicitly that "economic interaction is more intense within national boundaries than across them" (1983, 944) and implicitly that development occurs through reciprocal feedback among the sectors.

Such coherent or integrated economies are, in Leontief's words, "woven together by the flow of trade which ultimately links each branch and industry to all others" (1966, 15). Because of the interrelationship among the parts, economic effects all cumulate into a social transformation that, in this case, is economic development. From Leontief's perspective, the larger and more advanced an economy is, the more complete and articulated is its structure. And, conversely, "an underdeveloped economy can now be defined as underdeveloped to the extent that it lacks the working parts of this system" (Leontief 1966, 49). No doubt many national economies are coherent in this fashion. Dependency and underdevelopment theorists have cited at least two major inadequacies with theories making such assumptions: the existence of unconnected sectors within an economy, and the pervasiveness of links to the world economy. By utilizing concepts such as core, periphery, enclave, and dual economy, these theorists focused attention on asymmetric development within economies. Thus whether an economic system is one economy will greatly determine the extent to which any given case fits a development model that assumes a coherent economy.

Was the Portuguese economy a coherent whole in which there was articulation among the regions, sectors, and strata of society? Did growth in one sector have a significant impact upon others? No, the Portuguese economy at the turn of the century was so severely disarticulated that four economies existed within the boundaries of the nation-state. The roots of this economic disarticulation were located in the truncation of domestic economic linkages — a truncation that took place because of the semiperipheral location that Portugal held.

Within Portugal, it is possible to identify four barely overlapping economies. The largest of these economies was the agro-export economy. In 1910 agro-exports accounted for 85 percent of all exports: 10 percent in live animals, 21 percent in raw materials, and 54 percent in foodstuffs and drink. In 1926 trade was similar: Agro-exports contributed 88 percent of the total exports, and the three major categories were .2 percent, 25 percent, and 64 percent, respectively.

Farming for export can be considered a separate economy because of its isolation from other economic activities in terms of capital stock, labor force, and product distribution. First, the agro-export economy was an isolated economy because the capital stock was endogenous. In contrast to industry, for example, farmers made few purchases from other parts of the Portuguese economy. The principal capital stock of this economy was land and what was grown on it. Little machinery was involved in agriculture. In 1911 the commercial agent to the U.S. Department of Commerce and Labor wrote:

> The methods adopted in the cultivation of the land are almost primitive, the old Moorish plow still being in use on some farms. The people seem slow to adopt improved methods of cultivation and modern agricultural implements and machinery. The small farms in the north are too poor to buy agricultural machines, but there is undoubtedly a market for them in the south (1911, 42–43).

Production was self-reproducing — much could be reproduced from year to year without annual plantings (fruit trees, vines, and cork trees, for example). Naturally, some exceptions existed to this claim of minimal capital stock requirements. Wine producers and exporters had to purchase bottles and storage equipment from other producers, as did the producers and exporters of fruits and woods. Still, to the extent that harvesting and processing remained decentralized and rudimentary, capital stock purchases were minimal.

Second, the labor force of the agro-export economy was isolated from the rest of society. The agro-export labor force was not yet proletarianized—that is, it was usually not monetarily remunerated for its work, and where there was monetary remuneration, it was a supplemental wage. Generally, the labor force producing agro-exports was a population of small farmers working their own plots of land. On such rented or owned plots, they produced the export product in addition to their own subsistence. In other cases, seasonal workers harvested crops (especially grapes) on someone else's land and received wages in compensation, yet they also often worked subsistence plots. In short, workers in the agro-export sector generally relied less upon their wages for acquiring their daily necessities. All of their subsistence goods were not acquired in the market and therefore were not integrated into the rest of the economy.

Cutileiro's (1971) description of a southwestern village in the 1950s offers additional evidence on the question of the labor force. He found that only twenty-six of the 480 resident landholders were self-sufficient. The others worked as sharecroppers on someone else's land; conversely, many landowners employed sharecroppers that were at the same time landowners. He also argues that large estates had been farmed under a mixture of direct cultivation and sharecropping, but that sharecropping decreased with three factors: first, the increased cost of farming associated with a more generalized use of fertilizers; second, the 1929 subsidies to landowners that resulted in landowners wanting to work more land themselves; and third, the worsened contract for sharecroppers—they now had to turn over one-third of their produce rather than the customary one-fourth (*terras ao quarto*). In addition to paying more to landowners, sharecroppers had to pay landowners 8 percent for any threshing that they had done on their own crops. Shepherds also were not proletarianized. They could be paid in money or in entitlements to a share of the wool and lambs born to a pre-agreed number of ewes (Cutileiro 1971, 61). Still, into the 1950s, Cunhal found that small farmers renting land remained with one-third of the harvest, whereas in areas of corn and potatoes, the system of one-half remained (1976, 2:251).

Many aspects of olive oil production exemplify this model of production more or less isolated from other sectors of the economy. Olive oil production was not industrial; rather, it was an appendage to agricultural life. Olive trees were spread throughout Portugal, although some regions had a higher concentration than others. Each proprietor, no matter how small, harvested his own olives and used a rudimentary press to extract the oil. Even when more advanced machinery was introduced, it was underutilized by the proprietors, who continued to cultivate the same volume as they had before. In two districts with larger land expanses, Evora and Beja, a more industrialized operation was technically feasible, but it was not socially realistic (ACAP 1912, 177). The ACAP presented what it claimed was a typical case of an industrialist in Alvito. His shop had been in operation for ten years, contained a motor of 18 horsepower, eight presses, several machines to clean, grind, purify, and filter olives, and about twenty operators. However, because of the persistence of the traditional habits of the surrounding small growers—both regarding the volume of harvest and the practice of grinding their own harvest before selling it—the industrialist's efforts were directed toward increasing his own olive production. Ten years of industrial activity had transformed him into a full-time farmer. Olive oil continued to be an activity ancillary to farming, produced by farmers on small lots. Despite persistent backyard production, olive oil exports were significant: In 1910 Portugal exported 358,992 decaliters, 4 percent of the value of food exports.

Rental arrangements facilitated the extraction of produce for export from the land with nonproletarianized labor. A 1919 revision of the Civil Code required rural land contracts to be written but still allowed landlords to cancel the contract at the end of the agricultural year. Most important for this argument, it allowed the landlords to demand rent in kind.

The district data also support the interpretation that agro-export production took place on small farms and thus on less proletarianized and less capitalized units. Six districts had high proportions of land dedicated to agro-exports. One of these, Faro, had 21.14 percent of the surface area planted with fruit trees. Others, such as Oporto, Leiria, Aveiro, and Viana do Castello, had over 25 percent of the surface area dedicated to forests, whereas three of them—Oporto, Braga, and Viana do Castello—had the highest percentage of land dedicated to vineyards. And these districts, with the exception of Faro, had small farm units, all well below 1 hectare. Agro-export production, in other words, was carried out, above all, in small units. One of the more outstanding characteristics of the six principal districts where agro-export production was predominant was small average farm size (table 4.5).[2]

Third, the final destination of these agro-exports was, as the name implies, the international market. In this respect, the agro-export economy was also isolated from the rest of Portuguese economic activities. Although wine and olive oil, as well as fruit and many other exported products, were certainly consumed by the population, these products were wage goods only for the few urban workers. Many families consumed *caseira* (homemade) wine, cheese, olive oil, and the like rather than purchasing them. This practice was especially true of agricultural workers who produced the very items that were being exported. Not only was the final destination of the product outside of the economy, but prices were determined on the international market. Exporters with externally earned profits could repatriate them, consume them externally, or reinvest them in another country if they liked. In summary, whether one looks at the nature of inputs to the production process, at the labor force, or at the market destination of the products, one finds only minimal interchanges with other sectors of the Por-

Table 4.5. Principal Agro-Export–Producing Districts, 1902

Districts	Area Planted with Agro-Exports[a] (in percentages)	Average Number of Hectares per Farm	Farm Size[b]
Aveiro	30.09	.30	2
Braga	35.69	.47	6
Faro	31.64	1.81	13
Leiria	43.04	.42	5
Pôrto	56.49	.55	8
Viana do Castello	32.35	.30	1
Portugal	19.79	.85	—

[a]This count includes grapes, fruits, and forests but does not include areas with cork trees. They are dispersed throughout the countryside, and it is difficult to obtain an exact count.

[b]1 = district with smallest farms, and 18 = district with largest farms.

tuguese economy. With minor exceptions, the economy remained an isolated activity that had its cycle of production determined more by factors endogenous to the sector or external to the national economy and less by other sectors of the Portuguese economy.

The second identifiable sector, or economy, of Portugal was composed of the export-led industries (ELIs). This economy, like the agro-export economy, was isolated in many ways from other economic activities. A majority of the industrial inputs were imported, the labor force was only partially proletarianized, and the market destination of the products was external to the national market. The textile industry, which employed between one-fourth and one-third of Portugal's industrial labor, was not only the major industry of the country but also the major industry of this export-led economy.[3] Data from this sector constitute an example of how the ELIs worked and also constitute the principal evidence for their claim of being a nonintegrated sector.

Export-led industries, unlike agro-exports, required heavier capital investments both in raw materials and in capital stock. Yet these necessities did not link this industrial sector with the rest of the Portuguese economy; many of the inputs (raw materials, machinery, and energy) were purchased outside of the national market. The machinery for the cotton industry came from abroad: "The machinery in the carding, spinning and weaving sections is practically all of English manufacture. . . . The printing and finishing machinery is chiefly German" (U.S. Dept. of Commerce 1911, 49). In the other textiles, such as wool and silk, machinery was likewise foreign: "The knitting machines are German and French and the sewing machines are American" (U.S. Dept. of Commerce 1911, 55). Cotton also was imported: "The cotton used in the mills is chiefly American with small quantities of Egyptian and Brazilian for spinning the finer numbers of yarn. On account of the prevailing high prices asked for American cotton, some Indian is being imported" (U.S. Dept. of Commerce 1911, 50). Even the refinishing industry relied on imports for raw materials. "To supply this [African] market, which is practically monopolized by the Portuguese, print cloths are purchased abroad, bleached and printed in the domestic print works and reexported to the colonies" (U.S. Dept. of Commerce 1911, 46). And, finally, despite domestic alternatives to British coal, particularly hydropower, the textile industry, like many others, depended on other economies for fuel.

The workers of ELIs, again drawing from the case of textiles, were more integrated into the national economy than agro-export workers but still not totally proletarianized. Several facts support this claim. Some textile production came from cottage industries and some from factories. Small and medium-sized firms dominated textile production. In 1917 29 percent of the textile factories hired fewer than ten workers, and 71 percent of the factories hired fewer than fifty workers (Medeiros 1978, 75). Although it is difficult to assess the contribution from cottages, some estimates have put the cottage industry contribution in the wool industry at half of the labor force (Medeiros 1978, 79). The persistence of the cottage industry suggests, on the one hand, a reduced capital investment in factories and machinery on the part of owners and, on the other hand, an integration of the putting-out system with subsistence farm activities on the part of workers.

Further, many textile factories were located in rural areas and hired laborers from the surrounding countryside. Castro (1971, 75) estimated that in 1881 about 4,250 nonfactory workers, such as brick layers and carpenters, were peasants who came to their workplace for the work week and then returned on weekends to their small plots where they tended their livestock. Commenting on the adequacy of operatives to run the mills, an American observer wrote: "Some difficulty is encountered, however, in the grape-gathering season, when there is a large demand for laborers" (U.S. Dept. of Commerce 1911, 51). Other evidence that supports the claim of a semiproletarianized textile labor force is that 64.9 percent of textile workers were women and children (Medeiros 1978, 75). This labor force was composed largely of subsistence farmers, women, and children who only partially subsisted on the wages from the textile industries — wages supplemented subsistence farming. This particular system of labor organization was in transition, and the growth of the capitalist textile industry, which eclipsed the cottage artisans in both quality and quantity of spinning and weaving, would liquidate rural textile production as an activity complementary to the farm economy. This transition continued into the twentieth century (Castro 1973, 113–14).

The textile market was a foreign market not as a result of domestic market saturation but rather because the Portuguese textile market had been betrothed to the British. After the 1703 Methuen Treaty, which awarded the Portuguese textile market to England, Portuguese textiles never had a chance in the domestic market. For that reason, producers turned to the colonies. One of the largest cloth producers, Companhia Fabril Libonese, sent two-thirds of its production to the colonies. Given this market orientation, the Portuguese industry produced cheaper textiles than those imported for domestic use. And because the foreign market was a colonial market, the producers had a better chance of controlling prices through governmental restrictions on non-Portuguese imports.

One can only speculate on the direction of causality between product quality and market orientation, but this export-oriented industry was underdeveloped. The technology of the textile industry was old and progressively less competitive on the international market. The wool textile industry was outdated and not even capable of meeting the quality or quantity of local demand. With the World War I armistice (1918), growing currency devaluation, and an unprotected domestic market, even more foreign goods flooded the local market. Foreign textile imports jumped after the liberal 1923 tariff law (Decree 8741).

It is clear that ELIs such as textiles had a heavy exogenous component in profit determination. Prices of raw materials, machinery, and energy were beyond the control of the producers. By virtue of the colonial state, the prices of textiles sold to the colonies were partially within the control of producers, although the overall capacity of the African economy to absorb Portuguese production depended on its own welfare, which in turn was dependent on rubber and other agro-exports.

Although the canning industry appears to straddle the agro-export and ELI economies, I group it with the latter. The partially proletarianized labor force, the utilization of imported machinery and other raw materials (pressed tin), and the predominance of a foreign market argue for its inclusion in the export-led industrial sector.

Among the major inputs of the fish canning industry were fish, oils, and tin. The fluctuations in the industry depended on the supply of fish—the output could as much as double from one year to the next without any changes in the number of factories (Marques 1980, 227). The conserving process used either locally available oils or imported ones, depending on domestic prices and import taxes. Pressed tin, on the other hand, was always imported.

The canning industry hired an urban labor force that worked in factories. In that sense, the work force was proletarianized. Some 400 coastal factories employed around 59,000 workers (AIP 1926, 43). Compared with the salaries of other industries, canning workers were paid poorly. However, the low salaries obscure the fact that the canning workers were only partially proletarianized. Many workers moved in and out of the labor force between farming and factory work in the same fashion as the textile workers. In the case of the canning workers, this practice stemmed from the seasonal nature of the industry. Many of the employees were women and minors who returned to farming during the off-season.

Canned fish was sold on foreign markets. AIP complained that it had tried to introduce canned fish into the national market, but the preference for fresh fish posed an insurmountable barrier (1918–1920, 35). In addition to normal foreign consumption—in which Britain ranked first, followed by Germany—World War I radically increased the demand for canned fish, which was reflected by an increase in the number of factories and investments made in mechanical improvements (AIP 1926, 44).

In summary, in the export-led industrial economy, a substantial portion of the economic exchanges occurred outside the domestic market. Complete isolation was broken by a partially proletarianized labor force, which also appeared in the marketplace as consumers.

The third economy in Portugal was an industrial one, similar to the prototypical one portrayed in development theories. In this economy, the inputs were domestic, the products were destined for the domestic market, and the labor force was more proletarianized. Such a sector was built upon autocentric development: Expanding markets led to growing production, with subsequent profits reinvested in expanded production, and so on, into a spiral of growth. In Portugal, this sector included chemicals, cement, fertilizers, and metallurgy. Although the industries varied in the national content of their inputs, they shared the domestic market destination of their products. They were truly import-substitution industries (ISIs). They could not compete either abroad or at home with comparable foreign products, but with the help of protectionist legislation, they managed to capture and supply the local market.

Some of the raw materials for these industries were locally available. Although Portugal had mineral deposits, it exported the unprocessed minerals and imported processed metals such as copper, iron, and pulverized phosphate. Raw materials for industries such as ceramic and glass, cement, wood finishing, and chemicals existed within Portugal. Glass in Marinha Grande was made with nearby sand and heated with energy provided from the wood of nearby forests. Glass production was not totally local—soda was still imported from Britain, particularly the leaded soda for making crystal. In the Marinha Grande area, as glass shifted from an artisan to an industrial process, local labor was often paid at a piece rate. The glass sector had a tenuous integration with the agro-export sector, which was manipulated through tariff legislation. Although the wine crisis of 1921 provoked bankruptcies of glass factories, the stabilization and even improvement in the foreign exchange of the Portuguese currency (escudo) in 1924 made foreign products suddenly cheaper than local ones. This resulted in a threefold increase in imported plate glass between 1925 and 1930, and a twofold increase of glass bottles between those years (Monica 1981, 529).

The machinery for these "autocentric" industries varied tremendously in sophistication. One of the largest industries, the metallurgy industry, had a heavy artisan component and was relatively primitive in its level of machinery. Only 8 of the 784 shops reported on in the 1917 industrial survey hired more than 250

Table 4.6. Fertilizers Imported by Year, 1910–1929 (1910 = 100)

Year	Rate	Year	Rate
1910	100	1920	34
1911	94	1921	52
1912	88	1922	33
1913	69	1923	16
1914	64	1924	4
1915	52	1925	2
1916	43	1926	8
1917	8	1927	6
1918	18	1928	6
1919	18	1929	6

Source: Based on data from A. H. de Oliveira Marques, *História da 1a república portuguesa* (Lisbon: Iniciativas Editoriais, 1980), 121.

workers (Medeiros 1978, 84). Other industries, such as chemicals, required heavy investments in imported machinery. Although direct measures of capital investment are difficult to obtain, several ways to approximate investments across industries are available. Using average horsepower per worker by industry, one can confirm the lower capital investment in metallurgy as compared with chemicals (.28 and .68, respectively). Other factors also set this economy apart from the other two. Its labor force was more urban and more proletarianized than those of the other two economies. The largest chemical factory, which employed around 2,000 workers in 1916, was located just outside of Lisbon.

The production of ISIs was destined for the domestic market — either for consumers or for other producers. Portugal had, of necessity, imported many chemicals, tools, worked cork and wood, and consumer luxuries, and these industries began to penetrate the domestic market with the help of protectionist legislation and later of currency devaluation.

Many of these industries produced materials and utensils that were inputs for other economic processes, such as tools and machinery for agriculture. The metallurgy industry provided a range of items for home use, such as knives, tin items, balances, and candleholders, but it also produced articles for production, such as wine and olive presses, machines for distillation, and pumps (Marques 1980, 232). The chemical industry likewise looked toward the domestic market. It was estimated that 75 percent of the fertilizers used in wheat production had a phosphate base and that the CUF chemical company was in a position to provide for the necessities of domestic agriculture (Cabral 1979, 350).

The growing presence of these industries was matched in some areas by declining imports — for example, growth in the chemical industry was reflected in an appreciable decline in imported fertilizers (table 4.6). The ISIs varied in the extent to which they were successful in capturing the domestic market, but capturing it was certainly their objective.

One can find exceptions, but as a whole the ISI sector can be characterized as follows: The labor force receives a wage that is spent in the marketplace; raw materials come mainly from the domestic economy; and products are directed toward domestic consumption. At the beginning of the Republic, this sector was incipient, constituting only a small portion of total industrial activity.

The fourth economy was a residual economy—the domestic production of agriculture for domestic consumption. Farm sizes could be the large plantations of wheat producers in the south or small subsistence family plots spread throughout the country.[4]

By describing the economic activities in this fashion, I am offering a particular interpretation of the Portuguese economy, namely, a disarticulated economy. Specifically, the model asserts that the economic activities that occurred within the geopolitical space of Portugal coalesced into four sectors that were more or less independent of one another. The resulting disarticulation is diagrammed in table 4.7. This graphic representation follows the work of Leontief, who analyzes the flows from one sector of an economy to another in terms of such an input-output framework. For Portugal at the turn of the century, the lack of data makes this representation deficient in two fundamental ways: The matrix is not built upon individual industries or sectors—activities are grouped in terms of the four economies described above; and the matrix is not filled with quantities of exchanges but with indications of the presence or absence of exchanges. In short, it is more of a heuristic device than a data summary. Even in this form, it is useful for observing the extent to which Portugal was or was not a system of mutually interdependent branches of production and consumption. The rows of the matrix indicate how the output of each economy was distributed with an indication of final demand, and the columns indicate what goods and services each economy obtained from the others. An additional row and column record the foreign as well as colonial exchanges (imports and exports). Cells are marked where exchanges occurred. This graphic representation of exchanges emphasizes the nature of the disarticulation. The most salient feature of the matrix is the absence of exchanges among the economies—a claim that has already been made for each of the economies and now can be seen at the aggregate level.

ECONOMIC INDICATORS OF DISARTICULATION

In integrated economies, economic activities are not homogeneous, yet some sort of symbiosis takes place. This symbiosis means that in the long run, profits and wages tend toward common levels. In countries that have integrated economies, there should be less dispersion around the mean because there are capital markets and labor markets that promote the fluidity of capital and labor. Inversely,

Table 4.7. Exchanges of Goods and Services by "Economy"
for Early Twentieth-Century Portugal

	Intermediate Demand				Final Demand	
	Ag-Exp	Dom-Ag	ELI	ISI	Export	Household
Output						
Ag-Exp					x	
Dom-Ag						x
ELI					x	
ISI	x					x
Imports		x	x	x	x	x

Note: x = presence of exchange; Ag-Exp = agro-export; Dom-Ag = domestic agriculture;
ELI = export-led industrialization; ISI = import substitution industrialization.

disarticulated economies such as Portugal should have radically different rates of profit and wage levels.

Profit data are sketchy, incomplete, and without any assessable reliability or validity; thus I offer them as illustrative of the plausibility of the argument rather than proof in the narrow sense. They do not contradict the suggestion of a relatively wide dispersion between the lowest and highest profit rates. Although in 1900 the highest recorded rate is twice the lowest, the gap is four times in both 1921 and 1925 (table 4.8).

Although disarticulation does not predict the direction of profits in the four economies, the existence of four specific economies does imply directional differences in salary rates. Standardized national wage data do not exist, but it is possible to construct a single wage ranking, again from diverse sources. Here the validity and reliability of the wage data vary tremendously, so these figures, like the profit data, are only illustrative. I have used salary information for the period around 1910 to list occupations from the highest salaries to the lowest: electrical construction, sea transportation, tobacco, land transportation, metal, glass, chemicals, artisan shops, wood and furniture, clothing, construction and masonry, shoes, graphic arts, fish and salt mines, mines, food, skins, stevedores, ceramics, hotels and restaurants, beverages, textiles, paper, canning, and agriculture

This ranking is consistent with the disarticulated economy thesis. Industries classified as ISI are found higher on the salary ranking than industries classified as ELI. The economies varied not only in their profits and salary scales but also in their growth trajectories. The ISIs grew at a much faster rate between 1917 and 1930 than did other industries. One reflection of this growth is the rate at which new plants were established. In this aspect (table 4.9), ISIs (metals and chemicals) show a clear lead over ELIs (textiles and clothing).

On the basis of the economic sector descriptions and other evidence, we can

Table 4.8. Profit Rates for Selected Years (in percentages)

1900	1917	1921	1925
textile (12)	agro-livestock (22)	textile (70)	agro-livestock (64)
milling (12)	textile (18)	colonial banks (25)	finance (34)
agro-livestock (6)	finance (6)	finance (20)	industry (14)
finance (6)	milling (3)	commerce (16)	

Note: Profit is calculated as a percentage of capital assets. Where possible, I used industrial categories in the 1917 Inquerito Industrial [Portugal, Ministério do Trabalho, *Estatística industrial ano de 1917* (Lisbon: Imprensa Nacional, 1926)].

Sources: Armando Castro, *A economia portuguesa do século XX* (Lisbon: Edições 70, 1973), 190–91; Ramiro da Costa, *O desenvolvimento do capitalismo em Portugal* (Lisbon: Assírio e Alvim, 1975), 42; Bento Carqueja, *O capitalismo moderno e as suas origens em Portugal* (Oporto: Livraria Chardron, 1908), 186; U.S. Bureau of Foreign and Domestic Commerce, *Trade Information Bulletin,* no. 455 (Washington, D.C.: Government Printing Office, 1927), 49.

conclude that the Portuguese economy did not match the model of an integrated economy; rather, disarticulation existed and at least four different economies can be identified. What first appears as one economy was, in fact, multiple economies that coexisted in the same geopolitical space.

Levels of disarticulation are not given in the nature of economic production. They depend on the relative development of production in the world economy and on the domestic and international political situation. The state of the world economy that accompanied World War I forced some economic integration among these four economies. The war might as well have dried up the oceans. Importers lost access to many of their imported industrial inputs, and exporters to their traditional external markets. This wartime market condition was enhanced by tariffs that minimized imported consumer and capital goods while maximizing the availability of domestic products. Law 275 of 8 August 1914 expanded the president's powers to acquire foodstuffs, or raw materials, or to interfere in any way necessary. Local producers as well as local consumers were forced to turn toward the domestic market for their necessities. The export of wool was restricted (Decree 2149) and available for domestic manufacture. From 1914, legislation restricted the export of foodstuffs (such as onions and beans) and of medicines. Special attention was also given to foodstuffs that came from overseas possessions and previously had been reexported. On the import side, the free import of paper for journals was temporarily limited (Law 511). Wine exporters were forced to turn toward locally produced wine barrels because of restrictions on imported ones. Due to government prohibition on exports, shoemakers had access for the first time to light skins, which had always been bought up by the British (Alp 1915, 181). Merchants complained about export prohibitions, argu-

Table 4.9. Physical Plant Growth Rate between 1917 and 1930 (1917 = 100)

Industry	Rate in 1930
Chemicals	895
Electric	509
Metals	388
Clothing	286
Textiles	186

Sources: Adapted from Portugal, Ministério do Trabalho, Estatística industrial ano de 1917 (Boletim do trabalho) (Lisbon: Imprensa Nacional, 1926); and A. H. de Oliveira Marques, História da 1a república portuguesa (Lisbon: Iniciativas Editoriais, 1980).

ing that they would lose markets to competitors and, in the case of some goods, stockpiling would result in spoilage (onions) or devaluation (wool) (ACL 1915, 37; 1916, 119).

Wartime trade restrictions were de facto import quotas that forced an integration between domestic producers and domestic buyers. AIP admitted that the intensification and improvement of national production, as well as the establishment of new industries, had derived from those de facto quotas. Consumer durables, consumer nondurables, a few raw materials, and capital goods industries (such as tools and machinery) all experienced increases in production (AIP 1916, 145).

The government also intervened directly in the marketplace. Import quotas were supplemented by government distribution of critical raw materials such as fertilizers and sheet metal. In the case of coal, the government imported the material and turned it over to industrial users. Merchants lobbied against both the quotas and state intervention (ACL 1917, 142). On 20 August 1914, the government used special contracts to order the construction of two antitorpedo boats to help avoid an unemployment crisis in the state-run metallurgy shop (Peres 1954, 58). Law 493 of 3 March 1916 authorized the government to mobilize any industry when it was necessary for defense of the nation (AIP 1915, 40). With newly acquired executive powers, the eleventh cabinet of José de Castro (a cabinet composed of PDP members and independents) "mobilized" the fertilizer installations of Henry Bachoffen and Co. (Adubos do Póvoa), which had been brought to a stop (AIP 1915, 39). The government also requested increased production in the countryside to be channeled to Lisbon. Attempts to divert more production to metropolitan areas sometimes were met by peasant violence, which could only be subdued with the help of the GNR (Cutileiro 1971, 190). The government also became the exclusive purchaser (through its arm the Manutenção Militar) of certain agricultural products, such as beans. Thus the war increased economic integration.

ECONOMIC AND POLITICAL CONSEQUENCES
OF ECONOMIC DISARTICULATION

Multiple economic and political consequences emerged from the disarticulated economy. A key element of autocentric development is backward linkages. Autocentric growth with backward linkages implies a multiplier, or trickle-down, effect of import substitution that would eventually encompass not only domestic production of a product but also domestic production of machinery and other material inputs. According to Hirschman and others, such linkages multiply the effects of growth of one industry by progressively capturing more of the economy in their elaborated cycles of growth. Disarticulated economies, on the other hand, are economies in which such linkages are absent and, further, in which economic interest groups contest any attempt to create these linkages. If vertical integration and backward linkages are the consequences of successful autocentric industrialization, they are equally the precise locus of impediments to successful development.

In Portugal, resistance to backward linkages and to general economic integration was pervasive. Numerous grounds for conflict existed among the economies, particularly between the ISIs and others. The growth of the former meant a labor force redistribution, a capital shift, and the involvement of the state in the creation of an infrastructure.

A myriad of skirmishes arose at points where the economies might, in principle, have been articulated. This was particularly evident between ancillary producers of partially worked raw materials and raw-material producers. The Caime Pulp Co. wanted the freedom to export its paper pulp rather than being forced to sell it to the local newspaper industry, which, it claimed, preferred longer fibers rather than the short fibers of the pine and eucalyptus trees (AIP 1926). The textile industry contested the development of a Portuguese iron and steel industry, preferring to purchase its machinery abroad (AIp 1916, 366). The wool textile industry preferred foreign to local raw wool, claiming that the local wool was dirty and of low quality. One observer described the wool at the 1891 Industrial Exposition in Oporto as "very thick, badly dyed and with ordinary designs" (Mendes 1979, 42). Fish canners preferred cheaper foreign olive oil to the abundantly produced domestic oil, which, they charged, was dirty. Millers preferred foreign wheat, claiming that national wheat was only good for noodles (ACAP 1912, 148). And the metallurgy industry complained that the state bought railroad bridges from foreign producers at costs higher than the domestic equivalents (AIP 1926, 39). The hotel industry—to the detriment of the national furniture industry—fought for tax exemptions on imported furniture (ACL 1908,

102). When domestic wheat production was inadequate and wheat had to be imported, the foreign wheat would often be sitting in harbors (sometimes the Lisbon harbor), ready for purchase, before the word even arrived in Portuguese Africa and to the detriment of colonial producers (Lima 1925, 49).

Portugal produced half of the world cork supply but only transformed 22 percent of its own production. On the one side, AIP wrote that Portugal had to develop its bottle stopper and agglomerate industry (1921, 29). On the other side, when the government prohibited the export of raw cork, an editorial in the major commercial journal (*JCC* 9 November 1910) blasted the government's desire to sacrifice farmers for factory owners and workers. It claimed that such prohibitions violated international treaties, and it doubted that the world needed as many bottle stoppers as the Portuguese cork industrialists wanted to produce. Cork cutters struck in 1911, gaining concessions from the government that, the agricultural association charged, constituted an attack on the liberty of commerce and agriculture (ACAP 1912, 9). ACL refused to accept the premise that cork-producing countries had to be cork transformers as well (ACL 1919, 49). In a similar vein, policymakers anticipated that auxiliary industries, including furniture, processed wood, paper pulp, and toothpicks, could be developed by restricting the export of raw wood. Wood exporters and merchants objected, claiming that the domestic demand for wood was insignificant (ACL 1920–1921, 174). Businessmen from different economic fractions fought against economic integration; they preferred disarticulation.

Domestic industries also competed with colonial ones. This domestic dependence on the colonial market meant that they continuously had to contest autonomous colonial development. When developers proposed establishing alcohol, textile, or soap factories in the colonies, cries of protest were heard from ELI producers on the continent. Although ISIs—such as the soap industry run by Portugal's best-known industrialist, Alfredo da Silva—supported the development of *extractive* industries in the colonies, they would not support the development of *finishing*. For example, Silva endorsed the extraction of oil from seeds (an African raw material that he could use), but he opposed the competition that would ensue from colonial production of soap from the seed oils (Martins n.d., 7).

Because the majority of economic activity took place outside of the geopolitical sphere of Portugal, the question of foreign currency was highly contested. Foreign exchange was earned through exports, transfers from emigrants, and so on. The foreign exchange in turn had to be partitioned among those who needed it for importing. In addition to the import necessities for each economy, luxury goods were imported for the new, growing urban classes. Producers of capital goods had to compete with the purchase of foodstuffs and with luxury items for foreign exchange. No matter how much the agro-export economy grew, international earnings would have never compensated for the increase in the import bill resulting from increased capital goods consumption.

Conflicts about capital were evident in disputes over new tax structures. Each economy lobbied for the maximum taxation of the others. The antipathy that domestic farmers had for industrial activities was expressed in a northern newspaper, *O diário do norte*, in which farmers complained "that the value of the land and years of work can easily be destroyed in one moment of nature. Industry and commerce with relatively little capital and work can make a fortune, while the farmer does it very slowly and with high risk" (ACAP 1913, 81).

Another area of conflict revolved around the issue of frontiers and protectionism. Protectionist legislation was a recurrent request from ISIs that wanted to diminish the competition from foreign goods by keeping the doors closed both on the continent and in the African colonies. Producers of export products and international commercial houses, on the other hand, preferred open doors that would allow them to trade in all items, even cloth and threads that were domestically produced. Frontier policies were always an area of conflict between industrialists and merchants that flourished on high volume. Industrialists and farmers, on the other hand, split over the issue of protection. The historical record leaves no doubt that imported wheat was cheaper than domestic wheat. It was preferred not only by the urban population, the chief consumer of that product, and by milling industrialists who made flour and bread but even by other industrialists who understood that imported wheat could cheapen the wage bill.

The protection debate also had advocates for retaining raw materials for domestic use. Those policymakers who had hoped to develop the auxiliary wood industries, including furniture, processed wood, paper pulp, and toothpicks, by restricting the export of raw wood, suggested that export duties be weighted by the amount of national labor embodied in the items, thereby giving advantages to industrial exports (AIP 1921, 31). ACP objected to a similar tariff in 1921, arguing that the loss of exports would mean the loss of gold (1921, 75).

In similar fashion, farmers, businessmen, and industrialists disputed the welfare of workers. Although raising the salaries of workers and the urban classes was a mechanism for expanding purchasing power and thus the domestic market of some industries, to those who produced for export, it was nothing more than an increase in the prices of export goods.

Because of the disarticulation of the Portuguese economy, what at first appears as quite ironic turns out not to be at all. Portugal was, without a doubt, an agricultural country. Yet despite the fact that it was overwhelmingly agricultural, Portugal had to import foodstuffs. It consistently registered deficits in wood, coal, oils, plants and seeds, and livestock. Portugal, predominantly agricultural in its utilization of the land, in the occupation of its population, in the receipts of the state, and in the nature of its export activities could not feed its people. The total package of exports, which accounted for 27 percent of all commercial activity, could not compensate for the imports—debts remained. The second phenomenon that appears ironic is that, although Portugal possessed colonies, the wealth, raw materials, and so on were shipped to other countries for use in industrial production. For example, cacao was imported from the colony of São Tomé, but it was promptly reexported to countries such as Holland where it was converted into sweets. Portugal in turn imported finished chocolate products from other industrial countries. A *capital* (17 November 1915, 3) asked why Portugal, with its own resources of cacao and sugar, could not execute the transformation from materials to finished chocolates. Despite the fact that colonial supplies seemed adequate to provide at least 30,000 of the 38,000 long tons consumed on the continent, Portugal bought sugar beet from Austria while Mozambique sold its sugar to South Africa and Britain (*A capital* 2 November 1914).

These ironies disappear in the context of a disarticulated economy. Each sector behaved in a rational, cost-effective manner: Fish canners imported oil for their canning processes, and farmers produced oil for export. Although the consequence at the aggregate level (the export and import of oils) was inefficient, each economy, acting autonomously and efficiently, contributed to that peculiar situation. These observations are consistent with general characteristics attributed to disarticulated economies (De Janvry 1981; Marini 1973).

CONCLUSION

Two aspects of the Portuguese economy have been described: its semiperipherality and its disarticulation. Further, I have argued that the second was the domestic manifestation of the first. Using the functional definition of world-system zones, the semiperipherality of Portugal becomes clear. In fact, in this regard, Portugal probably comes closest to the ideal type. The second step was to argue that the disarticulated economy was the result of Portugal's location in the world-system. Does semiperipheral status perforce mean disarticulation? If Portugal had been, or aspired to be, nothing more than an entrepôt, taking cacao and the like from its colonies and reexporting it to Europe, as it had done for centuries, and if the revenue gained from that activity had satisfied the needs of the nation, semiperipheral status need not have produced a disarticulated economy. Put another way, if 80 percent of Portugal's commercial movement had been reexports, it would have been a country of merchants, not of a disarticulated economy. As we saw at the end of chapter 3, industrial production for export was replacing reexporting as the economic activity with the colonies. In this case, semiperipherality led to disarticulation.

Portugal's economic organization posed structural hurdles to the collective action of the bourgeoisie. What remains to be demonstrated is that the disputes among the bourgeoisie were neither trivial nor epiphenomenal. These conflicts did not originate in family feuds, stubbornness, lack of patriotic will, or even in minor differences of interest. They were based upon economies with different markets and different profit rates and wage bills—in short, upon different modes of organizing production. Portugal was not just an ensemble of economic sectors; fundamental fissures existed within its social organization.

Were such conflicts reconcilable? Could a bourgeoisie, so fundamentally divided, agree and unify? The need for unity stemmed from the economic and political crises described in the previous chapter. The alternative economic projects, described in the next chapter (chapter 5), called for unification of the bourgeoisie, albeit around each fraction's rallying cry. The alternative economic projects represent different interpretations of the crisis, of its solution, and in turn of the organization needed in Portuguese society to defeat the crisis. These projects were the embodiment of the economies described in this chapter. They were economic projects with their own political agendas. How those fissures, manifested in economic projects, were translated into political conflict and then into structural hurdles to democratic stability is treated in part 3 (chapters 6 and 7).

CHAPTER 5

Alternative Economic Projects

We have seen how the erosion of the agro-export and trade project contributed to the political crisis that brought down the Portuguese monarchy. We have also seen how that erosion was accompanied by the growth of incipient industrialization (both ISI and ELI). The erosion of the agro-export and trade project and the collapse of the monarchy unleashed a violent struggle among the advocates of contending economic projects. This chapter presents five projects — the principal alternative paths to economic development. Each alternative was a proposal for a new hegemonic organization of society that included a vision of future economic development, policies to achieve that level of development, and an ideology that presented the particular economic interests of the project advocates as the interests of the nation as a whole.[1] They were advocated by politicians, intellectuals, lobbyists for economic associations, and economic actors themselves. A description of the five projects is followed by a scenario of development based on the strongest candidate of the five — exporting industry. Next I give reasons why that project needed to coexist with domestic farmers in an alliance. I enumerate both the economic and political difficulties presented to such an alliance formation and preview the conclusion of the book, namely, that the political instability of the Portuguese Republic was rooted in the difficulties of executing this hegemonic project.

The three major economic paths were a return to a mythical agricultural past; a reaffirmation of the past (which had several variations); and a push for industrial development (again with variations). Described in world-system terms, these paths would be marginalization from the world-system, taking a more peripheral position, and movement toward the core, respectively. To the extent that mobility does exist in the world-system, countries move under certain conditions and via certain social transformations. There is some parallel between the projects and the alternative paths of mobility in the world-system described by Wallerstein (1981, 267–94). First, he suggests, countries can take advantage of world economic crises to promote their own development. For example, countries (especially semiperipheral ones) with an adequate industrial base were able to seize the opportunity during a depression and expand their own domestic market, especially for ISIs (Wallerstein 1981, 276). A second route involves opening the country to foreign capital. Development through self-reliance without crises or foreign capital is still another route. For semiperipheral countries to be upwardly mobile, they need an additional condition. Semiperipheral countries need a large enough market to justify their advanced technology (Wallerstein 1981, 282). Such an enlarged market could come from political protection of the home market, expanded political boundaries (including colonial ones), state subsidies to reduce production costs, or increased purchasing power to the internal market.

Five specific Portuguese projects that contain some of these paths and strategies can be identified. One project connected the self-sufficiency of Portugal to subsidies and political support for large-estate farmers. A second project, also predicated upon the conviction that Portugal could satisfy its own foodstuffs market, advocated agrarian reform. A third project lifted development squarely onto the shoulders of industry, whereas a fourth, the colonial project, argued that the supremacy of Portugal would rest upon colonial development. The fifth project was a continuation (or, perhaps more correctly, a resurrection) of the dominant nineteenth-century project: economic development through commercial exchanges. These projects are presented as ideal types, which assumes their mutual exclusivity. This exclusivity applies to the first three, less to the fourth, and not at all to the last. The fourth, or colonial, project coincides with the industrial export project. The trade (fifth) project coincides with one version of the industrial project (ELI) and with most versions of the colonial project. The only unique version of the trade project was its advocacy of agro-exports. In each case, I let the partisans of these projects and commentators of the time explain how the pursuit of each project would produce economic wealth for Portugal.

PROJECT 1: THE TREASURE OF PORTUGAL IS ITS SOIL

In 1918 Rebello of the agricultural association wrote: "The latifúndio [large landed estate] is the treasure of Portugal, the natural organization of our agrarian economy" (ACAP 1918, 245). This claim was predicated upon two essential notions: that agriculture was the mother of wealth in Portugal and that "the well-being of the agricultural class is not for its exclusive benefit but for the common good" (ACAP 1912, 2:34). From its inception to the end of the Republic, the ACAP heralded agrarian development as the hegemonic project. Portugal, an agricultural country by its very nature, had to be able to feed itself. The defense rested upon the claim that the soil was benign and fertile for the production of those products peculiar to temperate zones. ACAP claimed that history (which had been brought "to testify" more than once) bore out this argument — the principal wealth of a country had come from its land (*JCC* 4 September 1912). The country could and had to produce its own bread. Not to do so was wasteful of natural resources and detrimental to society, given that the bread shortage necessitated importing grains.

Despite its natural proclivity and the financial necessity of agricultural autarky, Portugal in 1912 was producing at higher per unit costs than any other country with similar conditions (*JCC* 4 September 1912). Rebello went on, however, to argue that because Portugal produced more expensively than other European countries, agricultural production needed attention. The restraints that had been placed upon it must be removed. But the republican government, instead of recognizing the need to nurture agriculture, launched a violent attack on that system, claiming that large landed estates encouraged absentee ownership. To the contrary, Rebello claimed, as the size of the farm unit increases, the incentives to live on the land and to realize profits also increase. Inversely, small farmers are less prepared to fertilize, choose seeds, or use machinery. Further, those activities require a capital investment that only the larger landowner is prepared to make. In response to the claim that large estates were the source of emigration and depopulation, ACAP alleged that such phenomena did not exist in the south where the large landed estates were found but rather in the north where land plots were excessively subdivided.

A project of domestic agricultural development would benefit the nation—a nation of farmers—and go far beyond the narrow interests of individual farmers. Because so many foodstuffs were imported—75 percent of the rice and 52 percent of the consumed wheat in 1913 (Cabreira 1916, 389)—this constituted a significant drain on Portugal's gold reserves. In this way, not only would the project of the *latifundistas* secure the gold reserves, but increased production would benefit all Portuguese.

To further this agricultural project, a certain social and political environment was desirable. Farmers had a political agenda with policies to improve the condition of large landowners and thus of agriculture. Their minimal requests to the republican governments were institutional ones: a Ministry of Agriculture and an agricultural survey. The first request was satisfied only in 1918, seven years after the declaration of the Republic. In 1920 the farmers lost their ministry when it was combined with the Ministry of Provisions. They protested, arguing that such a fusion distracted the minister from attending to the problems of agriculture. In 1924 ACAP lobbied for an "apolitical" minister who would be technically competent to handle agricultural issues (ACAP 1924, 26).

Farmers and their representative associations also requested governmental action that would guarantee them an adequate labor supply at harvest time. They blamed rural depopulation and the rise in rural wages on the higher wages paid to urban industrial workers. To ameliorate this, farmers advocated governmental policies that would minimize the loss of rural workers. They also requested policies that would inhibit the political organization of rural laborers. They believed that Portugal was perhaps the only country in which the revolutionary worker movement had spread to the rural classes (*JCC* 4 September 1912).

On the side of production, the farmers' association proposed a total exemption from import taxes on farm machinery and requested outright grants to farmers' cooperatives for purchasing machinery (ACAP 1920, 207). Policy requests also focused on the need for the state to underwrite the infrastructure of agriculture. Farmers wanted governmental support of experimental stations contributing not only to the betterment of seeds and plants but also to the improvement and cheapening of domestic fertilizers (ACAP 1918, 82). To facilitate future harvests, farmers requested state-organized farm credit that was independent of industrial credit banks.

On the side of consumption, farmers desired nothing less than a guaranteed market, which meant a border closed to foreign grains. Closed borders would immediately bring price increases in wheat, and this just remuneration would bring landholders back to the land. Prices were and had been seen as a viable mechanism of promoting agricultural autarky. Because most of the population had rural connections, farmers argued, an increase in the price of bread would not hurt inasmuch as both farmers and rural workers would experience increases in their income. As for urban industrial workers, farmers continued, increases in wheat prices would not constitute a hardship on them because Lisbon workers consumed sugar, wine, brandy, coffee, some codfish, and a little meat; when they ate bread, it was white, which was totally devoid of value (ACAP 1913, 92).

Protectionist policy had been used before in Portugal. Although the free trade era of 1855 to 1888 ruined the farmer, protectionism between 1838 and 1855 yielded such an increase in production that wheat was even exported (ACAP 1917, 160). History showed that in the last twenty years, only protectionism increased cereal production (ACAP 1922, 178). Protectionism, farmers argued, was not just for large landowners but rather was for 60 percent of the population— the farm population. Further, contrary to the consequences decried by the flour milling industry, protectionism would also benefit them. ACAP pointed out that in 1892 there had been thirty-seven flour mill factories; in 1897, after years of protectionism, there were sixty-nine (1917, 158). Therefore the advantages of this project would accrue not only to·farmers but also to the milling industry. By substituting domestically produced wheat for previously imported cereals, the import bill could be reduced and the whole nation would benefit. Thus farm protectionism would bring wealth and well-being to all classes, both rural and urban (ACAP 1922, 178). Finally, farmers argued, even with guaranteed markets wealth could be maintained if the state did not consume the meager profits by taxation. As can be inferred from the references, ACAP was the main voice for this project.

PROJECT 2: GARDENERS AND TRUCK FARMERS

The notion of a self-sufficient Portugal was not the exclusive domain of large landowners. Land reform advocates proposed an alternative plan for self-sufficiency. It began with the same assumptions held by supporters of large estates: that Portuguese soil was capable of yielding enough produce to meet the nation's needs and that the failure to do so resulted in a criminal drain of the national wealth through imports. Here the two projects parted company. This second agricultural autarky model was quite the opposite of the previous one. It advocated small agricultural units and, worse (at least for the estate owners), the appropriation of the larger units to be divided into small family ones. Thousands of families, it was estimated, could live on just the uncultivated part of larger estates.

This proposed redistribution would accomplish three goals: It would redistribute property; it would redistribute the population; and, by cultivating previously uncultivated soils, it would increase cereal yields. Increased production would mean higher income for a majority of rural workers and (again) a savings in the nation's import bill.

Agrarian reform proponents recommended policies of appropriation and redistribution. Policies varied in terms of the land targeted (common lands or uncultivated, privately owned land); the size and kind of payment to be made to the previous owners; and the technical and financial support to be offered to new inhabitants of farm property. Soon after the revolution, Constitutional Assembly deputy Ezequiel de Campos presented a project to incorporate all uncultivated land (held by owners who did not want to cultivate it) into the public domain. This land was to be sold in predetermined lot sizes to farmers who had sufficient capital to exploit it but who possessed less than 50 hectares. The bill was to increase the number of small and middle-sized rural landholders and thereby diminish emigration. The proposal never materialized (Marques 1980, 72). The following year, democratic deputy João Gonçalves proposed the division and auctioning of the vast property owned by Companhia das Lezírias. Stockholders would be able to purchase lots up to but not larger than the value of their current holdings. This proposal never gained the imprimatur of law either.

In 1913 the democratic cabinet of Afonso Costa managed to pass a law in which untilled common lands—which were not indispensable to the inhabitants or intended for forestation—were redistributed for utilization. The law gave heads of families and indigents preferential access, but the law was never implemented (Marques 1980, 75). In 1917 the democratic cabinet again tried to promote cultivation of private land, even to expropriate it when landlords refused to utilize it or rent it to the state (Marques 1980, 75). This November decree expired in 1918 under the interim military dictatorship that temporarily suspended the democratic regime. That same year, the minister of agriculture, himself a large landholder, revised the law. In the new version, municipal and neighborhood (*junta de frequesia*) authorities were given power to parcel out untilled common lands—in some cases, renting it to those who had in practice been cultivating it.

The cabinet of António Granjo, wishing to protect small property owners, issued a decree in 1920, calling for a division of land into family-sized lots. In particular, it favored families headed by World War I veterans (Marques 1980, 75). The targeted land was untilled common lands that belonged to the state or other administrative bodies. Still another decree in 1921 allocated the same untilled common lands to the same population and ended, like the others, without consequence. In 1922 the idea of the family plot formed part of still another cabinet proposal. Not only did the proposal give the state the right to expropriate lands and create agricultural colonies, it also committed the state to 50 percent of the installation costs. World War I veterans were indicated recipients, along with families, cooperatives, and farming syndicates (Fortes 1923, 97). Another plan was submitted in 1925 by Minister of Agriculture Ezequiel de Campos. His vision of parceling private property fell on 10 February 1925 with the cabinet of which he was a member. It had been the strongest version: It targeted private property. Provisions were to be made for reimbursing the expropriated landlords with treasury bonds that would earn interest after six years and could be redeemed in thirty-six years (Cardoso 1976, 18).

Although land reform certainly qualifies as one of the projects for economic growth, it was probably the weakest of all. It was not proposed by an organized economic interest group; rather, it was sponsored by intellectuals and various politicians of the PDP. The hegemonic appeal and policy recommendations were made by politicians who would not themselves practice the economic activity proposed. Even if weak, land reform remained a proposal for economic organization.

PROJECT 3: INDUSTRIAL CAPTAINS AND ARTISANS

"Could Portugal ever be an industrial country?" Anselmo de Andrade, a well-known economic commentator of the First Republic, answered the question with an emphatic "no." But many others answered "yes," including the industrial associations joined together for the purpose of advocating their development project. Their affirmative response was based on the belief that, although other development models would fail, industrialization could launch Portugal on a growth trajectory.

For these associations, the failure of the agricultural project was unequivocally registered in the trade statistics that confessed to the necessity of importing foodstuffs. According to the industrialists, the agricultural project did not work and its development potential was nil. Further, the AIp argued that an inflated apparatus for distributing agro-exports existed. Such disequilibriums could only be redressed by detouring investment from commerce and agriculture to industry (AIp 1924, 199).

Arguing the nonviability of all alternative development, industrial spokesmen claimed that national salvation depended upon industry. The proindustrial camp contended that Portugal contained sufficient raw materials (which could be supplemented by colonial mineral, animal, and vegetable materials) for industrialization. Further, Portugal had anthracite as well as hydraulic power. And, on the question of markets, its own domestic market could be extended by the Brazilian and colonial markets (AIp 1916, 325). Industry would create jobs for workers, who would then have an income, and it would produce goods for merchants to sell. Thus the wealth was not just for industrialists—it was for the whole society.

Protectionism was number one on industry's list of policies. The industrial spurt that followed the protectionist policies of 1892 brought prosperity to many sectors of the economy: It created some of the best textile houses of northern Portugal and thousands of new jobs, and it brought increased merchandise to retail houses and goods to consumers. Oliveira Martins, a famous historian, wrote in 1900, just eight years after passage of the first protectionist legislation, that it was possible to see marked industrial progress. Martins was referring specifically to the number of Portuguese participants in the 1900 Universal Exposition at Paris (AIp 1928, 1070).

The industrial associations were unequivocally convinced that the state had to nurture incipient industrialization with aid and protectionism. The state, they asserted, needed to override the egotistical aspirations of some of the less-than-patriotic groups, such as the merchants and the workers, who preferred to sacrifice national industry to foreign industry (AIp 1926, 602). Industrialists also requested that the state buy domestic products. For the metallurgy industry, it was crucial that the state buy "national." The AIP complained that the state preferred to equip the railroads with foreign bridges and cars and, worse, at prices higher than what national industry offered. The development of the Portuguese metallurgy industry was at the base of the development of all other industries. Assistance to it would translate into assistance to other industries because metallurgists produced tools used in farming and presses used in agricultural processing (AIP 1926, 35).

To assist capital accumulation, industrialists suggested a number of measures. They desired a reduction of import taxes on energy and primary materials and a reduction of taxes on domestic industrial profits. They also requested the development of industrial credit. The textile industries were having difficulty finding capital to maintain their production in 1923, and industrialists from the north observed that there were few banks linked to industry (*1ᵃ Congresso de Trabalho Nacional* 1923, 50). Thus they proposed the creation of an industrial development bank for which the Bank of Portugal would emit up to 250,000 contos for new industrial development.

Among the constellation of policies were those directed toward reducing production costs, which included wages. Industrialists needed the state to help keep down the wage bill. Although the expansion of the domestic market required amplifying the purchasing power of the urban masses, economic development also dictated some limits. Salaries could not rise unchecked.

Still other policies were aimed at cheapening marketing costs: requests for freight subsidies, reduction of shipping charges on Portuguese flag ships, reduction of postal rates, and the like (AIP 1926, 102). There were also proposals for the development of the hydroelectric industry, which would in turn support the development of the chemical industry (Silva 1982, 252) and the steel industry (Moniz 1919, 94). Last, because the extent of industrial development was unknown, industrialists requested that the state undertake an industrial survey. Here was another proposal for Portuguese wealth, development, and exit from the crisis. This proposal too had the hegemonic quality of offering the well-being of industrialists as the well-being of the nation. The two major industrial associations (AIP and AIp) claimed the superiority of this solution over the others.

PROJECT 4: COLONIES FOR PORTUGAL AND
PORTUGAL FOR ITS COLONIES

"The future of Portugal is in its colonies." With echoes from the past, the minister of colonies put still another economic project for national development on the agenda (Lima 1925, 30). The project captured the aspirations of colonists and would-be colonists. With several variations, this project and the respective advocates of the project saw the colonies as indispensable to the wealth of Portugal. "The beginnings of the Portuguese colonial policy dates from that period in which Lisbon sought to become the grand entrepôt with the Orient . . . [an] intermediary between the overseas empire and the foreign markets through Europe" (*JCC* 21 January 1910).

Roque da Costa (1916) claims that the colonial project was a necessary condition for an autonomous Portugal; in fact, it was a minimum for national survival. After World War I, colonial development took on heightened importance. The Portuguese Geography Society (the self-appointed continental guardian of the colonies, or the colonial spirit, as it was sometimes called) maintained that the colonies constituted the most valuable resource available to Portugal for its postwar reconstruction and take-off.

At the 1924 congress of the Geography Society, its president assessed the contemporary colonial empire: Neither Portugal's financial resources, population, culture, nor administrative action was sufficient to possess and develop its colonies. Consequently, state intervention would be necessary if Portuguese colonial development was to come to fruition. Lima, in a conference on Angola held by the Geography Society in 1925, advocated that the minister of education should create a program to inform citizens (including the Portuguese ambassadors to other countries, who he thought exhibited an appalling ignorance) about the colonies (Lima 1925, 44). He also suggested that attempts be made to channel emigration flows from Brazil to the colonies (Lima 1925, 10). Several proposals were made to get white European settlers to the African colonies. One specifically considered the possibility of using land grants to encourage an "Israelite" community in Angola (*JCC* 2 May 1913). The pros and cons of non-

Portuguese settlements were hotly debated in the Portuguese senate (1 May 1913), but these settlements never materialized.

Colonial exploitation had not required great amounts of capital. In fact, the level of economic development had been called primitive (Castro 1978, 37). Both mechanization and native salaries were minimal. Capital went mostly toward the slightly higher white salaries, minimal processing on agricultural products, and transportation. But, even so, more capital investment was mandatory to create the network to collect agricultural products and to explore for and extract mineral resources. Capital was clearly needed to build the infrastructure of colonial exploitation such as railroads and ports. The colonial project required a complementary national merchant marine because it would never thrive without a guaranteed transport line between the major Portuguese ports and the colonies (Correira 1916). Some advocated direct subsidies to a national navigation company, and others favored tax relief for domestic producers who used national flag ships.

Capital invested in the colonies came from private Portuguese entrepreneurs, Portuguese state loans, private foreign capital, and some local colonial capital. Each of these sources posed unique political conflicts. Encouraging private Portuguese capital was the simplest (and the most modest), and numerous financial and commercial companies invested heavily in the colonies. The second capital source — loans from the metropolitan government — often had negligible impact on colonial development. They were made under conditions unfavorable to the colonies, and, it was charged, the principal of the loans never made it to the colonies. Rather, it was absorbed in bureaucratic expenditures in the metropole.

Two less desirable sources of capital were concessions to foreign countries and loans contracted autonomously by the colonies from foreign companies. An example of the former was the large tracts of land in Mozambique that had been conceded to British firms for development. Foreign capital investment was concentrated: One company controlled the diamond mines in Angola, and one company controlled the rubber in Mozambique (Castro 1978, 39). In the case of foreign loans, the Portuguese congress in 1920 and 1921 passed legislation granting the colonies power to contract loans. Naturally, foreign countries were willing to grant loans under more favorable conditions in exchange for entrance into the colonial economy — for example, the British awarded credits to Mozambique in 1923 for the purchase of British products. Germany was interested in loaning money to Angola in 1925, with the constraint that Angola not borrow from other countries (Lima 1925, 16).

The colonial project was also built upon a strong base because it offered true potential for fulfilling its promises to Portugal. The colonies provided a rich source of mineral and vegetable exports. Optimistic plans for mineral extraction were made. Angola was known to possess magnificent sources of iron and coal. Some even thought that the Portuguese iron ore industry, which had been dependent upon foreign iron, could be established in Angola (Cabreira 1917, 12).

Table 5.1. Angolan Imports by Origin (in percentages)

| Years | Origin of Goods | |
	Portuguese	Foreign
1888–1891	21.5	78.5
1892–1896	36.8	63.2
1897–1901	63.1	36.9
1902–1906	62.8	37.2

Source: *Jornal de comércio e colónias* (*JCC*) (Lisbon, 1910–1926).

The colonial project was interpreted in several ways: as a project to extract and trade raw materials; as the material base of continental industry; and as a market for industrial production. Among industrialists were those who saw that continental industrial development built upon colonial raw materials. For example, if Africa would (and there was little doubt that it could) produce cotton for the Portuguese textile industry, reliance upon Britain (that is, on Egyptian and Indian cotton) and the United States could be eliminated. With lower-priced colonial materials, Portugal would not have to use its foreign exchange for importing raw materials such as cotton. In the metropole, defense of colonial products meant giving colonial raw materials preferential treatment over foreign products.

To the south of Portugal lay an extensive and untouched market that could solve economic problems by absorbing surpluses at home and could promote new industrial development. Here was a market that would permit domestic industry to expand beyond the limits of the home market (a predominantly agricultural population of 6 million). Here also was a market where Portuguese production, with the right legislation, would not have to compete with foreign production. The African market was split along color lines—the whites and the blacks. Although no one wanted the Africans to drink alcohol, the white colonists were considered an excellent market for Portuguese table wines. Colonial markets could compensate for the slack in wine exports that had appeared in European markets. Cloth also could be sold to Africans. However, as was already suggested, colonial markets were not a panacea for other industries (for example, livestock, port wine, and fruit) that had suffered economic difficulties (Pereira 1979, 78).

For the exporting industries, it was important to earn whatever concessions would facilitate colonial importing of Portuguese products. If any policy was pivotal, it was closing the doors to foreign goods. To protect the domestic alcohol industry, for example, a decree from the high commissioner in Angola was enacted in 1923 to prohibit importing beer, particularly German beer (ACAP 1923, 24). Tariff policies had been historically successful in increasing the Portuguese share of the Angolan market (table 5.1).[2] The alternatives—either foreign competition or colonial autonomy—posed clear threats to Portuguese industry and were transparent attempts, some thought, to convert Angola into the metropole and Portugal into the colony. In summary, the exporting industries depended heavily on tight colonial control.

PROJECT 5: TRADING INTO THE FUTURE

Early in the Republic, the Lisbon commercial association proclaimed that "the past is, perhaps, the best guide to the future" (ACL 1912, 35). Trade had been the secret to Portugal's wealth. Advocates argued that commerce was just as productive as agriculture and industry because it placed products at the disposal of the consumer; inversely, if products were not distributed, profits would fall and so would salaries (Ferreira 1923, 8). Commerce, then, was the real root of wealth. The well-being of all Portuguese lay with the nation's trading activities.

This hegemonic appeal was empirically verifiable. Advocates highlighted several factors. Merchant trade had brought wealth to individual producers and gold to the country. If it were not for that inflow of gold, they argued, Portugal would be unable to consume the luxury items and prime materials that it does. The nineteenth-century development of agriculture was based upon the trade of agricultural products to European markets. This wealth led to a rise in the level of consumption (Pereira 1979, 76). Moreover, the Lisbon commercial association pointed out that these economic activities generated revenues for the state. The state could not be rich for long if it impoverished its merchant class (ACL 1927–1928, 84). Thus not just the nation, nor just other economic activities, but the very fiscal solvency of the state depended on the wealth of the merchant class.

Trade consisted of four categories of merchandise: agro-exports, colonial goods, domestic industrial production, and foreign goods. As merchants were somewhat indifferent to the content of their trade, they made the supreme hegemonic argument: Whatever the economic activity of society, merchants were the realization of that activity. This fact meant that they were capable of making alliances with advocates of other projects, such as the agro-exporters or export-led industrialists. For this reason, some of the ideology and justification associated with the trade project overlaps that of other projects. Indeed the trade project could never be mutually exclusive of other projects because it needed something to trade. This undoubtedly explains why commercial organizations were so instrumental in trying to organize other sectors of the bourgeoisie for political action (chapter 6). The trading perspectives are presented below.

When the trade project was based upon the agro-export project, it promoted the idea that Portugal should produce and process agricultural products suitable for export.

The organization of our production must tend to develop Portuguese agriculture and its subsidiary industries — that of canning, of wines, of olive oil, of cork, etc.—because in spite of all the effort which had been made to produce articles of an industrial nature, Portugal is above all an agricultural country and it is the products of agriculture and the subsidiary industries, along with minerals, which constitute its exports (Cabreira 1917, 1).

Wines were the number one product, always constituting at least 35 percent of the exported value in the last quarter of the nineteenth century. The second trade project reflected the colonial project that advocated the extraction of raw materials. Although no longer fountains of gold, slaves, and spices, the colonies did supply a plethora of agricultural products (cacao, sugar, rubber, and coffee) that were sought on the international market. In this capacity, Portugal appropriated the products from colonial producers and resold them abroad. To merchants, colonial development meant expanding this reexporting of raw materials. For them, reexporting must have priority over the use of those materials by Portuguese industry or by any colonial industries that might develop in the future. The trade project also supported the shipping of foreign goods to the colonies.

Portuguese merchants wanted to be world traders, and they particularly held out hopes for stronger ties with Brazil. These hopes took on a strange, ideological justification: "Portugal's future lies in Brazil. . . . Portugal is the moral guarantee of Brazilian nationality. . . . Portugal cannot lose its moral dominion over Brazil" (ACL 1918, 274). Portugal's past did lie in Brazil, but Brazil had long ceased to be a Portuguese colony. In 1911 6 percent of Brazil's imports came from Portugal (Brazil 1911), whereas 15 percent of Portuguese exports went to Brazil (Portugal 1911). Yet historical and economic factors continued to make this commercial link seem natural to Portuguese merchants. Portugal, they argued, was a productive country and had a wealth of products to be exported. The market of Brazil was larger than Portugal's actual or potential productive capacity. The merchants thought that commercial linkages would flow easily because of historical ties, cultural identity, and linguistic similarities and that the Portuguese community in Brazil, when offered products from the homeland, would consummate these historical and cultural ties through their purchase of Portuguese products.

In 1913 ACL, shocked by the continual drop in exports to Brazil, examined the possibilities of recapturing the Brazilian market. Commercial societies judged that the high cost of freight had been the major hurdle to competitively priced exports. Merchandise from Lisbon, in spite of being closer to Brazil than merchandise from Liverpool, Hamburg, and other ports, paid more expensive freights, which in some cases rendered the Portuguese price 100 percent higher than the foreign price (ACL 1912, 140). Their proposed solution was a national Luso-Brazilian navigation line.

Since the declaration of the Republic in 1910, Portuguese exporters had advocated such a freight line. The 1913 freight increase outraged them to the point of their proposing the total nationalization of maritime commerce — that is, the creation of a powerful national navigation company with an allotted amount of capital, which would sustain regular traffic between the two principal ports of Portugal (Lisbon and Oporto) and Brazil (ACL 1913, 252). Nationalization was justified on the grounds that foreign merchants, with fleets heavily subsidized by their respective governments, eventually would capture Brazilian markets with their more competitive prices. The proposal for a national navigation line included a protectionist measure — a surcharge on national merchandise shipped from national ports on foreign flag ships.

Although some hoped for increased trade relations with Brazil, others looked toward new world markets such as Japan. One of those was V. Correia, a minister of commerce, who before he occupied that post had enumerated the advantages of having a national carrier link Portugal to the extreme East. He foresaw that Portugal could obtain raw materials and other necessities for industrial development more cheaply from Japan than from Britain. Further, he assessed highly the probability of placing Portuguese goods such as wine and canned foods in Shanghai (ACL 1916, 183). ACL petitioned the government to institute a shipping line that would encourage commercial relations in that zone of the world.

Retailers from Lisbon proclaimed that "the transformation of Lisbon into a world emporium is a noble aspiration of Portuguese patriotism" (ACLL 1909, 32). They lobbied for turning Lisbon into a free port with a trade exchange hall that would receive traders and merchandise from all over the world. In a series of proposals to create a trade exchange in Lisbon, they argued that it was one of the most important vehicles of international trade, that all major international ports had them, and that in practice it was the ideal mechanism for congregating buyers and merchandise. An emporium would not only facilitate the exit of domestically produced articles but, by virtue of the traffic in foreign goods, would generate income for both the economy and the state. In a proposal offered in 1911 to a conference given by the Commercial Association of Lisbon Retailers (ACLL), Tomás Cabreira, who later offered his suggestion as a bill on the senate floor, suggested a free port in which commercial exchanges with foreign countries would be free from customs duties and fiscal formalities (ACLL 1911, 112).

"There is a policy which we could call commercial," ACL argued in its annual report, and given that all powerful nations had adopted such a policy, it was time for Portugal to do the same (1913, 34). ACL continued to voice support for commercial policies throughout the Republic. It complained that the cabinet did not include a minister of commerce until 1919. Further, ACL wrote in 1920, it was necessary to reorganize the Office of Foreign Relations. They wanted the minister of foreign affairs to be more than a diplomatic representative — they wanted him to be a soldier of commercial expansion (ACL 1920–1921, 404). In pursuit of this stand, ACL argued for rapid renegotiation of postwar commercial relations with Germany (ACL 1920–1921, 411). In addition to setting up commercial attachés through the Ministry of Foreign Affairs, ACL requested that the government initiate commercial exchanges with Panama, California, and Brazil, to name a few. In short, ACL wanted the minister of foreign relations to procure markets for Portuguese trade.

Merchants preferred treaties over tariff policies. The 1892 tariff may have aided industry, but it seriously damaged the import-export business (ACLL 1909, 77). Merchants argued that industry, despite protection, remained irremediably condemned. In place of such policies, they advocated commercial pacts that would also benefit domestic agriculture. Bilateral treaties, which defined the legal status of merchandise according to the country of origin, were favored over rigid customs laws, which did not differentiate products by origin. Although the congress determined customs laws, merchants judged that an executive use of treaties could be more responsive to Portugal's crisis. Because treaties allowed a favored-nation status, they argued that a more flexible trade package could be fashioned. This strategy had worked in the past. In 1909 ACLL pressed for favored-nation status with Germany in the sweet wine trade. Because of the geographic proximity of French and Italian competitors to the German market, their transportation costs were lower than the Portuguese. Only a bilateral treaty giving Portugal favored-nation status in Germany would secure the port and Madeira wine market there. Naturally, in such a bilateral agreement, Portugal would have to reciprocate.

Many of the policies advocated in the trade journals were echoes of the liberal trade policies that had emanated from Britain. One advocate of this project invoked Adam Smith and called for the abolition of state intervention in trade, letting prices be regulated by natural laws (ACL 1923, 17). The major commercial associations favored unregulated commerce. Further, they argued that customs duties should not be the major source of state revenue to be augmented and decreased as the state needed. Rather, the state should extend only modest protection to industries capable of developing an internationally competitive position and withdraw support from industries incapable of survival without protectionism.

On the export side, merchants argued that the state should never hamper domestic production with export duties. They vociferously protested periodic attempts by the government to tax goods leaving Portugal. They lobbied instead for export bonuses. The export restrictions mounted during World War I (and repealed only in 1919) had been a constant annoyance to the commercial associations and, they argued, to the country because exports earned foreign exchange that the nation needed to resolve the crisis.

At home the commercial project also required noninterference in the regulation of work schedules for laborers. According to advocates of the commercial project, neither the work of commercial houses nor of docks could be regulated in the same way as that of factories. Thus governmental attempts at establishing an eight-hour day were nothing short of an outright assault on commerce (ACLL

1915, 117; ACL 1919, 26; ACP 1919, 73:97; ACL 1919, 198). Although merchants demanded noninterference in these areas, there were other areas in which they thought the state ought to have a more aggressive stand.

For example, commercial interests solicited state involvement in the infrastructures of exchange. New ports were needed in Lisbon and in the north where the existing port was so shallow that it was impossible for ships to load and unload there. Commercial associations as a group called for improvement of roads and rail lines to these ports. Also, ACL lamented the deplorable state of commercial education and suggested a complete remodeling (ACL 1912, 35).

Support of the trader and emporium project was found among the principal Lisbon commercial societies, the commercial newspapers, and the commercial organization of the north (ACP). These groups represented merchant interests, particularly in wine. They were less concerned about the balance of payments problem. One of the editors of the *Jornal de comércio e das colónias* wrote that it is wrong to think that the commercial balance must always be positive. Some of the richest nations in the world have negative trade balances (*JCC* 25 September 1912).

THE STRUGGLE FOR A NEW PROJECT

Was a struggle for a new project inevitable? Could several of these projects not have been implemented simultaneously? No, not all projects, not even a majority of them, could have coexisted because of potential interproject conflicts. Projects are not simply private earning schemes of individual bourgeois; rather, they are broad systems of social organization—of labor organization, uses of capital, state policies, and, most of all, economic organization.

First, the projects had mutually exclusive objectives for labor. They could not have operated simultaneously without some new infusion of labor because the growth of industry would have depopulated the countryside, leaving the farm owners with insufficient farmhands. As we have already seen, there were conflicts about freeing rural labor from the land, about labor organization, and about wages (ACAP 1913, 11). Although ISIs might have been able to pay higher wages, ELIs and employers of farmhands wanted lower wages. Whether in the form of higher pay or an eight-hour day, conflicts about labor stemmed from the different exigencies of these projects.

Second, the simultaneous implementation of all projects would have meant competition for insufficient capital, and without an infusion of foreign capital, the development of one branch would have meant the stagnation of another. Capital invested in the colonies could not be spent on increasing the productive capacity of industries on the continent or on building new ports for trade.

Further, simultaneous implementation of all projects would have proved difficult in the realm of state policies. Tax policies and tariffs advantageous to one project were disadvantageous to another. For example, protectionist legislation to industry would have been costly to agriculture, and merchants could not tolerate the loss of their market to protected domestic goods. Many components of development, such as labor, capital, and state policies, existed in the short run in fixed quantities and could not be stretched to accommodate all projects simultaneously. Thus disputes among industrialists, merchants, agro-export farmers, and domestic farmers were more than conflicts among individual capitalists; they were reflections of a more profound confrontation taking place among different ways of organizing the economy.

At the turn of the century, the agro-export and trade project had produced structural stagnation, and it was clearly necessary to fashion a new project of development to replace the discredited old one. Which project could replace the dying agro-export project and promote the development and enrichment of Portuguese society? We have just seen that many economic projects were possible. Some were certainly more economically viable than others, and some were more politically feasible than others. The rest of this chapter treats the economic viability of the different projects and their respective alliance-building potential.

Industry, albeit incipient, showed signs of being the most viable project of economic development. The textile industry, an exporting industry, was the most developed at the turn of the century. Other incipient industries, such as chemicals and metals (the ISIs), were the most promising for long-term economic development. Portuguese industry trailed far behind that of neighboring European countries in the organization of production, use of motor power, and levels of productivity.[3] Although the liberal Constitution of 1834 had formally freed the factors of industry, industrial development was extremely slow until the 1870s (Castro 1971, 36). This was due, in part, to a capital shortage and, more important, to the influx of British goods. Protectionist legislation finally kept some of these foreign products out of the domestic and colonial marketplace, thereby giving domestic industry a chance to grow.

Export industrialization posed one clear exit from the agro-exporting path to underdevelopment. Industrialists (initially textile industrialists) had to be the leaders of autarkic development because it was one place where capital accumulation could occur. This project required an expanded market through either an increase in the purchasing power of the population, a reduction in production costs, or an expanded foreign market. In the case of Portugal, this foreign market was to be the colonies. Perhaps it would have the same luck as Britain had had centuries before. "The cotton industry was thus launched, like a glider, by the pull of the colonial trade to which it was attached; a trade which promised not only great but rapid and above all unpredictable expansion, which encouraged the entrepreneur to adopt the revolutionary techniques required to meet it" (Hobsbawm 1962, 52).

Historically, industrialization had been the indicated project. Advocates had been fighting for it since the 1880s, and it was the one place where protection

Table 5.2. Portugal-Angola Cotton Products–Coffee Terms
of Trade (1897–1900 = 100)

Years	Index
1898–1904	114
1905–13	115
1914–23	226
1924–33	147
1934–38	168

Source: S. Sideri, Trade and Power (Rotterdam, Neth.:
Rotterdam University Press, 1970), 207.

yielded benefits. The 1892 protectionist legislation was an attempt to defend
and promote national industry by increasing the tariff on selected imported
goods. The textile industry and the grain milling industry were among those
that benefited. The growth of the textile industry and concomitant capital accumulation was particularly noteworthy after the earlier protectionist legislation
of 1882 and showed accentuated growth between 1887 and 1899. Although the
number of factories increased by only two between 1887 and 1891, both social
capital and capital stock doubled. This capital increase was intimately tied to
the textile market in the colonies. The industry of wool textiles also depended
heavily upon the colonial market.

However, many factors challenged the benefits of this legislation. First, the
legislation was undone over the years by shifts in the exchange rate and loop-
holes in the law (A capital 24 November 1915). Second, by increasing the price
of protected domestic wheat, the legislation lowered the real wages of urban
workers. In addition, because many industries, such as umbrellas, watches, and
matches, imported a majority of the elements utilized in their fabrication (Mendes 1979, 43), increases in the item price, import bill, and foreign debt resulted.
However, judging from the change in the TCI, the 1892 protectionist legislation
resulted in increased export of industrial goods.

The politically protected colonial market would allow profits and thus development of the textile industry. Here Portugal could exercise its "metropole"
attributes. The terms-of-trade index reveals the comparative advantage that Portugal enjoyed with its colonies and thus the prospects for their being the precise
place for capital accumulation. Whether exporting wine to Mozambique or importing cotton from Angola, the Portuguese had the upper hand in the terms
of trade. In Mozambique Portugal could even enforce price increases in wine
while it suffered price decreases on the British market (Sideri 1970, 209). Its
stronger position was also reflected in the cotton products–coffee exchange with
Angola (table 5.2).

The well-being of this colonial market and its contribution to Portuguese capital accumulation depended on two things. One was the general state of the colonial economy. "The African demand . . . is directly affected by the prices of rubber, cocoa and coffee, which are the chief products of the colonies. Owing to the recent good prices for these articles and the consequent demand for goods, the cotton mills in Portugal are now running on full time and some of them are even working until 9 o'clock in the evening" (U.S. Dept. of Commerce and Labor 1911, 49).

The second factor was the political support afforded the textile industry to exploit the colonial market. This support was a source of continual concern to textile manufacturers and to the AIp, in which textile producers had decisive weight. In 1913 they accused the government of jeopardizing protectionist legislation by allowing the Germans to steal the market from the Portuguese (Telo 1977, 68).

Thus, in terms of potential and viability, the textile industry certainly appears as the model for a new project in which the colonies would be an extension of the domestic market (forced cotton production was not introduced until the 1930s). But would that industry, which was in its infancy at the turn of the century, simply continue to grow, substituting the old project with a new one? Would the accumulation of this exporting industry have the "multiplier effect" and contribute in turn to the growth of other ISIs? For this to happen, cooperation with at least one other sector of society would be required. A hegemonic project had to be developed with industry as the leading force in alliance with another group.

The above discussion explains the economic and financial constraints to industry ruling alone. Industrialists were not in a position to force an industrial project on the rest of society; they had to establish their legitimacy through other means. For the industrial project to become hegemonic (in the sense of ruling with consent), it had to undergo modification—it could not appear as a purely industrial project. In the modification, the industrial project would exchange support from other fractions of the bourgeoisie for economic concessions to those fractions.

If exporting industry seemed like the best candidate to extract Portugal from economic stagnation, what alliances would be necessary? Which other economic interests could and would lend political support to industry, thereby allowing it to be the prime force of social cohesion and of development? Several candidates for an alliance with industry existed, but I argue that the economic exigencies pointed in one direction more than in any other. Promoting industrialization at the turn of the century would have meant shifts in the nature of imports and, more important, in the uses of foreign exchange. Industrial development meant more costly imports because newly developing industries had to import raw materials and machinery. This raised the question of foreign exchange to pay for these new purchases. The prospects of earning foreign exchange through exporting these new industrial goods were nil because Portugal was technologically unsophisticated and not competitive on the world market. Industrial development, therefore, was to be constrained by the foreign exchange earnings of other sectors.

The major foreign exchange earners were agro-exporters, but I have already shown how the terms of trade were turning against this source of foreign exchange earnings and how an increase in production would have resulted in even lower prices, not necessarily increased earnings. Even with the heavy export of agricultural products (wine, cork, and fruits), a negative balance of trade for agriculture still existed. Wheat and coal were major foreign exchange consumers. In the opinion of one ACL member, they were also responsible for the devaluation of currency because of the gold drain they provoked. He argued that the government should fix wheat prices so that farmers would plant enough to provide for domestic demand instead of planting barley or oats, which were more profitable and required less work and fertilizer. For energy, he suggested capturing the waterfalls (Barreiro, ACL 1922, 74).

Therefore one obvious and feasible solution to the foreign exchange problem would have been to increase the domestic production of foodstuffs, particularly that of cereals. Through the domestic satisfaction of the cereal demand, limited foreign exchange could be released for spending by the industrial sector. This might seem puzzling because the historical record leaves no doubt that imported wheat was cheaper than domestic wheat. It was preferred by the urban population, the chief consumer of that product, by the milling industrialists, who made flour and bread, and even more by the industrialists themselves, who understood that imported wheat cheapened their wage bill. But this cost factor had to take a back seat to the problem of the trade deficit. Wheat was one of the few imported items that could be replaced by domestic production, albeit at a higher cost. By promoting domestic cereal production, industrialists could acquire additional foreign exchange. For that reason, industry could only effectively overcome the crisis and put Portugal on a new path (given the constraints bequeathed by the nineteenth century) if it constructed its hegemonic project in partnership with domestic farmers.[4]

What would an alliance between industrialists and farmers look like? An alliance (following Gramsci's conceptualization of hegemonic projects in chapter 3) implies a mutually beneficial association between economic forces in which each partner is allowed to pursue a course of development that will prove fruitful without jeopardizing the other member of the alliance. In theory, an alliance between these two groups would have had to give birth to an economic project that would satisfy the developmental needs of each sector, thereby allowing both sectors to expand.

If an alliance could have been consolidated between farmers and industrialists, the condition of the project would have had to allow the growth of the constituent parts—no unilateral transfer of capital from one sector to the other could occur. For their cooperation, it would have been necessary to guarantee farmers satisfactory prices, which would mean profit levels sufficient for future investments and stable wholesale prices vis-à-vis nonagrarian prices (O'Donnell 1978, 9). This price policy anticipated (1) increasing productivity, (2) freeing foreign exchange, (3) encouraging investment that would spearhead modernization and capitalization of agriculture, and (4) allowing capital concentration in an industrial sector. Because total production typically undersupplied national need, cheaper foreign wheat was imported. Thus, to secure higher prices, farmers required a policy of wheat protectionism.

In a similar fashion, industrial producers would pursue good returns on their investment. These included closed borders (first colonial and then domestic) to shelter them from the competition of cheaper foreign products and domestic legislation that would minimize labor costs. In this alliance, the joined desiderata of the farm and exporting industries would have been high food prices and low wages.

What can be prescribed ex post facto, given the international and domestic forces, might well have not come to fruition. The scenario — the posited replacement of merchants and agro-export farmers by export-led industrialists and domestic farmers as the chief organizers of the economy — was, in fact, a proposal to transfer wealth from the colonial market to domestic industry. It could have been thwarted at several junctures. The vulnerability of this alliance would come from its application of the high-price and low-wage formula: first, in creating the partnership between two typically antagonistic groups; and, second, in realizing the anticipated capital flow over the opposition of those at whose expense the alliance was constructed.

The first hurdle would have been the initial difficulty in creating such an alliance. Historically, industry and agriculture have often been antagonists. "The businessman's specific demands might encounter resistance from other vested interests, and as we shall see, the agrarians were to erect one last barrier to hold up the advance of the industrialists between 1795 and 1846" (Hobsbawm 1962, 49). Nevertheless, this is not prima facie evidence that an alliance between farmers and industrialists could not materialize. The famous rye and iron marriage in late nineteenth-century Germany is one such alliance formed in the face of conflict. In Portugal, such an alliance was consummated under the postrepublican dictatorship (1926).

Problems could have come from particular attempts to consummate the alliance project. Difficulties could arise from the African market, which, as we have seen, was dependent upon world prices for its own export goods. Clearly, the costs could not be paid by either industry or agriculture because to do so would have annulled the alliance.

Several alternatives at the market end might have provided alliance members with buffers to economic problems, but, in the short run, other sectors of the economy would have to suffer. Taxes on international commerce might have helped pay some of the alliance bill. Taxes on reexports of colonial goods to foreign countries would have been an ideal source because they were consumed outside of the Portuguese economy. However, such taxation schemes were always limited by world prices. To be competitive on a world market, exporters of colonial goods wanted to minimize taxes, not increase them. These international merchants would have protested any such attempt to cut into their profits. This strategy was also dangerous given the alliance need for export earnings and for state revenues.

A hurdle to this alliance could have also been posed by any and all of those excluded from the pact. Two major groups were excluded: other fractions of the bourgeoisie and the workers. Exclusion was a costly status because the dominated groups would be the ones to pay the cost of the new social arrangement. First, problems could have originated with the working classes, who were to be maintained, according to the scheme, at lower wages. Workers too had an economic preference. They had a preference for a better life, that is, for higher wages and lower prices—the exact inverse of the alliance's high-price and low-wage formula. If there were some way of spreading this alliance cost around, worker opposition might have been minimized. Some revenue might have been extracted from the commercial sector, in particular, from the petty bourgeoisie—urban property owners and small merchants. For example, by legislating extremely strict rent controls, the hardships of the high-cost and low-wage formula might have been ameliorated. However, this solution was probably inadequate both because there was not much profit in housing to begin with and because electoral support of small property holders would not have been forthcoming under such conditions.

An attempt to recover alliance costs from retail merchants (excluded from the alliance) through transaction taxes was equally unproductive. Here, too, the actual volume of capital was reduced. Worse, those increments would have been passed back to the consumers, thereby aggravating the original problem by raising prices. The same result would have obtained with strict import taxes. They would have been assessed upon some part of the population—another more or less precarious solution depending upon the political power of the potential consumer of imported goods.

Opposition also would have come from other fractions of the bourgeoisie excluded from the hegemonic pact. Resistance to industrial development would come from the bourgeoisie and political representatives of alternative projects. Political proponents of the dying agro-export project and of alternative ones would erect barriers against the march of industrialists. Would the commercial activities that had been the basis for social organization for so many centuries give way to an alternate organization led by industry? To describe it as "giving way" would certainly be an oversimplification of the historical process, one filled with conflicts and disputes. As Rey points out, the articulation between the two modes of production is not a static affair; rather, it is a struggle with all of the confrontations between, and alliances among, classes that each of the respective modes defines (1982, x). The economic and political tenacity of the commercial and agro-export sectors suggests to me that if the industrial project were going to succeed, it needed to form an alliance with another sector in society to somehow overcome the residual political strength of an exhausted developmental project.

Such a fundamental shift in socioeconomic formation would not take place in a social vacuum. The institutional process of alliance formation still remained. To come to fruition, the farmer-industrialist alliance needed to consolidate that joint economic project in a political partnership, or a political coalition, that could make or influence governmental policy. The sociopolitical manifestation of the economic alliance between farmers and industrialists would have been a partnership or coalition among their political representatives. This political partnership could have been consummated within the ranks of one political party, in a political pact among two or more political parties, or under some other political actor such as the military or perhaps even the Church. Through political coalitions, farmers and industrialists could attempt to create and implement a nexus of legislation that respected their joint needs.

A STILLBORN ALLIANCE

The collapse of the First Portuguese Republic was the culmination of a political crisis. This crisis resulted from the same conditions that also prevented the farmers and industrialists from forming a ruling coalition within the democratic framework. The implications of the alliance scenario compel us to look for an understanding of democratic instability in (1) the inability of farmers and industrialists to construct a joint economic project; (2) their inability to translate that project into a viable and lasting political coalition; (3) the inability of the coalition to extract alliance costs from other sectors of society; and (here is the linkage to the political arena) (4) the inability of one or more of the above to occur *within the framework of parliamentary democracy*. This, then, is the second rephrasing of the question of why it was not possible for this alliance to form.

I have referred to the economic problems of the first condition several times already—farmers and industrialists had antagonistic interests. Further, the possibility was always there that some industrialists would try to go it alone or that farmers would try to hold back industrialization by undermining the coalition. Thus the success of the project would not rest solely on resolving the fundamental economic conflicts among the alliance members; it would rest also upon the ability of these members to establish a political coalition within the state (the second condition).

One potential threat to the coalition was that the agricultural sector had been intimately linked with the monarchy and might be unwilling to shift its representation to democratic forms, thereby precluding any democratic coalition. In fact, some farmers continued to dedicate both their hopes and resources to the frequent (almost annual) monarchist invasions. Yet, even though monarchist sentiments and ties remained strong, large farmers entered the republican parties and participated at all levels of the state apparatus. The first republican mayor and deputy mayor of a major city in the southwest wheat belt were the wealthiest (and previously monarchist) landowners of the area (Cutileiro 1971, 216). On the face of it, the lack of a democratic base among large landowners seems insufficient to explain the inability of farmers and industrialists to jointly promote an economic project.

Any policy, economic project, or alliance would face the problem of legitimacy. Policies could not be imposed upon dominated groups without their approval. Thus the coalition would have had to persuade other members of the bourgeoisie of the universal benefits of the project. Political representatives of an agrarian-industrial project would also have to negotiate some compromise with the working classes or risk anything from an electoral withdrawal of legitimacy to a revolution. A third hurdle would have been an inability to put together an economic package adequate to neutralize the dominated classes.

Was there something about the democratic form itself that foreclosed the possibility of a political coalition between farmers and industrialists? Or was there something in the nature of the democratic system that precluded a compromise between the remaining classes and a farm-industry coalition? According to democratic rules, coalition policies could not be imposed upon the population in the form of an ultimatum—they had to be offered in a political platform and had to be approved electorally. A political coalition that represented farmers and industrialists, or any coalition for that matter, had to secure the consent of all the citizens who could vote. Democracy is characterized by the fact that workers as citizens can make individual or collective claims to goods and services through the political system (Przeworski 1980, 28). Democracy encourages interest organization: It offers facilities for the expression of economic interests and their conversion into policy demands. Because individuals had voting power equal to that of any capitalist, the policies of the coalition were subject to review through an electoral process that not only contained a high degree of uncertainty but also provided a forum for propaganda, organizing, and agitation against the coalition. Unorganized but acting as individual citizens, the working classes could reject the economic project simply by not reelecting political representatives who sponsored or defended it. Acting collectively, the working classes could strike and perhaps even organize a revolution. We must look here for a final hurdle to the success of an economic project, a project that was born in a democratic republic.

The 1926 military dictatorship (and its civilian successor, the Estado Novo) solved the problem of compromise with the working classes by making its autonomous organization illegal. It thereby removed one of the major hurdles to bourgeois unity and the organization of hegemony. The authoritarian regime also gave a mortal blow to the old merchant-farmer alliance while nurturing the adolescent alliance between industrialists and farmers. Whereas industry had formerly been subordinate to commerce and agriculture, commerce now became subordinate to them both. Merchants were threatened with military penalties, even deportation, for activities normal to commercial practice such as hoarding. Industry extracted profit from agricultural activities as commerce had previously done.

There are different accounts of which capitalists did well under the Estado Novo. Some refer to the general growth of monopoly capitalists (Antunes 1978, 64), whereas others argue that opportunities to develop Portuguese capitalism were missed. Bragança-Cunha laments the missed opportunities of developing heavy industry to provide needed floating stock (both for war and for colonial trade), which Salazar turned over to a British firm (1937, 230). The work of Clarence-Smith suggests that ELIs benefited from Estado Novo economic policies. The introduction of exchange control (converting foreign currency that entered the colonies into Portuguese currency) enabled Portugal to acquire foreign exchange without reexporting its colonial products through Lisbon and, perhaps more important, facilitated the colonial purchase of Portuguese goods (Clarence-Smith 1985, 16). Colonial industries (such as fish meal) were permitted to the extent that they would not compete with Portuguese industries and would have either a colonial or African market (Figueiredo 1975, 80).

Other industries that did particularly well were integrated with domestic agriculture: fish canning, olive oil, milling, fertilizers, and farm machinery. Where industry encountered conditions for continued accumulation of capital, it had to accept certain concessions for the domestic farmer. From February to June 1928, some sixty-six decrees were issued that authorized municipalities to sell off common lands (Cunhal 1976, 2:231). In 1929 support was given for the wheat campaign (*campanha do trigo*) through a state-controlled federation that as sole purchaser of grains maintained them at an adequate price (Cutileiro 1971, 217).

Income was transferred away from the lower classes and the real salaries of the working classes dropped (Amaro 1982, 995–1011). The masses were denied essential purchasing power and malnutrition was widespread (Bragança-Cunha 1937, 233). Under the Estado Novo, the socioeconomic organization was rearranged.

PART THREE

The Political Consequences of Structural Propensities

The structural contribution to the explanation of the Portuguese collapse consists of (1) analyzing the way in which Portugal experienced an economic crisis (because of its location in the world economy), and (2) alternative solutions, or packages of social organization and public policies, to the crisis (also derivative of Portugal's location in the world economy). These candidates were going to battle it out on the Portuguese economic terrain, landscaped by the development of the world economy, and on the political terrain of the Portuguese Republic, landscaped by the rules and regulations of a democratic state. In a disarticulated economy, economic interests act as a centrifugal force, propelling groups as far away from each other as possible, given the minimal exigencies of coexistence within a common geographic territory. On the other hand, it is clear that although the structural characteristics of disarticulation may predispose the bourgeoisie to disunity, these structural characteristics are not completely deterministic. Situations do occur in which the bourgeoisie of a disarticulated economy remains sufficiently united to maintain a political system. This raises two fundamental questions: When are economic cleavages transported into the political realm? And how does the consequent political disunity result in political crisis?

In this section of the book, I use analysis of the cabinets to insert analysis of the disarticulated economy into the problematic of the democratic collapse. In the first step (chapter 6), I extract as much as possible from a formal organizational analysis of cabinets. This formal organizational analysis highlights the unstable cabinet forms and points to a dominant and perpetual arena of conflict that stands out above the others, namely, that between cabinets and the parliament. In the second step, I repeat the cabinet analysis with policy profiles. This policy analysis highlights the association between policy profile and cabinet fate. The fate of cabinets varied by their policy profiles: Pro–domestic agricultural cabinets succumbed to popular uprisings; populist cabinets fell to military coups; and cabinets that attempted to put together the industrial-agricultural coalition fell apart from internal dissension or from parliamentary opposition. My presentation and analysis remain within the structural framework by arguing that given Portugal's place in the world-system and the exigencies placed on each sector of Portuguese society, these conflicts of interest were carried into the political arena.

In chapter 7, I push the structural analysis into the conjunctural crisis of the late 1920s. In the final chapter, I discuss the findings, evaluate the strength of the interpretation against alternatives, and offer a general theory of democratic instability.

CHAPTER 6

Political Coalitions in Structural Crisis

Why should the bourgeoisie be united? Why is it a problem if elements of the bourgeoisie pursue their respective interests without concern for unity? Some general situations do exist that require unity, although societies by virtue of their level of development vary in what are minimal conditions for bourgeois rule. At a minimum, the bourgeoisie needs to have sufficient unity to maintain stable conditions under which it can conduct business affairs, establish some compromise with the working classes, and make foreign policy. Situations that required Portuguese bourgeois unity are presented, along with historical epochs, such as World War I, when such unity was achieved. In this chapter, actual cabinet instability is described. A first glance reveals two axes of conflict: between parliaments and cabinets, and between the military and single party cabinets. A socioeconomic analysis of cabinet instability points to ongoing conflict between cabinets that embodied mainly domestic agricultural policies and the masses, and ongoing conflict between cabinets that had a populist flavor and the military.

In considering the minimum conditions of production, it is easy to see the need for a unified currency. Without one, it would be difficult for any economic fraction to execute transactions. Continental Portugal had achieved currency unity, but multiple currencies, including one from South Africa, still circulated in the African colony of Mozambique. Portuguese bankers complained of the competition to their currency (Paixão 1964, 2:225). Several years after expelling foreign currencies, colonial bankers came to lose their note exclusivity to an indigenous currency, again making continental-colonial exchanges more difficult.

Unification among the fractions of the bourgeoisie is also necessary for negotiating a social compromise with the working classes. Inversely, lack of political unity poses problems for conducting business. When two "enlightened" cabinets offered social security and insurance to workers along with shortened work weeks, one cabinet was brought down by a military coup and the other by parliamentary opposition. The 1915 law, which was opposed by all of the major business associations, was never implemented.[1] Again, in 1919, a democratic (PDP) cabinet attempted to legislate an eight-hour day for workers. Two general complaints circulated among businessmen about a reduced work day. First, they argued, industries varied in their annual as well as their daily schedules. The continuous-process industries (olive oil and chemicals) worried about forcing an irregular industry into a regular work schedule. Harvests also varied by seasons and could not be restricted in this manner. And what about filling large orders? Retail merchants wondered how they could do business (ACLL 1915, 65).

Second, industrialists argued that in a time of economic crisis, the production of workers should be increased, not decreased (AIp 1915, 359), and that the effect of this legislation would be reduced production (AIP 1918–1920, 56). They argued that workers could not afford the loss of salary commensurate with a drop to an eight-hour day, and owners could not afford to pay three eight-hour shifts instead of two twelve-hour ones. Some claimed that the number of employees would need to be doubled (AIP 1911, 126). AIp thought the eight-hour day a fine idea for developed nations, but for nations in crisis an eight-hour day and free trade were nothing more than strategies by developed countries to handicap less developed ones (AIp 1926, 604). Similar complaints were voiced by ACL, ACLL, UACI, ACP, plus the cork and boat owners trade associations. Regulation, finally coming six years after the 1919 legislation, did not make AIp any happier (1925, 474). These conflicts over how much to "give in" to working-class demands stemmed from intrabourgeois disagreements and the inability of political representatives to reach consensus on a social pact.

The lack of bourgeois unity complicated Portuguese international relations, making it difficult, for example, to consolidate bilateral agreements. Bilateral agreements typically favored one sector at the expense of another and thus were a focus of conflict. Sweet wine producers from the south opposed a treaty that favored port wine producers in the north.[2] This intrabourgeois battle delayed ratification of the treaty with Britain and hindered international negotiations.

Some fractions of the bourgeoisie saw the impending need for intrasectoral unity. In its 1916 trade journal, *Trabalho nacional*, AIp predicted that the end of the war would bring unfavorable economic consequences. With peace, they foresaw the end of the guaranteed market, particularly the loss of demand for uniforms, combat equipment, and foodstuffs. World peace, wrote the editor, would not bring peace to the economy; rather, it would bring an intensification of battles among industrialists and merchants. In such a situation, the industrialists had to unite and to close ranks (AIp 1916, 226). This was the basis for the 1916 meetings between the two major industrial associations, AIP and AIp. Lack of economic interest group unity was also blamed for inadequate political representation in the congress. Instead of acting with indifference, ACL argued, groups should work together for electoral victories (ACL 1919, 36).

Despite such economic exigencies for unification, the unity of the bourgeoisie is not given automatically; it has to be constructed. The diverse economic interests and orientations of the various fractions have to be reconciled, either through force or consent. Thus one fraction of the bourgeoisie, if it had the power to do so through civil war, the military, a dictator, or strong executive, could force "unification." In a society in which the unity of the bourgeoisie is achieved through consent, the economic project that orchestrates that unity is viewed as dominant or hegemonic. Because domination by consent needs to be continually recreated, one should look at the places and ways in which political unity is achieved.

Where can this consent be fashioned? There are numerous places where the bourgeoisie can reach a compromise: various branches of state, religious organizations, private clubs, political and economic associations, or even extended family networks. Perhaps the most common place for bourgeois unity to occur in democratic capitalist societies is within the state itself. For Marx, the quintessential character of the democratic state was that it represented the potential unity of the bourgeoisie — "on which the two factions of the French Bourgeoisie . . . could dwell side by side with equality of rights" (1969b, 96). So, although the July Monarchy was characterized by the exclusion of some from political rule, the French Republic was characterized by the inclusion in political rule of all contenders to the throne: "The bourgeois class fell apart into two big factions, . . . the big landed proprietors under the restored monarchy and the finance aristocracy and the industrial bourgeoisie under the July Monarchy. . . . The nameless realm of the republic was the only one in which both factions could maintain in equal power the common class interest, without giving up their mutual rivalry" (Marx 1969b, 88). Despite their preferences for restoration, "each faction of the bourgeoisie had to assert their joint rule, that is, the republican form of bourgeois rule" (Marx 1969b, 89). In this sense, Marx argues for democracy as the arena and motivation for unification. The prospect of obtaining power is precisely what keeps the different sectors committed to democracy.

The democratic state serves as a place of unification because the state allows each and every fraction of the bourgeoisie (as it allowed each and every franchised citizen) to participate in the political process. The democratic state facilitates the unification of the bourgeoisie by providing an arena in which the bourgeoisie can work jointly on the *conditions* of unification. Democratic institutions — elections, political parties, legislation, and cabinets — are all mechanisms through which the bourgeoisie works out hegemonic pacts and achieves unity. According to democratic rules, no political faction has exclusive possession of power; when any one faction gains that power, it is guaranteed only until the next election. Thus the bourgeoisie has the opportunity, the arena, and some incentive for unification.

Other places exist where such unification could occur. Gramsci attributes the lack of unification among the bourgeoisie to the fact that the common denominator of bourgeois rule was already met by an alternative institution: "The communal bourgeoisie did not succeed in transcending the economic-corporate phase, i.e. in creating a state 'with the consent of the governed' and capable of developing . . . since it was rather the church and empire which constituted states" (1971, 54).

To the extent that any other institution meets the necessities of common rule — whether it be a standard currency, an arena for making and enforcing contracts, or the freeing of labor — the unification of the bourgeoisie within the state is unnecessary. Outside the walls of the Church and the formal apparatus of the state, the bourgeoisie may construct unification within organizations and associations set up by elements of the bourgeoisie or its representatives. These may range from clubs, which are nothing more than social manifestations of overlapping and intermarrying elites, to trade and intertrade associations, in which the bourgeoisie works out the terms of its unification.

The Portuguese bourgeoisie encountered difficulties in unifying, both in the state and in interest associations. Eventually, those democratic institutions turned into caricatures: Stability became instability; participation became monarchist invasions, popular uprisings, and capitalist lockouts; and public order became military intervention.

BOURGEOIS UNIFICATION WITHIN THE STATE

Historically, there were times when the unity of the Portuguese bourgeoisie was constructed within the state apparatus. One such situation appears to have been at the outbreak of World War I. In this extreme case, unity was constructed above the interests of individual groups. This unity is typically referred to in the literature as "autonomous." As Skocpol argues, "A state's involvement in an international network of states is a basis for potential autonomy of action [of the state] over and against groups . . . even including the dominant class and existing relations of production" (1979, 31).

During World War I, Portugal found its African territory and its own sovereignty challenged. In 1914 the Portuguese Expedition in Africa had its first conflict with German troops. The period just prior to unification was politically tumultuous. A series of democratic or democratic-leaning cabinets (the fifth through the eighth) had been terminated by a military coup staged in January 1915 with the complicity of President Manuel de Arriaga. The militarily installed prime minister, General Joaquim Pimenta de Castro, filled his cabinet with military men and attempted, with the help of the military, to suspend parliamentary sessions. In May of that year, a republican uprising reinstalled the democratic regime, which in turn convened parliamentary elections.

In this instance, international events imposed a unification upon this epoch of political disunity. Many agreed on the necessity of military action following German attacks on the African colonies. Disagreements arose, however, over a Portuguese presence on the European front where there was no actual threat to Portugal. The prointerventionists argued for Portugal's participation on the grounds that such participation would restore Portugal's international prestige, which had been so tarnished by the humiliating loss of part of its African empire to the British in 1890.

The general debate over Portugal's entrance into the war reflected divisions among the bourgeoisie. Although the PDP was most anxious to join its ally Britain in the war effort,[3] the PRE was less enthusiastic but eventually agreed to join the allies. Intervention was also supported by exiled King Manuel, who was in Britain. Nonintervention was the position of the Miguelist branch of the Monarchist party (followers of the descendants of the absolutist contender, Miguel), which longed for a Portuguese restoration under a victorious German protectorate. The PUR, the party of large landholders, argued for neutrality. They hoped to rely on the British alliance for any necessary protection on the continent and in the African colonies. The large landowners were inconvenienced by the war: Imported machinery and fertilizers were nearly impossible to get, and wheat prices, production, and sales were controlled by the government. Further, war participation meant that the farmers were going to lose laboring hands to the army. In the end, however, nationalist sentiment won, and the PUR and others joined the interventionist coalition—the Sacred Union. Political unification meant the political parties temporarily suspended normal interparty disputes and agreed to pressure the British to request Portuguese participation in the war.

Public reaction to this political unification was overwhelmingly favorable. The *Jornal de comércio e das colónias* (20 September 1914) summarized the position of other journals: "The collapse of the cabinet in this conjuncture would not be an error, it would be desertion (*A capital*, 9/18/14). This is the first time since the provisional government that there has been unity among the three parties (*A intrasigent*, 9/18/14). [António] Ginestal Machado hopes that the parties continue to put aside their divisions even after the war is over (*A lucta*, 9/18/14)."

The opportunity to intervene arrived in February 1916 when the British asked the Portuguese to seize the German and Austrian merchant ships anchored in the Lisbon harbor. This naval campaign was said to have taken place on a straw sea (*mar da palha*; Vieira 1926, 371). Although trivial in military terms, it produced the desired results. In March 1916, Germany declared war on Portugal. Austria's declaration followed shortly. Portugal was finally granted its much sought after opportunity to defend its national sovereignty.

The problem of bourgeois unification or political coalition formation depended on resolving (even temporarily) the fundamental economic antagonisms. It also depended upon the ability of the coalition representatives to persuade other bourgeois members and the working classes of the value of their project. Cabinets were the political entities in the state that constituted, promoted, or destroyed economic projects. They were also attempts to form a ruling coalition with the consent of the ruled classes. With the fate of agreement and consent went the fate of cabinets.

What accounted for Portuguese cabinet instability? Cabinets fell for a variety of reasons: cabinet resignation, presidential dismissal, parliamentary vote of no confidence, military *golpe*, and popular uprisings. In cases in which cabinets fell for more than one reason, they have been assigned the least constitutional cause.[4] Parliamentary conflict accounted for 51 percent of cabinet collapses,

Table 6.1. Cabinet Types and Average Cabinet Duration (1910–1926)

Cabinet	Number	Days
Single party	17	156
Military	3	163
Independent	1	172
Coalition	21	91
Concentration	3	162
Total	45	

which means that a good part of cabinet instability was due to some conflict between the cabinets and the parliament (either an explicit vote of no confidence or elections that led to cabinet dissolution). This category is followed by cabinet resignations (20 percent) and military *golpes* (13 percent).

Perhaps some cabinet configurations are inherently more stable than others. To consider this possibility, I first classified the cabinets by type: single party, military, independent, coalition, or concentration (table 6.1).[5] Almost 50 percent of the cabinets were coalition cabinets (two or more parties) compared with 38 percent that were composed of a single party. We might expect that concentration cabinets (those representing all parties) and coalition cabinets to a lesser extent would be more stable than single party ones because they offer the prospects of political tranquility with broader parliamentary support. However, such cabinets also bring into their corpus the possibility of interparty conflict. Inversely, if parliamentary hostility from opposition parties (those excluded from cabinet rule) accounted for cabinet instability, single party cabinets should have the least longevity. The findings are just the opposite: Coalition cabinets had the greatest parliamentary opposition (and therefore the greatest turnover). The average duration of coalition cabinets was only two-thirds that of single party cabinets.

Some facts seem self-evident. It is possible to understand, for example, the duration of the military cabinets by virtue of their use of force and simultaneous denial of channels of protest to the opposition. However, there were only three such cabinets. Likewise it might appear that independent cabinets owed their survival to the increased legitimacy derived from their installation in times of crisis. Concentration cabinets also might have survived longer by virtue of the fact that they were composed of representatives of all groups. But why were coalition cabinets so unstable compared with the others? Looking at cabinet type by causes of termination gives initial clues (table 6.2).

Stability did not seem to follow necessarily from a broader parliamentary base. Certain cabinets were more vulnerable than others to specific terminations. Of parliamentary votes of no confidence, 65 percent (15 out of 23) were directed against coalition cabinets. Inversely, coalition cabinets, more than the

Table 6.2. Cabinet Types by Causes of Termination (1910–1926)

				Cabinet			
Cause	Party	Military	Independent	Concentration	Coalition	N
Popular uprising	2	2	—	—	1	5
Military *golpe*	4	—	—	—	2	6
Parliament	6	1	1	1	15	23
President	—	1	—	—	—	1
Cabinet	5	—	—	2	3	10

Table 6.3. Cabinet Types by Five-Year Periods (in percentages)

Cabinet	1911–1915	1916–1920	1921–1925
Party	36	12	59
Military	9	12	—
Independent	9	—	—
Concentration	18	6	—
Coalition	27	69	41
Total	99 (11)	99 (16)	100 (17)

Note: The numbers in parentheses refer to the number of cabinets.

others, owed their termination to parliamentary actions (whereas the rate for termination by parliament was 51 percent for all cabinets, it was 71 percent for coalition cabinets). Three other important facts are demonstrated by cross tabulating cabinet type and cause of termination: Military *golpes* were most often directed against single party cabinets; two of the three military cabinets were terminated by civilian uprisings; and the most frequent event was a coalition cabinet terminated by parliamentary opposition (33 percent of all cases).

Linz suggests that the passage of time is itself a variable; thus we need to look at these associations from 1911 to 1925. Cabinet stability over time showed a general deterioration. Earlier cabinets had better longevity prospects than later ones. Other over-time trends are also detectable. During the first five years, 1911–1915, the cabinet formula most prevalent was the single party cabinet. That formula was abandoned for the most part during the five-year period 1916–1920 when coalition cabinets were predominant. In the final years, 1921–1925, single party cabinets again became more common (59 percent), whereas the remaining cabinets were composed of coalitions (41 percent) (table 6.3). In short, although the war years provided sociopolitical conditions for the governing of coalition cabinets, the early 1920s provided other conditions that led to the resurgence of single party cabinet rule.

Two important historical shifts also played a part in the causes of cabinet termination (table 6.4). (The termination of cabinets by the withdrawal of parliamentary support was not among these shifts. It consistently accounted for half of the cases throughout the period.) The first shift was that cabinet terminations by popular uprising rose slightly after the first period. The second was more dramatic — the influence of military *golpes* in cabinet terminations doubled from the beginning of the Republic to the end.

In conclusion, important patterns were observable in the political arena. Constant antagonism existed between coalition cabinets and the parliament; single party governments and military interventions; and military rule and civilians. Over time, a general increase in the level of instability and a heightened participation of the military in civilian rule ensued. However, these are not natural

Table 6.4. Causes of Cabinet Termination by Five-Year Periods (in percentages)

Cause	1911–1915	1916–1920	1921–1925
Popular uprising	9	12	12
Military *golpe*	9	12	18
Parliament	54	50	53
President	—	6	—
Cabinet	27	12	18
Death of prime minister	—	6	—
Total	99 (11)	98 (16)	101 (17)

Note: The numbers in parentheses refer to the number of cabinets.

antagonisms any more than growing instability is endemic to democratic regimes. Such analyses do not provide answers, but they do help pinpoint a number of questions such as, Why were civilians in opposition to the military cabinets? and, What were the objections of the military to single party cabinets? To answer these questions, one must look at cabinet projects and policies and thus at the interaction of cabinets as embodiments of both economic projects and democratic rules.

THE FAILURE OF COALITION POLITICS

Many cabinets had relatively clear statements of their agenda, which can be inferred either directly from their inaugural addresses to the parliament or indirectly from their policies.[6] In grouping cabinets in terms of their agendas, four major orientations can be identified: proagriculture, proindustry, proindustry/worker, and proagriculture/industry. Cabinets grouped in this fashion are analyzed in terms of variations in cabinet policies, in cabinet type, and in reasons for cabinet termination.

At least three of the forty-five cabinets were devoted to pursuing policies that would benefit domestic agriculture, a devotion notable in their policies and declarations. These three were led by Sidónio Pais (the fifteenth), by António Granjo (the twenty-sixth), and by António Ginestal Machado (the thirty-eighth). They all promoted policies favorable to landholding farmers. The one-year dictatorship of Pais, installed by a military coup that threw out the previous democratic cabinet, had the financial backing of some of the largest *latifundistas*. His government promoted planting prizes, contracts for exploration and construction of irrigation, cheaper fertilizers, and parceling of common lands. It also established an advanced agricultural school and added a minister of agriculture to the cabinet. The other two cabinets were democratically installed. The Machado cabinet, during its one-month tenure, proposed measures to develop the fertilizer industry and to improve agricultural credit. The Granjo cabinet, which lasted four months, decreed bonuses for increased planting and production; fixed wheat prices; gave grants for the purchase of agricultural machinery; established agricultural credit; and eliminated the duties on imported fertilizer. In addition, it decreed that untilled land be divided among families, especially families of World War I veterans.

Did these cabinets succeed in establishing the dominance of an agricultural project via an agreement with other fractions of the bourgeoisie and the dominated groups? In short, did these cabinets establish their projects as hegemonic? Representatives of the farm project were sometimes violent in their attempts to install the agricultural vision as the national one.

Under Pais, peace among parliamentary parties was achieved by closing the parliament and restructuring it along proto-corporatist lines. Twenty-five parliamentary slots were allocated to representatives of major economic interests: farmers (10), industrialists (5), merchants (4), civil servants (3), liberal professions and artists and scientists (3). There were no places for workers because they were represented, allegedly, by their respective sectors. This was the design of the hegemonic project, and although economic interests were given formal representation, some were to suffer under the farm project. Pais's actions pitted urban workers against merchants. In response to complaints about food prices and hoarding, Pais sent some of his staff to search the large warehouses. Hidden foodstuffs were appropriated and sent to a state garage. Sérgio Principe, who had united store owners in protest against this action, was sent to jail. Botelho Moniz, working on behalf of Pais, attempted to secure support from the National Workers' Union (UON) by proposing that foodstuffs be sold through the union organizations themselves (Martins 1921, 201–3). During the Granjo cabinet, measures designed to help agriculture were opposed by commerce. Temporarily allowing farmers to directly import fertilizers evoked protest from the commercial associations.

Were any of these cabinets successful in reaching agreement with the working classes? The urban masses appeared unwilling to make social pacts with these cabinets, and riots and strikes marked the tenure of all three. In turn, these cabinets treated the workers harshly: The Granjo cabinet entered into war with the anarcho-syndicalists; the Machado cabinet plotted against the "radicals and communists"; and the Pais cabinet closed the National Workers' Union (UON) and exiled its president along with 200 other civilians and military men to Africa. Pais had made some pretense of concern for the urban and lumpen masses. He set up soup kitchens throughout the country, and long lines of hungry people waited for free soup. In Lisbon alone, some 15,000 bowls of soup were distributed daily. But quasi-populist measures like free soup and open warehouses were not sufficient to form the basis of a social pact with the workers, who in the meantime were forbidden to congregate.

The violence of these times comes closest to class warfare between the urban masses (including the workers) and the landowners represented in those cabinets. Prime Minister Pais was assassinated on 14 December 1918 by a man who had declared his willingness to die for democracy. His death was followed by a great republican uprising in defense of the Republic, which was under attack by a military revolt in Santarém and a monarchist rebellion in Oporto. Granjo was killed in a 1921 uprising after his governance as prime minister in the thirty-first cabinet. And the Machado cabinet was forced out of office in 1923 by a joint popular and marine uprising.

The Granjo and Machado cabinets had parliamentary minorities (44.5 percent and 19.4 percent, respectively). The cabinet with the lower parliamentary backing succumbed to a popular uprising, whereas the one with stronger parliamentary support was expelled from office by parliamentary opposition. Advocates of the farm project seemed unable to rule hegemonically under the democratic system. These three cabinets were unable to hold on to power for any length of time. The fifteenth suspended democratic rule; the two others lasted four months and one month, respectively.

A second project, an industrial one, was promoted by the policies of the third, seventh, and twenty-first cabinets. The twenty-first was composed solely of democrats, the seventh of independents, and the third of a coalition of PDP and other parties. The third and twenty-first offered industry protectionist legislation. Legislation varied from prohibiting imports of foreign goods to requiring payment of import duties in gold or gold equivalents. The seventh proposed the development of a steel industry and suggested certain privileges, such as tax exemptions, assistance in transportation, and the like. It also provided a subsidy for national construction of two antitorpedo boats.

The proindustry policies and legislation were praised by the two major industrial associations that had fought consistently for protectionism. These cabinets were just as unsuccessful as the others in getting the cooperation of other fractions of the bourgeoisie. Import restrictions and gold payments were opposed by merchants and their associations. The seventh cabinet may have offered proposals to develop the infrastructure, but other measures, such as allowing import exemptions on materials needed for the hotel industry (Decree 1121), were opposed by domestic furniture producers.

The payoff of these industrial projects for domestic and agro-export farmers was negative. Farmers objected to industrial protectionism because it meant purchasing national, and therefore more costly, farm implements. These proindustry cabinets clearly antagonized the nonindustrial economic groups and some of the industrial ones. The policies of the seventh cabinet were, of course, fused with war-related ones.

These political representatives of industrial projects did no better than those of agricultural projects in obtaining the support of the working classes. Strike activity was also heavy during these cabinets, which in turn dealt harshly with the workers. The third cabinet closed union headquarters in the rural area of Evora and arrested many of the workers. In response to a railroad workers' strike, the twenty-first cabinet shut down their union headquarters and placed strikers as hostages on the front of remaining in-service trains to protect those trains from sabotage (Peres 1954, 246). The twenty-second cabinet was more lenient with the railway strikers but threatened striking civil servants with dismissal if they did not return to work. The thirty-seventh cabinet neither helped nor hindered the working classes. The fortieth cabinet, in a move not directed explicitly against the working classes but affecting them nevertheless, diminished their purchasing power with a new stamp tax.

It appears that none of these cabinets obtained the consent of the other fractions of the bourgeoisie or of the working classes. These cabinets ranked highest in terms of their parliamentary support. Although the twenty-first was a democratic cabinet, having a 52 percent majority, the third (coalition) cabinet formally had a majority support of 90 percent, and the seventh was an independent cabinet. Nevertheless, these cabinets fell to parliamentary opposition. The third cabinet, despite being a cabinet that concentrated most parties, had internal problems resulting in the resignation of the minister of colonies. This cabinet resigned due to parliamentary opposition (Ferreira 1973, 1:82). The seventh was boycotted by the opposition parties in protest of the excessive democratic character of this "independent" cabinet. Parliamentary opposition to this cabinet included democrats. The twenty-first cabinet, despite formally winning the vote of confidence (*Diário da câmara dos deputados* 1 July 1920, 55), chose to resign because it saw that the parliament would not let the work of the government continue.

Did the industrialists and their representatives have to be so uncompromising? Could not they have implemented their project with the support of the working classes by offering them some concessions? Why did these parties not form a pact with urban consumers and workers against the farmers, thus simultaneously terminating rural political dominance and acquiring the power to effect a capital transfer from agriculture to industry? Precisely such a project was approximated in a number of cabinets (the fifth, eighth, fourteenth, twenty-second, and twenty-fifth). The first three were single party rule by the PDP; the last two were a coalition of the PDP with members of the Socialist and other parties. The policies of these cabinets were modestly favorable for industrial development. Most of them proposed improvements in the infrastructure, import restrictions (the twenty-second in Decree 6391), and a loan program for industrial development (the twenty-fifth).

These cabinets can be distinguished from the industrial ones described above by their policies maintaining the real salary levels of the urban masses. Major overtures of this sort included the control of cereal, milling, and bread production, resulting in lower bread prices. The twenty-second cabinet fixed the price of sugar and olive oil. Policies of price control or restrictions on the export of foodstuffs were opposed by both the landholders and merchants.

These cabinets also authored legislation to protect workers in a number of ways. The fifth cabinet decreed in 1913 that owners had to take responsibility for workplace accidents (Law 83) and created a minister of public education. The eighth cabinet, days before it was cast out of office by a president acting under the influence of a military Movement of Swords, decreed a seven-hour day for office and bank workers, an eight- to ten-hour day for factory and other manual workers, and a ten-hour day for shop workers (Marques 1980, 355). This law, which gave civil servants a shorter work week than other workers, disproportionately benefited the urban masses. The fourteenth cabinet showed its favor for urban consumers, who were its electoral mainstay. The twenty-second cabinet inscribed 17,000 new employees on the civil service roll and proposed nationalizing insurance (Decree 6636). As urban residents, workers also enjoyed other benefits.

At the same time, these four cabinets also used some repressive measures against strikers. The fourteenth and twenty-fifth cabinets both used public force against strikers, resulting in some deaths. Although these cabinets incorporated workers into the coalition as voters and consumers, they reacted against them when the workers pushed their own interests against the other part of the coalition — the capitalists.

For the most part, the peasantry did not participate in these coalition cabinets. In the electoral reforms of 1913, 1915, and 1919, the PDP had withdrawn the franchise from illiterate voters (who had been included along with women in the original 1911 electoral law). Such literacy requirements eliminated from the electorate most of the rural peasantry and a good deal of the urban working classes. In 1900 80 percent of the population was illiterate. Although in the district of Lisbon (which included the capital) the rates of illiteracy were 62 percent, in rural areas they went as high as 86 percent. Still, hegemonic rule required some overtures toward the peasantry, even if only an attempt to split them from the landowners to whom the peasantry had been politically tied for centuries. The fifth cabinet had a plan to divide and distribute common untilled lands, and the fourteenth proposed to divide private lands that were not being worked. The plots envisioned by the PDP were subsistence size, which in practice would leave their holders dependent upon additional income. Even though this probably would not have deprived large landholders of a stable source of harvest labor (and one with no off-season maintenance costs), landholders trembled at these "utopian" plans of the PDP and mobilized against them.

These cabinets, based on a project that combined the urban consumers and an industrial bourgeoisie, designed a transfer from the farm sector to the industrial sector via: (1) lower farm prices that would have forced down farm profits and kept up the real income of the popular sectors; (2) steeper taxes on farm land (fifth cabinet)—even going so far as to tax potential income as a means of encouraging production; (3) prohibiting export of foodstuffs that were also wage goods; and (4) redistributing uncultivated land.

These coalitions had moderate parliamentary support—42 percent, 42 percent, 67 percent, 98 percent, and 52 percent, respectively (corresponding to the weight of the parties in the parliament at the time). Even with such apparent support, the cabinets were turned out of office. The fifth left office because the parliamentary elections indicated that another party should direct the cabinet, and the twenty-second and twenty-fifth left office under a parliamentary vote of no confidence. The remaining two, moderately redistributive coalitions of Vítor Hugo de Azevedo Coutinho and Afonso Costa, fell to army coups. Little evidence exists that these cabinets had the agreement of other fractions of the bourgeoisie. To the contrary, the opposition was ready to enlist the support of the army to extract these coalitions from office.

Perhaps the political tenuousness of these projects reflected the impossibility of democratic survival for single-interest cabinets (representing pure economic projects either of industry or of agriculture). Would the same fate have befallen cabinets that embodied a coalition composed of both farmers and industrialists, and could that coalition succeed where others had failed? At least three cabinets attempted a coalition of farmers and industrialists: the twenty-eighth (1920–1921), a cabinet concentration of four parties led by National Guard Lieutenant Liberato Pinto; the thirty-third (1921), also concentrating four parties led by Carlos Pinto; and the thirty-fourth (1921–1922), containing some members of the previous cabinets led by Cunha Leal.

The policies of these cabinets addressed the development of both domestic agriculture and domestic industry. The twenty-eighth proposed protectionist legislation for import-substitution goods, with duties to be paid in gold, and state development of energy. The thirty-third accompanied protectionist legislation with tax exemptions for farm machinery and fertilizers, whereas the thirty-fourth proposed an external loan to develop both industry and agriculture. These cabinets all advocated, with variations, state intervention in industrial development.

Their policy approaches to the working and urban classes ranged from indifferent to moderately positive. These cabinets did not repress working-class organizations to the extent that other cabinets had done. Populist policies to expand the domestic market or to subsidize the wage bill were absent. There was little need to build a coalition with either workers or the middle classes because these coalitions of industrialists and farmers presumably could bring the peasantry along with them. Further, to the extent that policies succeeded in raising agricultural productivity, the prices of foodstuffs could decrease (theoretically), thereby offering in the long run the possibility of a hegemonic solution that included the workers and the urban masses.

Parliamentary support made these cabinets of concentration appear secure.

Table 6.5.   Ability of Projects to Solve the Developmental Problem, Obtain the Consent of Other Capitalist Fractions, and Maintain Electoral Support

Project	Solved Developmental Problem	Other Capitalist Support	Electoral Support
Domestic			
Agriculture	–	–	–
[15, 26, 38][a]		(mass uprisings)[b]	
Industry	–	–	–
[3, 7, 21]		(parliamentary opposition)	
Industry-Populist	–	–	+
[5, 8, 14, 22, 25]		(military coups)	
Industry-Agriculture	+ [c]	–	–
[28, 33, 34]		(cabinet resignations)	

[a]Numbers in brackets refer to the cabinets that sponsored the project.
[b]Data in parentheses explain why the cabinets fell.
[c]This positive valence for the industry-agriculture coalition summarizes the argument developed at the end of chapter 5, namely, that given the structural and conjunctural problems of Portugal at the end of the nineteenth century, this coalition would have been most efficacious for development.

Each had a sufficient parliamentary majority to secure their programs (52 percent, 87 percent, and 87 percent, respectively). They were composed of all groups represented in the parliament and included some splinter groups not yet electorally legitimized. Yet these cabinets were as unstable as the others. Their failure fell upon the shoulders of the cabinets themselves: Dissension within the cabinets, that is, opposition from their member parties, put these cabinets to rest. Only one left office because the elections gave an overwhelming victory to the democrats and thereby indicated the appropriateness of an all PDP cabinet. The others disintegrated from internal dissension.

Analysis of collapses by policy orientation reflects certain patterns. Many political disputes were derivative of the inherent conflicts described in chapter 4. In other words, although political parties made and unmade the various cabinets, many political conflicts were actually the economic conflicts of projects. The government arena is one place where politicians might have worked to mitigate those conflicts and negotiate a compromise; however, the evidence shows that there was little success. Portuguese bourgeois unity was not attainable within the arena of government.

OTHER LOCI OF BOURGEOIS UNIFICATION

If bourgeois unity was difficult to construct within the government, was there some nongovernmental place where the inherently conflicting interests given by the disarticulated economy could have been integrated into a hegemonic project? I have already suggested that unification need not take place within the state if it can take place in some alternative institution such as the Church or nationwide business organizations.

The Catholic Church was an integral part of Portuguese society. But despite its influence, it could not have served as a locus of unity for either the nation as a whole or for fractions of the bourgeoisie; to the contrary, it contributed to the disintegration of the Portuguese Republic. The Church was so intertwined with the monarchy that anticlericalism had become one of the vehicles of republican opposition. In 1909, one year before the republican revolution, ACLL in its monthly bulletin praised several associations for their anticlerical tendencies. One of them was the Republican League of Portuguese Women, which appeared before the parliament to protest the intervention of the Church, particularly the Jesuits and the Sisters of Charity, in civilian life (ACLL 1909, 94).

As soon as the opposition to the monarchy became the democratically elected Republican party (under the leadership of Afonso Costa, its first minister of justice), it promulgated the 1911 Law of Separation and predicted the disappearance of the Church in two or three generations (Relvas 1977, 161). This law was met with intense jubilation by the urban masses, with applause by ACLL, and with disdain by former monarchists and republican conservatives. It expelled the Jesuits; prohibited priests from meeting together under penalty of arrest; banished bishops from their dioceses; abolished the religious oath and saints' days; forbade religious teaching in national schools; appropriated religious buildings; and promulgated a divorce law. The anniversary of the law was celebrated in the streets in 1912 and again in 1914, sometimes provoking disorders and confrontations between religious and civil groups. In 1914 the sixth cabinet, a predominantly democratic cabinet, closed down one of the Catholic centers, the Centro Académico de Democracia Cristã (CADC).

This anticlerical policy was reversed in 1918 during the interim dictatorship of Sidónio Pais. He reopened schools and pulpits to the Society of Jesus; reinstated deposed bishops; reestablished diplomatic relations with the Vatican; and generally mobilized proclerical sentiment while arousing the animosity of the anticlerical population. Catholic parties had participated in politics since the 1915 elections when only two Catholic representatives were elected. By 1921 six representatives were elected to the congress (Salazar, the future head of the Estado Novo, among them).

The conversion of the Church into a political actor reflected the emergence of a Christian solution to the political and economic crisis, and these Christian politicians showed no sign of repudiating political power. The Church was intimately involved in political cleavage and could not have been the institution that unified the nation. Anticlericalism was associated with the urban masses (the supporters of the PDP), whereas clericalism was associated with some fractions of the bourgeoisie (such as the PUR). Thus the Portuguese Church was an unlikely place for national unification.

What about bourgeois unity within its own organizations? Numerous business organizations existed and offered the prospect of being the *modus vivendi* for resolving the problems of bourgeois rule. Many members of the bourgeoisie realized that intrabourgeois agreement or some pact was necessary for economic solvency.

The organization of classes is the unmistakable direction which modern societies are taking. . . . The organization of classes does not mean battles between them but only the reciprocal recognition of their rights. They will have trajectories distinct, not convergent. So that their paths do not cross, it is necessary that the constitutive elements of each class are united and disciplined, then after discussing the general tendencies of each class, the directors can work out the legislation which will protect all and will be violated by none (ACAP 1918, 210).

The writers for ACAP were perceptive about the need for unity and the need for compliance to the pact once agreement had been reached. ACL also thought that economic corporations needed a united front to defend the economy and social interests against the wave of destruction and to give new force to an epoch of expansion (1922, 41). Because unification seemed to be an aspiration for many, and achieving it was difficult within the state apparatus, could it not have taken place within the intertrade associations that unite a series of business associations?

Soon after the declaration of the Republic, capitalists began to use the right of association that had been granted to them by the republican constitution. In 1911 ACLL organized a multiple-interest association called the Union of Farming, Commerce, and Industry (UACI). In 1912 ACAP joined (1912, 155), but ACP decided against affiliation (1912). UACI participated in the 1914 congress of commercial and industrial associations, whose themes included state involvement in: creating the country's economic infrastructure; collecting adequate statistics; providing technical education; developing the iron industry and cold storage; creating industrial credit and an export bank; and promoting colonial navigation. The rhetoric centered on national regeneration.

The second congress called under similar auspices had a decidedly different character. Here positions were much more specific and directed against the government's fiscal and monetary policies on the subjects of free trade, foreign exchange, capital flight, monetary circulation, and the like. The working classes were mentioned only in one presentation in which the increased cost of production was tied to the rise in stevedores' wages. This second congress is noteworthy because of the low profile of large landowners and the absence of ACP and AIp, the major commercial and industrial associations from the north. In 1916 the two major industrial associations, AIP and AIp, initiated contacts that were to lead to further association. Representatives from each association made official visits to the other. AIp later wrote that the factory tours, discussions, festivities, and fraternization of the two associations awakened a long-slumbering indifference (AIp 1916, 205–26). This unity, however, was intraindustry unity and not interbourgeois unity.

In 1918 prominent merchants and industrialists created an alliance that, according to some observers, was only collusion to raise prices and combat the eight-hour day (Castro 1925, 169). The 1921 founding of the Confederation of Employers was another attempt to unify the small and middle-sized commercial and industrial bourgeoisie. Its mandate was to defend itself against the rise in the cost of living and increases in salaries. It promoted lockouts, spying on workers, and hiring strike-breakers. It disappeared in 1923 after the stabbing of its leader Sérgio Principe (Antunes 1978, 66).

In 1921 UACI held a congress that was attended by all of the trade associations. UACI differed from other associations in its representational breadth, for it included the farm and the northern commercial organizations. The working classes were barely mentioned among its deliberations. Major recommendations were directed toward the government, requesting among them the immediate suspension of the law that taxed merchandise as it traveled over district boundaries within Portugal. The congress also requested government investment in infrastructures such as ports and roads (AIP 1921, 23; ACAP 1921, 414). The second congress, held one year later, concluded with complaints about the repressive commercial taxes, demanded reorganization of the railroads, and made requests for an industrial census and for industrial credits. Again, there was little mention of the working classes (AIP 1922, 18). A third congress, in Braga in 1922, resulted in the same kinds of recommendations: improve communications lines (in this case, a telecommunications line between Portugal and the colonies in Africa and between Portugal and Brazil); take better advantage of river transportation; simplify customs regulations; and take advantage of national coal to promote national independence. In addition, this congress recommended some fiscal reforms: reduce state expenses, consolidate the floating debt, and institute tax reforms. This conference added a mention of the need for public order (AIP 1922, 24; ACAP 1922, 123–26).

None of these umbrella organizations succeeded in unifying the bourgeoisie. Even though they were created by the business associations of the bourgeoisie, they failed to develop a joint project beneficial to all. Perhaps these ephemeral associations that produced fleeting unity were inadequate for the task demanded by the economy of the time — that of avoiding an economic crash. Their inadequacy, it seems, was because their most dynamic element (founder and mover) was the merchant class—a class tied to a dying project.

In 1913 ACL had taken the initiative in forming the Association of Commerce and Industry (ACI) (Gomes 1919). ACLL rejoiced in the event of the first congress, which was held in May 1914. ACL members said that they had tried to unite with other associations since 1903 in defense of economic resurgence, thus the 1914 meeting signaled an important watershed (1914, 37). Of the sixty associations that participated in 1921 in the first (and only) congress of the Confederation of Employers, twenty-two of them were merchants' associations and fifteen of them were mixed merchants' and industrialists' associations. ACL also promoted the constitution of a group to study the economic and financial problems of the country and to elaborate a reform of public administration. This proposal was submitted to the meetings of UACI (ACL 1922, 3). ACL, through UACI, was also the instigator behind the first national economic congress as well as the subsequent ones in 1922 held in Braga and Coimbra. Again, the 1923 congress of commercial and industrial associations was promoted by ACL to study the economic and financial situation of the country (ACL 1923, 81). Finally, the commercial-industrial political party, the Union of Economic Interests (UIE), which was founded in 1924, was due in large part to ACL organizational work.

These organizations were characterized by a defensive posture that made it more difficult to unify the rest of the bourgeoisie. For example, an initial circular to UACI membership, of ACL authorship, promoted the necessity for producers to combat political clientelism and other political hindrances to national development. They also argued for a reduction in state intervention, a position less convenient to sectors wanting state assistance. The Confederation of Employers sought to protect merchants and industrialists who were caught between the rising cost of production and rising salaries. When the owners' association promoted lockouts and other measures against the working classes (Antunes 1978, 66), it became nothing more than an organization to battle these classes.

The defensive actions promoted in these associations paralleled the political actions of the commercial interests. In 1920 Pina Lopes, finance minister of the twenty-third cabinet, proposed reforming the industrial tax and the stock exchange taxes. ACL, ACLL, ACAP, and the Colonial Center (CC) joined to request a withdrawal of the proposed tax reforms, but their request was made obsolete by the departure of the cabinet. The December 1920 proposals of Leal were protested even more vigorously, but they were passed into law anyway (Law 1096). The defensive nature of the associations was also obvious in the positions of the first national economic congress held in 1921 under the initiative of the UACI. The congress sent off a telegram to the Portuguese congress asking for immediate suspension of Law 999, which had authorized municipal taxes on goods moving in and out of municipalities (AIP 1921, 23). In that congress, ACP advocated more governmental attention to the transportation network in the country. It argued that trade was made more difficult because of nonstandard-ized railroad beds. ACL likewise orchestrated protests against Law 1368, which fundamentally restructured the tax system. In one of its amended forms, Law 1368 applied the transaction tax to import-export negotiations. Another aspect of Law 1368 was the tax on capital investment, which would be levied on corporations.

In 1922 ACL called for a united front against the advancing "wave of destruc-tion" and for a renewed emphasis on economic expansion (1922, 41). In 1923 ACL submitted motions to the Portuguese congress on monetary circulation and the exchange and development of economic relations between the colonies and the metropole (1923, 81–87). ACL met its real challenge in the 1924 stamp act. First, the merchants and the shopkeepers held back tobacco and bottled bever-ages until the government agreed to a more lenient tax payment schedule. At numerous ACL meetings, members made resolutions of nonpayment. Then, on 14 October 1924, in protest against Decree 10166, ACL spearheaded a move-ment of commercial establishments to shut their doors for one day (1924, 99). Their actions resulted in some modifications to the law, but ACL considered them insignificant. By 15 July 1925, ACL again was complaining about the stamp taxes.

It appears as though the leaders of these ephemeral organizations were repre-senting a project that was no longer hegemonic. Through their associations, mer-chants tried to salvage that program by further integrating their economy with the British. In that spirit, the editor of the ACL monthly magazine wrote that progressive nations, like Britain and Germany, should adopt countries like Por-tugal and promote their growth, especially through trade and more and more through industrial development (1913, 484). The commercial association, then, was advocating liberal trade policies that it offered as hegemonic. Merchants, through these interbourgeois organizations, were trying to salvage the dying hegemonic project more than offering a place for the bourgeoisie to unify in constructing a new one.

The omen for the failure of ACL in both endeavors (bourgeois unity and mer-chant project resurrection) was portended in government reactions to ACL. The defensive campaign that ACL led against government policies was noticed by the respective cabinets.[7] The merchants charged that the government had suf-focated commerce. The governmental reaction ranged from legislation against the interests of ACL to finally closing down the commercial association. Two government agents attended the 27 December 1920 meeting of ACL. Although ACAP had met to discuss the same finance proposals, its meeting passed with-out such harassment (ACL 1920–1921, 535). At the 21 February 1921 meeting, ACL members decided not to pay taxes levied on them by the new Law 1096. Shortly afterward, ACL became the target of governmental repression and the association was shut for five months. On 6 February 1924, the government or-dered the dissolution of ACL (Decree 10515). It was dissolved because it rebelled against the laws of the Republic and it criticized a decree that intended to reform the bank system (AIP 1924–1925, 80). Finally, after much protest, on 29 June 1925, the forty-second cabinet permitted the association to reopen.

Although the most outspoken advocates for these positions against state intervention and of support for a "commercial Portugal" were organized commercial interests, the front lines of the rhetorical battle were filled by members of ACLL. They were the ones who uttered the lofty phrases, "Portugal's future is found in its past," and "Portugal could again be a great nation, resuming its stature of the sixteenth century."

Other Portuguese organizations might have provided some coherence and unity and helped in the reconstruction of a national program. One such society that joined many members of the "cream of society" was the Masonry. Among its 2,528 members could be found ministers of state, senators, deputies, professors, diplomats, army officials, doctors, judges, journalists, merchants, industrialists, colonists, and so on (Carvalho 1976, 99). Members of many city councils and fifty members of the 1925 Portuguese congress belonged to the Masonry.

Sometimes political pacts were made among brothers of the Masonry. Afonso Costa and José de Almeida, two political party leaders who joined their respective parties (PDP and PRE) in the União Sacrada (Sacred Union), a political pact formed during World War I, were Mason brothers, as was Bernardino Machado, the president under whom this union was formed (Carvalho 1976, 84). Nineteen hundred eighteen was a difficult year because of the attacks it brought on the liberty and democracy that Masons cherished (Carvalho 1976, 88). Although President Sidónio Pais reestablished relations with the Vatican, he also put Masons in prison. During Pais's presidency in 1918, Mason headquarters around the country were attacked by civilians and the military (Carvalho 1976, 89). All Masonry adversaries were not outside the organization, however. In 1919 and 1920, the animosity and hatred from outside was brought into the Masonry. In a 1920 report, the state of disunity was lamented: "It has to be admitted that an institution, which must be one of love, good-will and caring, of sincerity, solidarity and tolerance, has the hatred which poisons, and the slander which kills" (Carvalho 1976, 90–91).

In March 1926, the Masonry finally managed to reunite the branch that had split off in 1914, only to be attacked afresh by a new regime, the Estado Novo, a mere two months later (Carvalho 1976, 100). Obviously, the Portuguese republican Masonry by itself could not overcome the divisions extant in society; therefore it could not have been the place of unity.

Unity in a Bourgeois Party

Finally, in 1924, the bourgeoisie gave concrete form to its desires for unity by creating its own political party, the UIE. ACL, again at the front of this initiative, solicited support from the other associations in Portugal: ACP, AIP, ACAP, AIp, and UA (Agricultural Union). Although financial subsidies seem to have come mostly from ACL (ACL 1924–1929), the annual budgets of the other associations, such as AIP, also recorded contributions (AIP 1926). UIE differed from earlier attempts to bring the economic associations together in that it joined these groups under an umbrella organization for the explicit purpose of political intervention in government. UIE was a new vehicle for the organized capitalist classes that were previously handicapped by association charters that denied them a direct role in politics. It justified its 1924 founding and mandate on the fact that "parties had stopped being what they normally are . . . that is the expression of the great currents of public opinion" (AIp 1928, 974). Also, "the lack of attention on the part of the government for the votes of Congress, the general disorganization in the country, all this leads us to think that it is necessary to fight in parliament for our interests and aspirations" (ACAP 1924, 316).

The party position reflected the constituent position: The parliament should not be based on the selection of representatives by citizens; rather, it should be based on representatives chosen by organized economic interests. In this way, politicians who had allegedly been marching to their own tune—party politics and self-aggrandizement—and who had been deaf to the voices of citizens and business leaders would be replaced by politicians who had technical competence and could hear those whom they represented (AIP 1924, 316). The Lisbon commercial association and the retailers association, along with the federation of farm unions in central Portugal, all had agreed earlier upon the need to have their own representatives in the senate (ACL 1920, 6). This aspiration finally materialized in the UIE.

The bourgeoisie's requirements for national salvation were inscribed in the UIE declaration of 1925. They included maintenance of social order; defense of economic liberties and national interests; condemnation of "statism"; the non-retroactivity of laws; the arbitration of disputes between capitalists and workers; and obligatory governmental consultation with relevant economic groups before proposing bills or decrees that would affect those groups. By January 1925, the UIE had managed to organize 104 electoral commissions at the county level. Their electoral success that year was substantial—six in the house of deputies and three in the senate. UIE influence was also evident in the countryside. In 1925, in the district of Portalegre, UIE members sent the GNR to break up a rural workers' meeting; eleven peasants were wounded. Although both *latifundistas* and the GNR had already practiced violence against peasants, UIE seemed to give some political legitimacy to such actions. Whereas other political parties had failed to express the waves of public opinion, UIE would come to represent the interests of its members (AIp 1927, 974).

The unity constructed within this new political party seems to have been constructed at the expense of the democratic regime. UIE was not a typical democratic party; rather, it was a party of unmasked capitalists who had as their goal the betterment of their own economic condition. It was antipoliticians, antiparliament, and antidemocracy. It had cast off the pretext of a hegemonic appeal and had abandoned the necessity for parliamentary democracy (although it was prepared to work within that electoral scheme until the changes it wanted had been made). UIE was, in Linz's words, disloyal opposition.

The shifting ownership of the independent daily *O século* shadowed the diminishing tolerance that the bourgeoisie had for republican institutions. *O século*, founded in 1881 as the official organ of the Republican party, was used until the end of the monarchy in 1910 as the main public expression of republican opposition (Teles [1905] 1968, 16). After the 1910 revolution, the journal continued to campaign for republican causes. Although squarely within the republican camp, it sided often with democratic party politics. In 1922 its direction was offered to Cunha Leal. Leal's republican credentials included prime minister; minister of finance and interior under three other prime ministers; founder of at least three splinter groups; highly vocal deputy in the parliament; and, to some, a bête noire republican politician. He accepted direction of the press under several conditions: that no stockholder be allowed to gain access to a majority of the stocks; that no one hostile to the Republic (namely, monarchists) be given administrative positions in the holding company, the National Typography Society; and that he as director have complete autonomy in the political direction of the journal. By his own account, Leal directed with the "greatest impartiality," giving the newspaper a "clearly republican" orientation ([1926], 159).

Bread politics was one of the major issues in the postwar period, and *O século* planned to publish opinions by two congressmen critical of the cereal industry. Anticipating the reaction of milling interests (which were also stockholders in the company that owned the newspaper), Leal offered them an opportunity for rebuttal. Their rebuttal was to gain controlling interest in the stocks and to fire Leal from direction of the newspaper in 1923. *O século* remained with interim directorship for one year.

Directors of ACL had felt for some time the need to diffuse their political opinions beyond the readership reached by their membership bulletin. With the unification of the bourgeoisie under the umbrella of UIE, the need for an official organ became even more acute. The opportunity to acquire *O século* was unanimously supported and subsidized by the member organizations. In 1924 ownership passed into their hands (ACL 1924, 113). Thus *O século*, which had been launched by the Republican party, later coming under the more sectarian influence of the Democratic party, became in 1922 a less partisan republican press. Leal, a self-declared free-floating intellectual, had attempted to maintain a critical distance from both parties and specific economic interests. When that critical distance put the newspaper in opposition to one of the stronger industries, the purely republican press was snuffed out. As the mouthpiece of the UIE, the paper railed against disorder, political parties, and the democratic state and courted the military in hopes of gaining control over society.

THE FAILURE OF UNITY

Because Portugal at the turn of the century suffered an economic crisis that could only be solved by a new development project, the bourgeoisie needed some agreement, some unity, or some social pact. During the sixteen years of the Republic (1910–1926), the Portuguese bourgeoisie failed to realize any sort of social pact. For peculiar historical reasons, neither the Church nor the monarchy could serve as the locus of unification. For structural reasons, the executive, particularly the cabinets, was equally unsuccessful. The politically empowered bourgeoisie, rather than defending a common denominator (namely, economic production and growth), disintegrated into individual corporate groups.

Only the UIE party approximated the unity of economic groups. Yet we have seen how that unification through a political party could be considered a failure. The bourgeoisie revealed its desire to substitute parliamentary democracy with a pseudo-democratic form in which it would be guaranteed political control. Because the democratic constitution did not admit to a corporatist parliament based upon economic classes instead of citizens, the bourgeoisie had to look outside of the constitution for justification. In this context, it turned to the military. The military had intervened more than once in the political process. In most cases, it had displaced the Democratic party from power and turned the government over to non-PDP republicans. Thus, in 1926, fractions of the bourgeoisie again placed their hopes with the military to effect a transformation of the state. A corporatist parliament could both unify the bourgeoisie and consolidate a pact with the working classes. The failure was not a failure of unification per se but rather a failure of unification within the democratic regime.

Having posited political instability as a conflict among fractions of the bourgeoisie, I presented an analysis of cabinets that claims that the conflict was the political manifestation of underlying economic conflicts. My description of the Portuguese economy laid the foundation for understanding the difficulties that the bourgeoisie had in uniting by arguing that different projects represented different interests given by the disarticulated economy, which in turn was the product of Portugal's semiperipheral location.

Up to this point, I have shown how structural constraints must be added to the "purely political" and "personal volitions" explanations of democratic instability. Although the structural constraint contribution to democratic instability is quite significant in this case (and perhaps in all semiperipheral cases), the existence, however transient, of democratic regimes in semiperipheral countries indicates that the structural constraints are insufficient conditions. Certainly, all economic conflicts do not exercise such a centrifugal force on democratic institutions. Perhaps under different historical circumstances, even the Portuguese democracy would have been able to weather this political disunity. In the 1920s, however, the disarticulated economy organized within the rules of the democratic state encountered insurmountable historical circumstances. This is the subject of chapter 7. Rather than combine the structural and conjunctural analyses into one chronological analysis, I present them separately. This separation reflects my judgment about their conceptual separateness and their overall importance in the explanatory model. Without the structural constraints, the conjunctural crisis of the 1920s might have had minimal impact on the political system. But this was not the case for Portugal.

CHAPTER 7

Political Coalitions in Conjunctural Crisis

It is time to arrange the house.—(ACAP 1923, 244)

The economic and political instability continued throughout the Portuguese democracy. Perhaps under other conditions, it might have survived in that unstable state beyond 1926, but that possibility was precluded by a number of factors. An extreme economic crisis rendered the gaps between the fractions of the bourgeoisie even more difficult to bridge, the hegemonic project even more difficult to construct, and the political exigencies of a democratic state even more difficult to attend. Other democracies were able to survive the postwar economic crisis, so, clearly, the crisis factor alone is insufficient to bring down a democratic regime. However, in Portugal it appears that the conjunctural crisis superimposed upon conflicts endemic to the disarticulated economy was responsible for bringing down the democratic state. This chapter presents the crisis and superimposes it on the political conflicts outlined in the previous chapter. The already divided bourgeoisie took on new divisions as the causes and solutions of the crisis were debated. In the end, the disunified bourgeoisie was incapable of absorbing the crisis. Although neither the structural nor the conjunctural factors by themselves were sufficient conditions for democratic collapse, the interaction of the two appears close to a sufficient condition.

A conjuncture is a set of conditions that determines the consequences of a limited set of actions. Several sets of constraints have been elaborated that can be summarized in declining order of specificity. First, Portugal was a semiperipheral country and constrained, above all, by its neocolonial relationship with Britain. This constraint remained in the form of debt, trade agreements, and the like. Second, Portugal had a disarticulated economy, which signified that individual fractions of the bourgeoisie and the working classes had alternative strategies that they preferred to pursue. Third, the country's old economic project was in crisis and there was need for a new economic order. Fourth, the first three factors in turn constrained the range of economic alternatives available for managing the postwar crisis. Finally, all of these factors were constrained by the rules of the democratic state. Could there be a solution to the economic crisis *within* the Portuguese democratic state?

One disclaimer must be repeated to reinforce the argument of embedded crises. This is not a "series of crises" explanation that loads one crisis on top of another until the list is so weighty that one could hardly challenge the implicit assertion that it provoked the collapse of the democratic regime. Such alleged association between a series of crises and the democratic collapse is difficult to refute, in part because one does not know where to begin. The interpretation offered here, although it speaks of two or three crises, cannot be reduced to a volume of crises or to a crisis threshold. Political crisis or democratic collapse should not be reduced to a unidimensional and linear economic scale on which some threshold can be identified.

Przeworski describes conjunctures by first asking whether continuing accumulation generates a crisis of consent under conditions of economic crisis. He argues that a crisis ensues if wages are below a certain minimum level and/or profits are not sufficient to reproduce consent and to allow future profits. This analysis of hegemony and the material basis of consent uses two actors—capitalists and workers—and locates workers as the major threat: "A breakdown of consent is not a sufficient condition for a breakdown of capitalism, since its effect is first to bring to the fore the coercive mechanisms which underlie the reproduction of capitalist relations. Hegemony is 'protected by the armour of coercion,' and when consent breaks down coercion can still hold the system together" (1980, 56).

In a hegemonic system, there is a material basis of consent that workers give to capitalists and that some capitalists give to other capitalists. In a hegemonic democratic system, consent is given through the electoral apparatus of the state. Workers consent to work for a certain wage and let capitalists draw their profits, understanding that investment and future growth will be the long-term consequences of those profits. If the workers ask for wages that are too high, they threaten the profits necessary for future growth, and if they receive too low wages, they are insufficiently rewarded for their sacrifices. Somewhere between these two limits, the workers consent to the system in which they remain dominated by capitalists. Movement beyond either of these two limits (by excessive worker militancy or by excessive capitalist accumulation) provokes a crisis.

It is necessary to expand the set of actors to include fractions of the bourgeois classes and to broaden the analysis to include the possibility that profits are not sufficient both to reproduce the consent of nondominant fractions of the capitalist classes and to grant the future profits of the hegemonic fraction. Also, this analysis broadens the problematic from protecting hegemony to installing it. Conditions do exist under which the different fractions of the bourgeoisie, unable to form a hegemonic pact (and thus unable to agree upon a compromise with the working classes, rate of taxation, and so on), may see that disunity constitutes a threat to the reproduction of capitalist relations in general.

Expanding this analysis to fractions of the ruling classes requires consideration of the material basis upon which some fractions of the bourgeoisie consent to be dominated by others, the limits of their consent, and the possible origins of crises. Each project had its corresponding design for a myriad of fiscal and economic policies, including tax plans, levels of monetary circulation and foreign indebtedness, and government spending. For the nondominant fractions of the bourgeoisie, those policies had limits beyond which their own projects would be hampered and their consent to the dominant project would become tenuous.

Thus the question of democratic stability operates in two directions: horizontally among the fractions of the bourgeoisie and vertically between capitalists and the working classes. For hegemonic rule and thus democratic stability, the major antagonisms operating in both directions need to be resolved. That might appear an onerous task for a hegemonic project, but Gramsci's interpretation of stable democracies is precisely that they have achieved such a two-dimensional pact.

In this sense, the Portuguese democratic collapse (as distinct from the preceding instability) can be interpreted as recognition of the inability to create bourgeois unity under a democratic regime. The willingness to forsake political rule in the democratic regime was arrived at painfully and slowly, but its arrival was tantamount to a withdrawal of legitimacy from the state (the concept that analysts find so pivotal in regime collapses).

Previous to the postwar economic crisis, various projects had captured the state, and each cabinet consequently implemented its respective project until it was pulled out of office by force or by the constitutionally empowered opposition (chapter 6). Following the postwar crisis, this use of the state was altered. The severity of the crisis was forced upon cabinet holders, and it became necessary to treat not only their narrow economic interests but also to address the more pressing question of Portugal's economic solvency. Ministerial declarations paralleled the changing emphasis. From 1910 to 1919, ministerial declarations to the congress stressed issues of public order, political crisis, social reforms for the masses, and territorial defense. From the twenty-first cabinet onward (30 June 1919 until 1926), ministerial declarations specifically mentioned the state deficit, need for fiscal reform, loans, the problem of foreign exchange, tariff reforms, and monetary circulation.[1] The pressing crisis also resulted in the creation of political pacts. The new challenge was to install a hegemonic project, broaden its mandate to resolve the economic crisis, mobilize consent of the dominated interests (the horizontal dimension), and do so within the democratic state with the consent of the dominated (the vertical dimension).

ECONOMIC CRISIS FOR THE BOURGEOISIE

The conjunctural crisis was the havoc of the postwar economic crisis. In Portugal it was manifest in a debt crisis, a production crisis, a market crisis, a currency exchange crisis, and a state deficit crisis. Numerous signs attested to its overall severity. Inflation became rampant in the postwar years. This can be seen in the rise in the cost of living indicator (table 7.1) and in the precipitous devaluation of Portuguese currency, especially in the postwar years (table 7.2).

Table 7.1. Cost of Living by Year, 1914–1927

Year	Index	Year	Index
1914	100	1921	817
1915	112	1922	1,128
1916	137	1923	1,720
1917	162	1924	2,652
1918	293	1925	2,286
1919	317	1926	2,148
1920	552	1927	2,430

Source: Portugal, Ministério Finanças, Anuário Estatístico de Portugal (Lisbon: Imprensa Nacional, 1927), 269.

Individual plants and shops were forced to close, and banks declared bankruptcy. This reduction in production was paralleled by a reduction in exports. Whereas in 1910 exports constituted two-thirds of the international trade, in 1925 that portion had fallen to less than one-third (AIp 1925, 394). Despite the devaluation of Portuguese currency, foreign market crises were still severe for some of the principal agro-exports. The crisis of wine exporters varied with the kind of wine. Port and Madeira wines had relatively stable export markets but were threatened by a wave of prohibition that spread through Europe after the war. The boost that the table wine trade had received from the mobilization of the French army fell when those soldiers returned to the fields. Cork also suffered a loss in exports due to the paralysis of major importing countries such as Holland, Russia, and Scandinavia. From 1918 until 1922, cork exports were down (ACL 1918, 212). This negative balance of trade both reflected and aggravated the general economic crisis.

Among industrialists, there was consensus that the economy was in crisis. By the end of 1924, the crisis was described as very grave, and shop and factory closings had put thousands of workers out of work (AIp 1924, 377). Wool, canned sardines, textiles, cork, and metallurgy were among the industries that suffered reduced productivity from the early to mid-1920s. The crisis occurred in the textile industry in 1924, when the colonial administration conceded foreign producers easier entry into African markets (AIp 1925, 397).

From the perspective of individual capitalists, such as those represented by the Portuguese industrial association, the crisis followed from a loss of credit, a high tax burden, foreign competition, and high labor costs (AIP 1924–1925, 70). The metallurgy industry put particular blame on the recent improvement of the exchange rate. The brusque improvement permitted the invasion of all sorts of foreign articles, destroying the tenuous defense that the customs barriers had provided while devaluing exports of prime materials. At the same time, workers were pushing for better working conditions (AIP 1926, 40). A similar

Table 7.2. Value of the British Pound Sterling in Portuguese Escudos (1910 = 100)

Year	Exchange	Year	Exchange
1910	100	1920	396
1911	96	1921	804
1912	97	1922	1,377
1913	101	1923	2,169
1914	105	1924	2,661
1915	126	1925	2,272
1916	140	1926	1,899
1917	153	1927	1,884
1918	157	1928	1,922
1919	167	1929	1,963

Note: Average based on average monthly escudo–pound exchange.

Source: A. H. de Oliveira Marques, *História da 1a república portuguesa* (Lisbon: Iniciativas Editoriais, 1980), 512–13.

thing happened in the glass industry with the 1924 currency revaluation. Foreign glass became significantly cheaper and the quantity of imported plate glass tripled; the quantity of imported glass bottles doubled between 1925 and 1930.

Such fluctuations in foreign exchange constituted a crisis for the business classes, although the effects were unequally distributed. From the inception of World War I, merchants and merchants' associations protested governmental inactivity in the face of the declining exchange rate. ACL had written in its 1915 annual report that "the constant oscillations of the exchange rate, its exaggerated rise, caused enormous damages to commerce" (1915, 67). The report went on to request that the government either fix the rates or absorb the losses by acting as a buyer and seller of foreign exchange. The oscillations only worsened.

The problem that seemed to call the most attention was the postwar debt crisis; it entered frequently in the redefinition of hegemonic projects. Instead of arguing that agriculture or industry was the best for the country, project advocates argued that it was best for the country *and* for resolving the debt crisis. Historically, a general capital shortage had forced many political leaders to request loans from foreign creditors. In the 1880s, Portugal defaulted on its external loan and declared bankruptcy. The record of the Republic was better. In 1914 Afonso Costa, prime minister of the fifth cabinet, converted the external debt into an internal one; further, the residual prewar foreign debt was secured through customs duties and the tobacco monopoly (*TE* 28 March 1921, 1173). Though the population had in no way been relieved of the debt, Portugal had reestablished its foreign credits.

This favorable credit rating proved useful sooner than anticipated. In 1916 Portugal entered into World War I with a British loan, granted at 6.5 percent interest. That debt was to be repaid within two years of the declaration of peace with another external debt that Britain would help Portugal to secure. At Versailles Portugal requested a sum for damages caused by the war and the war expenses, which would have been more than adequate to repay the debt. However, Germany deducted the cost of its boats, which had been confiscated while sitting in the then-neutral harbor of Lisbon, reducing the original reparation of £342 million to £37 million. In reality, Portugal only received a small part of the war reparations.

A country may deal with its outstanding foreign debt in several ways. However, the solutions for Portugal were limited, given its particular integration into the world economy and that most of the possible solutions were contested by one group or another. Portugal could have defaulted (the solution of the late 1800s), paid with gold, borrowed more, or increased its exports in hope of gaining more foreign exchange. Default was out of the question because it would destroy confidence in a country that wanted to continue foreign borrowing. Paying with gold was equally implausible for a country that had neither a mineral source of gold nor a willingness to relinquish its gold reserves (ACAP 1921, 95).

Two other solutions — exporting foodstuffs or manufactured goods — were unlikely to earn enough foreign exchange to ameliorate the debt crisis. The intention of the agro-export policy was to increase foreign currency receipts, but foreign barriers prevented this solution. The foreign debt coexisted with a trade deficit. Because Portugal imported more than it exported, there was no foreseeable way to mitigate the debt crisis by manipulating the trade balance. In fact, everything pointed to a worsening trade balance. Exports were dropping, and the cost of imports was rising. Nineteen hundred twenty and 1921 were particularly bad years for the balance of trade. If the international agro-export market had not been so elastic, and if it had been within the power of Portugal to increase its agro-exports, it would not have had a trade deficit in the first place. Despite this reality, agro-exporters lobbied for state facilities to help them in their "patriotic" task of debt reduction.

Earning foreign exchange through increased exports of manufactured goods was equally unrealistic because so much of the production inputs, capital goods, and raw materials was imported. Unfavorable terms of trade between machinery and exports would have cost more foreign exchange than it created in value, sending Portugal on a downward spiral of worsening foreign debt. In principle, an increase in exports — say, of textiles — might have provided needed foreign exchange. However, Africa was the chief market, and there the demand for textiles revolved around the prices that Africa obtained for cotton, cacao, and coffee. Several cabinets attempted to capture needed foreign exchange either by demanding that exporters deposit 75 percent of their foreign earnings in the state-controlled bank or by selling import licenses. Such mechanisms earned cabinets the wrath of the exporters.

Reducing imports was an equally unviable alternative, for a project of industrial growth had a heavy reliance on imported capital goods and raw materials. This left additional borrowing. Securing foreign credits or foreign borrowing were the most favored solutions of cabinets in the 1920s. How serious could this or any debt crisis be? Keynes, in his commentaries on postwar Germany, treated a similar situation as a conjunctural crisis.[2] Keynes saw both social and political consequences to the economic crisis. He remarked on "how near Germany is to a nervous breakdown" (1978, 28); "the public is pessimistic and depressed and has lost all confidence" (1978, 29). But more than general malaise, Keynes foresaw a specific problem for the government:

I find, therefore, widespread apprehension that general unemployment and difficulties about food will be regarded by the masses as indicating the failure of the present regime, with the result that they will be lukewarm in its defense. In such circumstances a new Putsch from the Right or from the Left might overwhelm the Government in Berlin. It is not uncommon to hear it said in Germany today, "We are on the edge of civil war"(1978, 30).

Although I would not lay the collapse of the Portuguese democratic regime at the feet of the debt crisis, it made forging a hegemonic development project more difficult. Not only did structural conflict exist among the economic interests, and among their projects, but any hegemonic project arrived at had to be consensually installed in the presence of an economic crisis. Or, put another way, the disunified bourgeoisie confronted a double conjunctural crisis—the postwar economic crisis and the hegemonic crisis of development.

Debt and Growth

Several tools were available to promote industrial development. Choosing from the constellations of policy alternatives for industrial growth is not a technical act: It is a complicated, sociopolitical process. Further, each policy implies a different constellation of economic alliances and thus different bases of support and of opposition. In this section, I map out some of the policy constellations that are directed toward industrial development and growth, indicating which alliances would accompany them.

Many policies are geographically specific and often short-term responses to the universal dilemma of how to promote economic growth. For economic growth to occur, some of a country's total product must be withheld from consumption and channeled into investment (Lewis in Meier 1976, 256).[3] How does this deferred consumption take place? In LDCs where capitalists have not yet been consumed by what Lewis calls a passion for saving and productive investment, several other sources are available: taxation, compulsory loans to the government, inflation, foreign capital, or restrictions on imports. The mechanism or combination of mechanisms chosen will depend on the historically specific economic endowment as well as the sociopolitical formation.[4]

Frequently, growth is not just quantitative, it is qualitative — a shift from the agricultural sector to an already existing or forming industrial one. Farmers have often supported industrial development and economic growth, though seldom by their own design. In fact, historically, farmers have tenaciously resisted such transfers with all the economic and political resources at their disposal. Yet agriculture remains a principal source of surplus transfer through: (1) supplying foodstuffs to the expanding urban sectors; (2) providing a surplus of savings and taxes that can be transferred and invested in other sectors; (3) selling a surplus for cash and thus increasing the size of the domestic consumer market; or (4) earning foreign exchange through the export of farm products (Meier 1976, 280, 563). Although surpluses may theoretically be transferred to any sector, growth often requires a transfer to the industrial sector. Nevertheless, without directive policies, the transfer will not be to industry in general but to specific industries. For example, the transfer via terms of trade that are unfavorable to agriculture encourages the growth of manufacturing industries aimed at the domestic market; yet, it is often those industries that are less efficient in their use of capital and labor. Consequently, the agricultural sector ends up subsidizing an industry incapable of competing in the international market. Therein lies the role for the state — to determine the source, the destination, the quantity, and the medium of capital transfers.

International trade policies can be lethal or vital to the development of a domestic industry. Historically, international trade policies were mortal for Portuguese industry up until the end of the nineteenth century. This was precisely the intent of the Anglo-Portuguese treaties. The literature on development and trade points to five trade policies that specifically promote domestic industrial development: currency devaluation, import quotas, import tariffs, export subsidies, and export taxes on raw-material inputs. Each is evaluated in terms of its likely impact upon different fractions of the bourgeoisie, on the debt-devaluation problem, and on the likelihood of mass democratic support (table 7.3).

Currency devaluation, the first trade policy, does not affect all economic interests equally. Policies that raise the domestic currency prices of imports and exports favor domestic industry because they discourage the purchase of more expensive foreign items and encourage their replacement by domestic ones. Devaluation may also return a higher income to exports. Because industries with lower prices have a market advantage that could lead to increased profits, the assumption is that capital would eventually move into those sectors, leaving the other sectors with capital and labor shortages. This model assumes that wages are not allowed to follow prices, for if they did it would produce an inflationary spiral negating the advantages of the devaluation.

Currency devaluation was not received favorably by all industries. Those producing with imported inputs for a domestic market opposed devaluation. Indus-

Table 7.3. Potential Coalitions and Consequences for Democratically Solving the Developmental and Debt Problems

Developmental Policy[a]	Coalition			Effect on Debt	Democratic Support
1. Currency devaluation	ISI + Ag-Exp	vs.	ELI + Dom-Ag + WC + IntlCom + State	0	–
1a. Currency devaluation with wage goods subsidies	ISI + Ag-Exp + WC	vs.	ELI + Dom-Ag + IntlCom + State	–	+
2. Import quotas on agricultural and industrial wage goods[b]	ISI + Dom-Ag	vs.	Ag-Exp + IntlCom + ELI + WC	+	–
2a. Import quotas on ISI goods	ISI + WC (ISI)	vs.	Dom-Ag + ELI + IntlCom + Ag-Exp	0	–
3. Import tariffs on all wage goods	ISI + WC (ISI) + Dom-Ag + State	vs.	Ag-Exp + WC + ELI	+	–
3a. Import tariffs on ISI goods	ISI + WC (ISI) + State	vs.	Dom-Ag + Ag-Exp + ELI + WC (non-ISI)	0	0
4. Export subsidies	AG-Exp + ELI + IntlCom	vs.	ISI + WC + State	–	–

[a]Excludes trade policies aimed at maintaining the status quo or resurrecting an old project.
[b]A possible developmental alliance.

Note: ISI = import substitution industries; Ag-Exp = agro-exports; ELI = export-led industries; Dom-Ag = domestic farm sector; WC = working classes; IntlCom = international commerce.

tries producing for a domestic market with imported components were squeezed by such devaluations because their importing costs had to be paid in gold equivalents, but their domestic revenues were earned in escudos (CUF 1921; AIP 1921, 24; AIP 1926, 39). According to one company, "Sometimes the currency devaluation is such that what currency exists is not sufficient to produce the same amount of quantities sold" (CUF 1921). Devaluations caused many houses to declare bankruptcy (AIp 1926, 605). Retail merchants had to absorb the higher prices and were also accused of hoarding and speculating. Retail merchants, in particular, were the targets of popular, journalistic, and legislative attacks in 1922.

On the other hand, industries that had benefited from the devaluation (because they were less dependent on either imported inputs or the domestic market) vehemently protested a rapid currency appreciation. Industrial association interests charged that improvement of the foreign exchange deeply wounded national industry because strengthening Portuguese currency would lead to an invasion of foreign goods and the consequent destruction of industries such as metallurgy (AIP 1926, 40). The AIp voiced an identical concern regarding the consequences for textiles of a brusque revaluation of the escudo (AIp 1924, 378).

Currency devaluation could favor both import-substitution industrialization and agro-exports while prejudicing domestic agriculture, international merchants, and the working classes. However, one modification of the devaluation policy could change its economic ramifications and thus its support coalition. By accompanying the devaluation with subsidies on imported wage goods, it would be possible to ameliorate the burden falling upon the urban and working classes. Because such a modification requires state expenditures, the coalition model would be revised in two ways: currency devaluation benefits ISIs, agro-exporters, and the urban and working classes to the disadvantage of domestic agriculture, domestic commerce, industrial exporters (with imported inputs), and the state. How well does devaluation address the two major problems, that is, debt and economic growth? Devaluation, with or without wage-goods subsidies, could be a mechanism for promoting capital formation and economic growth. However, if the debt obligation were made in gold, devaluation would not solve that second problem. Devaluation with wage-goods subsidies also would further aggravate the debt by increasing the state deficit.

Import quotas are commonly used to promote domestic development. The policy tool of the potentially most successful developmental coalition could have been import quotas. Import quotas, unlike devaluation, act only on the import side. Import quotas would produce alliances quite different from those produced by devaluations. If quotas are raised against wage goods (industrial and agricultural) (number 2, table 7.3), the working classes would side with other opposition groups that prefer imported goods against the industries being protected. If, on the other hand, the import quotas are directed against capital goods (number 2a, table 7.3), the working classes may give support, but the users of imported capital goods would side with the opposition. The ISIs and domestic agriculture, both users of imported capital goods, would join other opposition interests such as agro-exports, the working classes, and international merchants. Import quotas offered possibilities of growth through a reduction of the trade deficit but were problematic in terms of popular support.

World War I imposed trade conditions that were de facto import quotas that benefited many national industries. AIP admitted that there had been an intensification and improvement of national production, as well as the establishment of new industries. Consumer durables, consumer nondurables, a few raw materials, and capital goods (tool and machine industry) all saw rises in production (AIP 1916, 145). In 1920 the twenty-second cabinet, a coalition of democrats, liberals, independents, and a socialist, passed a decree that prohibited the import of luxury items (pearls and gems) and a host of domestically produced consumer goods (textiles and threads) and limited the imports of still other goods. To the chagrin of the chemical industry, fertilizers were not protected. Thus this cabinet, author of many populist measures, such as the eight-hour day, passed a measure that was in opposition to the needs of the chemical industries and consequently to many workers. The commercial and retailers' associations protested that this legislation would severely harm commercial houses.

Agro-exporters disliked import quotas because they feared retaliation by exporting countries against Portuguese wines. ACP argued that Portugal must not restrict French imports because the French would reduce accordingly the quantity of the port wines they imported (ACAP 1920, 16). Such retaliation would result in growing wine stocks that would in turn drive down the prices. Wine exporters objected to 1920 legislation designed to protect the domestic barrel industry. Such protection increased the cost of wine production by requiring the purchase of new barrels instead of used ones. Like other import quotas on industrial products, this one favored manufacturers (and workers if the benefits were passed on in higher wages or steady employment) and disadvantaged wine producers and merchants.

Tariffs (number 3, table 7.3) constitute a tool by which governments can influence the direction and velocity of industrial growth, and they produce revenue for the state. As with import quotas, tariffs benefit the domestic producers of whichever product is tariffed. An industrial-farm coalition for development could use the tariff policy to protect their respective industries and accumulate revenue for the state. It would be beneficial for development and instrumental for terminating the debt but, as with quotas, would have resulted in higher consumer prices for domestic agriculture, agro-exporters, and the other nonprotected industries. By raising their purchase prices, tariffed products can be made scarce in the domestic market, thus benefiting protected industries. Because of higher returns on scarce capital and potentially higher wages in the tariffed industries, nontariffed activities (other industries, agro-exports, and domestic agriculture) could suffer shortages in capital and labor. International merchants would suffer directly from the reduced trade volume and perhaps indirectly from retaliation by exporting countries. In general, tariffs offered protection to some domestically produced goods, alleviated the debt burden, and provided revenue to the state.

Much of the debate in Portugal centered around tariffs and their collection. The proposed collection of all or part of a tariff in gold rather than in escudos agitated divisions among the economic interest groups. Industrialists, on whose behalf the legislation was framed, were first on the line of defense. Initially proposed in 1911 by the minister of finance of the provisional government, the tariff proposal was supported by industrialists, who claimed that it would bring tranquility to industrial life (AIP 1911, 25). In 1922 AIP called the revised customs schedule the salvation of the economy. The enthusiasm of the industrialists for tariff revision matched the animosity of the merchants, who claimed that tariff payment in gold was a "nondemocratic" measure (*JCC* 9 December 1910). They objected to these duties on the grounds that they would raise the price on both imported and domestically produced items (ACP 1912, 84). In 1918 merchants—whose stores had been broken into by consumers reacting to the harsh conditions of life—expressed concern with the new legislation that proposed to collect half of the tariff on imported items in gold. When the updated duties appeared in 1921, the chagrined Lisbon commercial association condemned this legislative attack on the economy (ACL 1920–1921, 250–52). The complaints were cloaked in a perfunctory defense of the consumer.

State-awarded bonuses to industries that produce for export can also promote growth. Alternatives to direct subsidies—which require state spending—include state-awarded tax discounts on public services (such as freight discounts on national carriers) or on import licenses for raw materials (Cody et al. 1980, 69). There are several reasons why industrial capitalists may find a domestic market insufficient and therefore encourage export-facilitating policies. A home-market orientation depends a great deal upon the size of the economy and its level of development. In small economies, the full exploitation of economies of scale and benefits obtained from the division of labor may be precluded. State officials may support exporting for the foreign currency that it yields despite the necessity of state subsidization.

Export subsidies can produce quite unique economic alliances. First, export subsidies benefit only a few industries. Second, exportation normally creates a domestic scarcity of the exported products, which in turn makes them more costly for urban and working-class consumers. On the other hand, domestic merchants receive export subsidies more favorably. However, if subsidies involve the transfer of real income, the state would be forced to collect additional revenues, resulting in the use of indirect subsidies over direct ones.

Republican debates, projects, and conflicts were generally around indirect or negative subsidies—export surtaxes. Subsidies, direct or indirect, constituted a drain on the treasury and would have reflected unfavorably on debt resolution.

There are other minor variations of trade policy manipulation to promote industrial development. A government could tax the export of materials that likewise serve as inputs to domestic industry. For example, by taxing the export of raw cork, the cork-processing industry would have first chance at those raw materials. Alternatively, by taxing exports of foodstuffs that also entered the domestic wage bill, the government could hope to cheapen the wage bill and thus indirectly subsidize domestic industry.

These are general ways in which trade policies can be effective tools in promoting industrial growth. The trade policies and their impact on both the debt problem and democratic stability are summarized in table 7.3. This summary highlights several key points. Most important for this discussion, the policy that jointly favors industrialists and domestic farmers is not a policy that represents a strong solution to the debt problem, nor is it a policy that gains strong democratic support. In fact, there seem to be few developmental policies that can address simultaneously the debt crisis and the political crisis. The complexity for any given coalition of solving the developmental problem, the debt crisis, and maintaining democratic support is uncovered in my analysis of several cabinets in the next section.

POSTWAR CABINET COALITIONS THAT FAILED

Two formulas stand out among the policy attempts to deal with the crisis: an expansionary one and an orthodox one. The cabinets that most often pursued expansionary and inflationary policies were those administered by the PDP. Of the last ten cabinets, the thirty-fifth through thirty-seventh followed these policies to a great extent, whereas the forty-first, forty-third, and forty-fourth followed them to a lesser extent. The PDP's interpretation of the origins of the economic and fiscal crisis focused on the trade deficit that Portugal had accumulated over the years. By rectifying this imbalance, it hoped not only to ameliorate the economic crisis but to promote economic growth as well.

The notion that PDP policies were expansionary, inflationary, and populist stemmed from PDP policies regarding the civil service payroll, the operation of state enterprises, the colonial policy, and the general mechanisms for obtaining state revenues. Payroll expansion was commonly undertaken by PDP cabinets. During the thirty-fifth cabinet, for example, Prime Minister António Maria da Silva rehired 90 percent of the employees of the State Maritime Transportation Company (TME) who had previously been fired (ACL 1922, 124). He also enlarged the GNR. Likewise, the forty-first cabinet under Prime Minister José Domingues dos Santos nominated new state employees. Such populist measures were one way to augment the ranks of the middle classes from which the PDP garnered its political support.

PDP cabinets complemented new hirings with salary increases. Again, it was Silva of the thirty-fifth cabinet who granted salary increases to state employees.[5]

This was repeated in the fortieth cabinet. The prime minister of the forty-first cabinet tried to keep civil servant salaries at parity with the levels of inflation.

Although it was not within their power to increase the wages of all their potential supporters, PDP cabinets did pass a series of measures that reinforced real wages. Trade policies were enacted that reduced the cost to urban consumers of important wage goods such as foodstuffs. This reduction was accomplished by restricting the exit of some domestically produced foodstuffs and by minimizing the tariffs on imported foodstuffs. Export barriers were erected for common produce, such as potatoes and olive oil, and were a source of great irritation to farmers who produced for the export market (ACAP 1924, 156). Export barriers on domestic products were sometimes enforced jointly with lowered import taxes on foreign merchandise, in order to force down the prices of local products. In this way, trade policies were used to fortify the real wages of the urban classes. Other policies, such as municipalized social insurance, public assistance, and subsidized housing, helped the urban masses.

Some PDP cabinets also forged policies directed at garnering the political support of the peasantry. Proposed land redistribution to peasants was a populist PDP scheme in the sense that it envisioned appropriating uncultivated land from large landholders and distributing it, along with other parcels of municipally held land, to World War I veterans, peasants, and families who desired to farm. In addition to the political payoff, such land redistributions could have contributed to increased domestic production of food.

A certain similarity existed between the expansionary domestic policy and the colonial ones. The colonial budget supported large administrative staffs, and, according to some, the ordinary budget had to bear the expenses of luxuries totally out of proportion to their utility. Salaries were excessively high, and the bureaucracy was extended under various pretexts. Attempts were also made to help the middle-class colonial consumers defend their real wages. When Norton de Matos was appointed high commissioner of Angola in 1921, he set up a state warehouse of foodstuffs for the civilian (white) population in the colonies. Weak import restrictions on items like foreign textiles meant lower prices for colonial consumers and the ire of metropole industries. In questions of colonial debt and inadequacy of capital for development, the PDP cabinets followed a plan of increasing monetary circulation for the former and sought external loans for the latter.

Finally, these PDP cabinets used the state to promote economic growth. They advocated the enlargement of existing state enterprises and the creation of new ones. The state owned and operated enterprises such as an explosives factory and a metallurgy shop. Beyond outright ownership, the state also participated in the profits of other monopolies, such as the tobacco company and the match company. Silva advocated programs for roads, bridges, and hydroenergy—support designed for industry in general.

The expanding state payroll added to the state budget deficit. The prevailing solution for the PDP was the inflationary one of printing money. All of these PDP-controlled cabinets increased the monetary circulation to cover the state debt. Law 1424, one among many, contracted the Bank of Portugal to put new money into circulation (up to 140 thousand contos), but a majority of it went to pay off the state debt.

The conjuncture of a negative balance of trade, governmental deficit, and devaluation led these cabinets to attempt to control the exchange rate at least against speculation. The cabinets used political mechanisms to defend agro-exports, albeit with the intention of transferring capital elsewhere. Portugal threatened to put a tax on imports from Belgium if Belgium put restrictions on Portuguese wines. It protected wines in Angola by forbidding the import of foreign wines. The PDP cabinets required exporters to deposit 75 percent of their foreign currency earnings in the state bank, which in turn paid exporters at a predetermined exchange rate and controlled the use of foreign currency for imports. Regardless of their success at bettering the exchange rate, these policies irritated the nondominant fractions of the bourgeoisie.

There was also an orthodox response to the economic crisis of the 1920s. Cabinets employing the orthodox response constructed an economic solution that, although not quite recessionary, was rather orthodox: It attended the state deficit and debt crisis to the detriment of the cabinets' own democratic support. Advocates of the conservative policies had a different interpretation of the economic crisis than that held by their PDP counterparts. The latter blamed the crisis on trade deficits, whereas the former laid the burden of the crisis on state deficits and therefore on PDP policies that encouraged flagrant state spending. Their solution was to reduce state expenditures. These policies were drafted by members of the Republican Liberal party (PRL) and its descendant, the Republican Nationalist party (PRN), which attempted to implement them in the thirty-first and thirty-eighth cabinets, respectively. Other cabinets that followed, and were part of the PRL-PRRN-PDP political pact, applied the policies in a progressively diluted fashion. [The pact had been signed by the leadership of the PRL, the Republican National Reconstitution party (PRRN), and the Portuguese Republican party (PRP) in recognition of the need to jointly solve the crisis (Barbosa 1922, 236).]

The policies of these orthodox cabinets included restricting both state expenditures and the money supply. In its inaugural speech to the house of representatives, the thirty-first cabinet promised to attend to public opinion regarding the reduction of expenses and the extinction of the budget deficit (*Diário* 31 August 1921, 16). In his inaugural speech to the house of representatives, the thirty-eighth prime minister, António Ginestal Machado, addressed both government deficit and the great number of state receipts listed in the budget that had never been collected (*Diário* 19 November 1923, 7). He also promised to address the "irregularities of public administration" in the TME and the bairros operários (public housing) (*Diário* 19 November 1923, 8). The minister of commerce was going to propose the total liquidation of TME. The thirty-eighth cabinet opened a credit of £3 million in Britain (Law 1.272) in order to acquire capital goods necessary for the state (*Diário* 19 November 1923, 12).

For a number of reasons, both of these responses were inadequate to solve the double problem — development and debt — within the democratic framework. Both populism and orthodoxy were in crisis. The populist cabinets of the PDP elicited a strong reaction from opposition parties and economic interest groups. Complaints were registered against high governmental expenditures, state deficits, corruption, ruin, and the rise of bolshevism. One politician accused the PDP of being nothing more than a *sociedade de socorros mútuos* (mutual benefit society) in which it was necessary only to present one's political party card in order to obtain help (Leal 1966, 2:463). Even the size of the naval and military schools was criticized. AIP complained that state salaries absorbed 84 percent of the receipts and that it was impossible to have a rich state in a poor country (1918–1920, 63, 22). The northern traders preferred restricting public expenses over paying import duties in gold (ACP 1921); Lisbon traders agreed (ACL 1922, 124).

Opposition to these populist cabinets was really opposition to the PDP's spending on the vertical social pact. A majority of PDP legislation was directed toward cementing that pact, and to the extent that it could also address issues of development and debt with additional loans or increased monetary circulation, it did. The reputation of the PDP as a perpetuator of inflationary policies and excessive spending stemmed from such activities. The general line of the opposition was for the PDP to spend less. ACAP wanted the PDP cabinets to reduce the state's payroll and operating expenses, suggesting that they decrease governmental use of automobiles and telephones (1923, 244). Government increases in the number of state employees put pressure on the public debt (AIp 1920–1921, 281). In a similar tone, ACP complained about the size of the state budget in its 1921, 1922, and 1923 annual reports.

Objections were registered to most of the policies. Reacting in 1925 to lowered import tariffs, a representative from CUF complained that foreign digestible oils paid fewer taxes than those produced in Portugal, thereby granting them an unfair advantage. Reacting to the proposed land reform, ACAP objected to this violation of property rights as the beginning of bolshevism (ACAP 1922, 63). Restrictions on agricultural exports were likewise protested (ACAP 1924, 156). State-owned and -operated factories were the basis of complaints from private producers of both gunpowder and metallurgical products (AIp 1925–1926, 76). AIP aspired to have productive industries as well as infrastructural ones returned to the private sector, including the military manufacture of vehicles, railroads, ports, the mail and telegraph services, and the merchant marine. It saw these activities as a drain on the budget and unfair competition for the private sector (AIP 1926, 107). Referring to the colonial policy, one critic argued that large quantities of materials of little practical use were purchased, and allowances and subsidies were distributed to undeserving causes (Bragança-Cunha 1937, 242). The commercial associations viewed with great hostility the cabinet plan to capture part of the foreign exchange. (ACP, the chief exporter of port wines, later succeeded in getting an exemption from the state-fixed exchange rate.) They protested the "unpatriotic" assumption underlying Decree 8280, namely, that exporting houses would deposit their earnings in foreign banks (ACP 1922, 55).

Although criticism of the TME was formally made by a member of the Monarchist party, it expressed the sentiment of the orthodox reaction. The TME was attacked by the Monarchist party in 1922 for six years of capricious and corrupt neglect. Speaking for the Monarchist party to the house of representatives, Cancella d'Abreu argued that because the TME had been administered so badly and in a manner so costly to the nation, it was time to disband it and sell the balance of the fleet to private buyers. In his five hours of speeches, he presented evidence to support his claim of bad administration. The loss of money he attributed to neglect in bookkeeping, falsification of billing charges, corruption (which always led to Portugal receiving unfavorable exchange rates) (Abreu 1922, 27), irresponsibility in the coal service (which resulted in such losses as double payment for the same load of coal) (Abreu 1922, 30), and absurdities such as the use of one boat for a cabbage patch (Abreu 1922, 21). In addition, Abreu pointed out that the boats maintained excessive personnel (1922, 34). Abreu lamented that the TME had existed under too many administrations—in six years, there had been twenty-six ministers and eight diverse pieces of legislation, ranging from Law 480 in February 1916 to Decree 7814 in October 1921. The TME was considered typical of the PDP's wasteful spending. By dissolving such state companies, he argued, the country would free itself of financial burden, and private capital would flourish.

The expression of this opposition, both within and outside of the congress, eventually led to the collapse of the PDP cabinets. Although these cabinets had a parliamentary mandate—the thirty-fifth cabinet was appointed following the 1922 election in which the PDP received 49 percent of the popular vote—they did not have an absolute majority. The ardent parliamentary opposition to their expansionary policies led to some rearrangements, which accounted for the appearance of the thirty-sixth and thirty-seventh cabinets.

Leal was adamantly opposed to the violation of the legal limits of increased monetary circulation. Others were equally vociferous in their challenges to the PDP, and parliamentary opposition finally ended the run of populist cabinets led by António Maria da Silva. The forty-first cabinet was extremely unpopular with many of the capitalists' organizations for its February 6 decree (10515), which dissolved ACL (ACL 1925, 42). These cabinets were populist and generally committed to industrial development; however, their responses to the trade deficit put them at great odds with agro-exporters, and their reaction to the state deficit put them at odds with more conservative politicians. A clear connection existed between the complaints of the economic interest groups and the parliamentary opposition.

Were opposition interests behind the conservative economic policies of the orthodox cabinets? Were the orthodox cabinets the political expression of bourgeois opposition to populism? Was there a PDP-opposition political polarization that reflected a class polarization (the working classes versus the bourgeoisie)?

The bourgeoisie enthusiastically endorsed the reduction of the state budget and the reprivatization of state-owned enterprises. The conservative cabinet (the thirty-eighth) that followed the three populist cabinets was composed of ministers like Cunha Leal (minister of finance), who had led the parliamentary opposition. The new cabinet, composed of PRN members (descendants of the PRRN), had the support of a parliamentary minority. The PRN was unsuccessful in persuading the president to dissolve the congress and call new elections, from which it had hoped to gain a majority. The cabinet was challenged by the PDP and particularly by the two previous finance ministers, Vitorino Guimarães and Portugal Durão (Nogueira 1980, 260). However, it was not just PDP opposition that portended failure for the thirty-eighth cabinet. The orthodox cabinets were unable to rule because, just as the populist cabinets had encouraged the wrath of the bourgeoisie, the orthodox ones in turn encouraged the wrath of the urban masses. Their financial policies assaulted the urban masses, who responded with civilian uprisings (Nogueira 1980, 260). On 10 November 1923, a tenants' protest was staged, and the following day a revolutionary attempt by the marines took place when they fired shots from boats anchored in the Lisbon harbor. Although the minister of war managed to contain the uprising with loyal forces, the president, again revealing his lack of support for the cabinet, visited the marine quarters and disputed the existence of any revolutionary outbreak. A parliamentary motion of approval for the cabinet's handling of the incident was defeated 53 to 42 (Peres 1954, 370). One month after it took power, the thirty-eighth cabinet fell (*O que eles* 1945, 16).

On the one hand, cabinets representing landed interests tried to do what no cabinet relying on the consent of the majority could have done—namely, promote the domestic agricultural project, address the debt problem with orthodox fiscal policies, and maintain democratic support—thus some were thrown out of office. On the other hand, cabinets representing workers' interests tried to do what no cabinets dependent on the cooperation of capitalists could have done—namely, solve the dual problem of development and debt with democratic support—thus they encountered parliamentary opposition. Was this the internal contradiction of democracy that Marx had forecasted coming to roost in Portugal? Was the democratic regime finally showing itself to be unstable because those with economic power were not satisfied with less than a monopoly of political power, and those with political power but no economic power were striving to appropriate economic power?

Accounts of the cabinets and their opposition make it clear that the political representatives of the capitalist class (even when in control of the cabinets) were unable to implement their economic policies and deal with the economic crisis because of popular opposition. Further, political representatives who offered some concessions to the working classes were unable to implement their economic policies while solving the economic crisis because of parliamentary opposition. Thus neither group was capable of carrying out a mandate within the democratic framework—at least neither could do it alone.

This difficulty most likely led cabinets to compromise even with their own base of support. The thirty-fifth cabinet, despite its populist measures, reacted to a transport strike by having the military take over public transportation. Because of corruption within the GNR (Marques 1972, 172) and GNR-led insurrections, António Maria da Silva disarmed the GNR and then moved to legalize this disarmament by depriving it of its machine gun potential and of its infantry and cavalry facilities. This rendered the GNR a negligible force not only in terms of its intervention in politics against the Republic but also in terms of its ability to defend the democratic regime. In his memoirs many years later, Leal wrote that this transfer of military capacity left the monarchist elements in the army elated (Leal 1966, 2:364). Here were two acts of betrayal against their own bases of support.

The realization that neither political group alone was capable of carrying out a mandate within the democratic framework gave birth to the *pacto partidário* (political pact) of the PDP and the PRN. Cabinets thirty-nine through forty-two were "pact" cabinets. For the PRN, the pact represented hope of implementing more orthodox economic policies without the civilian uprisings that had accompanied them in the past. For the PDP, the pact represented hope of implementing its own economic policies without parliamentary opposition. The PDP took a minority position in the first cabinet but progressively regained its political weight in subsequent cabinets. In general, these joint cabinets combined some orthodox economic policies with expansionary ones. They were less inflationary regarding revenues, and they took advantage of the more orthodox tax reforms and revenue collection policies that had constituted part of the conservative plan for fiscal reform. However, over time the expansionary aspect seemed to regain dominance.

The fiscal aspect of the pact was articulated most clearly by the prime minister of the thirty-ninth cabinet, Castro. He was a member of a splinter group from the PRN that later became an official party, the Republican Action party (PAR). Policies announced by Castro included a reduction of state expenditures, state divestment of such enterprises as the infamous TME, and authorization of the working-class housing project (Castro 1925, 66). The Castro cabinet also eliminated the Ministry of Labor and purged many administrators from the Social Insurance Institute. These firings affected ministries that executed the institutionalization of the populist vertical pact. Other ministries also suffered personnel reductions totaling around 2,500 (Paixão 1964, 4:474).

Although antiinflationary politicians decried the PDP's scandalous practice of increasing the money supply, Castro himself claimed that his party was not in favor of rapid deflation because a rapid and painful readaptation would hinder growth. Still, restraint on the money supply accompanied reduction of state expenses. This, Castro hoped, would reequilibrate the state budget and rekindle the confidence of financiers to invest in the Portuguese economy.

Castro's exchange rate policies had a conservative orientation. The objective of his policies was to maintain the value of the escudo, gain foreign investor confidence, and secure foreign credit. Several decrees were passed to battle against the devaluation of the escudo. Even consulate fees were pegged to the exchange rate. Although the PAR approved of the PDP policy of governmental control of 75 percent of the foreign currency earned through exports, the PAR lobbied for stiffer control of imports. The PAR gave the minister of finance the power to restrict or forbid the importing of merchandise or foodstuffs that were dispensable to the continuation of life and work. These policies did have some effect on the exchange rate, and revaluation between July and October 1924 was significant (a drop from 157 escudos to 100). Castro also proposed banking legislation that would have taken central banking functions out of the hands of the state bank and turned them over to private banks. Spending cuts were insufficient to balance the budget, however, and Castro looked toward a more general tax reform. He was convinced that the wealth produced in the country could support a more rigorous taxation than had been practiced in the past. His tax reform policies, particularly the stamp taxes on luxury items like perfume and liquor, enraged merchants.

Castro's cabinet was the product of a political pact, albeit one of contradictions. Its recessionary policies were in conflict with the expansionary and proworker tendencies of the PDP members. However, the PDP joined the bloc because the experience of earlier cabinets showed it could not rule alone. In addition to the two parties (the Democratic party and the PAR wing of the PRN), the thirty-ninth cabinet was joined by two members of an intellectual group called Seara Nova. Thus, in the compromise of the bloc each party had in a way co-opted the others. The thirty-ninth cabinet (December 1923–July 1924) did last longer than the thirty-eighth cabinet (November 1923–December 1923) and was freer from uprisings.

Conflict within the pact and between the cabinets and labor emerged over labor policies. Disagreement over wage-granting concessions to striking postal workers prior to other major cuts in the budget provoked one of the cabinet members to resign (Seara Nova 1971–1972, 1:136). At the same time that the party-pact cabinets suffered from intracabinet conflict, the democrats of the pact alienated themselves more and more from their working-class base. As these cabinets pursued expansionary policies, they also invaded union meetings and arrested labor leaders. These cabinets (such as the forty-second) incurred worker hostility because, despite an expansionary orientation, they could not offer sufficient guarantees of labor peace to the capitalists. The forty-first did a bit better in this regard and with the slogan "bread and work" received support from the socialist newspaper, O batalha. Within the constraints of the pact, however, even the more populist cabinets found they had to contain labor.

On the other side, the pact, which allegedly represented the bourgeoisie, promoted legislation that was against their economic interests. Cabinets of 1922 and afterwards attempted to institute profound tax reforms that would have not only increased the amount of savings taken from income but would have shifted the direction away from indirect taxes toward direct taxes. Although the early tax laws did not get much further than the Diário do congresso, conflicts over them spread throughout the capitalist class. Farmers complained that farm incomes had not risen as much as the new tax legislation presumed. The new assessment was to be seven times that of 1914, but, farmers claimed, production had not increased to that extent. For example, cork was selling for only three times its 1914 value (ACAP 1922, 118). Farmers also complained that industry was not paying its share. Merchants in return argued that the income generated by agriculture was much greater than its assessed value (Castro 1925, 17). In 1924 merchants launched a full-scale tax rebellion against a pact cabinet. The discussion during the forty-first cabinet regarding banking reforms was so intense that the session was called off.

In this conflictual environment, state enterprises remained a politically viable source of state revenue. The forty-first cabinet promoted state enterprises (such as the state gunpowder factory) over private companies. When cabinets lowered the price of certain products, they forced private companies, such as the Sociedade Africana de Polvora, to sell below production costs (AIP 1926, 116). Instead of being reduced, state enterprises were being increased to the detriment of private industry. Further, state use of military personnel for labor was considered by private industry to be unloyal competition (AIP 1924–1925).

The pact had simply brought the conflicts from society and the legislature into the cabinet. Interparty congressional disputes and civil society disputes were now intracabinet disputes. These cabinets were brought down by opposition of parties that themselves were part of the pact. Because of intense parliamentary opposition to the forty-first cabinet, the nationalist opposition had expected cabinet power to be passed to them. Instead, in February 1925 the president passed the cabinet back to the democrats, who continued with the earlier policies. This time the nationalists manifested their opposition in a stronger voice—they walked out of the senate when the cabinet arrived to deliver its ministerial program. Although least constrained by the policies of Castro and the original pact cabinet, the forty-second cabinet also had to contend with attacks from the right. On 18 April 1925 military and other organized conservative elements attempted to overthrow the government.

Although the bloc may have been planning for long-term economic development, many capitalists found such recessionary policies detrimental to their short-term well-being. During the cabinets of the bloc, economic interests banded together to form UIE. UIE was preoccupied with the possibilities of direct taxation. During this same period, the Communist party was reorganized and participated in the 1925 legislative election (Quintela 1976, 68). More and more, economic interests were finding representation outside of the established political parties. Capitalist and worker parties replaced the republican parties that had tried to represent their interests. Instead of consecrating a compromise, bloc politics increased class warfare. Bloc politics earned the opposition of public employees, the working classes, and capitalists. The PDP was cutting itself off from working-class support, and the bourgeoisie was cutting itself off from its traditional political parties.

The first post pact cabinet (the forty-third) was democratic, devoid of any illusions of a pact. The next cabinet, a composite of various PDP tendencies, received a close vote of confidence from the house of representatives (52 in favor and 51 against). This cabinet's sole mandate was to oversee the upcoming elections. It resigned after the elections only to be replaced by another all-democratic cabinet (indicated by a strong PDP victory of 54.6 percent at the polls). With such an overwhelming democratic majority, the prospects for a long rule should have been good. Money was earmarked for education, the hated municipal sales tax was reinstated, and the government planned to increase its revenue from the tobacco monopoly. This was the cabinet that was brought down by the military coup of 28 May 1926.

CONCLUSION

I have maintained that Portugal's location in the turn-of-the-century world economy determined both the economic groups in that country and their projects. These projects were responses to the crisis of the decaying agro-export project and to the postwar economic crisis. Factors that created one project simultaneously created its opposition. In the democratic state, these conflicts were carried into the cabinets and produced the observed democratic instability. Chapter 6 described political coalitions embedded in structural conflict — it showed a state occupied by various economic interest groups that attempted to translate their projects into legislation. The occupation of the state apparatus by economic interest groups is conceptualized in various ways — most common, however, is the notion that the state lacked autonomy. If a state lacks autonomy, it will never be in a position to supply collective goods (Evans et al. 1985, 60–61).

In the Portuguese case, the lack of unity and the lack of autonomy have the same empirical consequence. The lack of unity meant that no project could install itself hegemonically with the consent of other groups. There was no viable project (in the socioeconomic and sociopolitical sense) to direct the economy. The consequence was that each group, using state institutions, fought for its own project.

The lack of autonomy reflected the absence of any agent or group independent of these individual project alternatives that could have put together a workable coalition. When fractions of the bourgeoisie attempted their own version of joint rule (coalition cabinets), they were pulled apart internally. Although that first crisis — the decline of the agro-export project — was a conjunctural crisis, and although it was recognized as a crisis, it did not have the urgency of the later debt crisis. In fact, we saw that some of the solutions offered to that first crisis were simply versions of the same old project. Thus, until about 1920 it was possible to identify cabinets that were political representatives of projects and, inversely, to identify the alternative projects in the political opposition.

Rueschemeyer and Evans think that a divided dominant class favors state autonomy:

> The most obvious social structural condition favoring greater autonomy is division within the dominant class . . . . Increased pressure from subordinate classes is a second source. The most likely conditions for increased state autonomy are constellations in which the pact of domination has serious cleavages within it, in which threats from below induce the dominant classes to grant greater autonomy to the state, or in which subordinate classes acquire sufficient power to undo monolithic political control by the dominant classes (Evans et al. 1985, 63).

In the first phase of the republican struggle, we saw that neither the intrabourgeois divisions nor the threat of the subordinate classes was sufficient to create a unified bourgeoisie or an autonomous state. The structural conflicts (resulting from the disarticulated economy) prevented the bourgeoisie from sustaining the few coalitions that it did form and contributed to the Balkanization of the state. Does this mean that the processes cited by Rueschemeyer and Evans did not obtain in Portugal?

Although the disunity coming from the structural conditions was not a sufficient condition for democratic collapse, the conjunctural crisis gave greater impetus to coalition formation. The second discussion of the republican struggle describes political coalitions embedded in the conjunctural postwar economic crisis. After the outbreak of that crisis, the installation of a hegemonic project required, in addition, attending to the new economic crisis. This expanded the terms of political discourse to include references to the debt, the deficit, the trade balance, foreign exchange, and the like. The urgency imposed a recognizable need for unity on the economic interest groups and their political represen-tatives. Thus the political pacts, such as had been seen during World War I, re-appeared. Again, as during World War I, these political pacts attempted to make policies somewhat independently of individual capitalists. The policies of the pacts were a compromise between economic reform (addressing the two con-junctural crises) and redistribution (sustaining the vertical pact).

This unity was no more successful than single policy rule. Expansionary politi-cians had provoked the opposition of the bourgeoisie, and conservative parties had provoked the animosity of the working classes. The pacts, which represented moderate versions of both expansionary and conservative policies plus attempts at long-term economic reform, attracted the animosity of both sides, including the very economic groups that they intended to benefit.

One could interpret the Estado Novo of Salazar as a more autonomous state. By abolishing political parties and class unions, Salazar created a vacuum into which he inserted his corporatist structure (Marques 1972, 2:181). With increased autonomy from economic groups (beneficiaries of the Estado Novo are described at the end of chapter 5), the state became more interventionist — even to the ex-tent of generating a state budget surplus by 1934, "an achievement for which Por-tuguese history could show but few precedents" (Braganca-Cunha 1937, 230). One spokesman for the Estado Novo, testifying on its behalf, listed the following ac-complishments: social peace; financial stability, namely, a balanced state budget and elimination of the internal and external debt; and infrastructural works such as roads and ports (O que eles 1945, 45, 50, 56–57).

The legitimacy of the state was no longer rooted in the citizenry. The state now derived its power foremost from force but also from the Catholic Church. The Church, which suffered ideological demotion during the Republic, was restored to its former position of ideological centrality under Salazar. Salazar and the Church agreed on traditional rural values, a highly centralized authori-tarian state, and the prominent role of the family. More extreme groups, such as the Portuguese Catholic Action, took the reconquest of society as their main mission.

For Portugal, the democratic breakdown process began with reduced state autonomy. Attempts by fractions of the bourgeoisie to grant increased auton-omy to the democratically elected state were unsuccessful. Here the authori-tarian regime of the Estado Novo would succeed.

CHAPTER 8

Sources of National Disintegration

For some time, it had been recognized that it was necessary to put an end to the situation in which the country struggled, a situation which could only be called anarchy.—(Almeida [1936], 244)

The First Portuguese Republic thus fell. Democracy is a trifaceted phenomenon. In conventional wisdom, democracy resides in a cluster of freedoms—freedom of speech, freedom of religion, freedom of organization, and so on. At the juridical or procedural level, democracy is the division of state power into a number of branches and the sharing of power among them. What characterizes the political aspect of democracy is the placement of individuals into positions of power through an electoral mechanism activated by political parties. Not only are political parties the principal mechanism by which individuals are placed into slots in the government; they are also the formal link between the will of individual citizens and the representative government. Democracy, in contrast to other types of political systems, such as monarchy, corporatism, or dictatorship, is characterized by political parties that organize, articulate, represent, and act upon the aggregated will of citizens. State institutions guarantee that political outcomes are to some extent indeterminate and that "no one can intervene to reverse outcomes of the formal democratic process" (Przeworski 1986, 56–57).

In addition to its juridical and political components, democracy has a social aspect: Democracy is a social compromise among classes that have inherently conflicting interests (Przeworski 1980, 21–66). The notion of social compromise answers the dilemma of why the asymmetric distribution of economic and political power might not have brought the downfall of democracy as Marx thought it would. Further, the horizontally extended version of vertical social compromise used in this analysis shows how divisions among those who held economic power could have brought the downfall of the democratic state. A social compromise is a mechanism that can mitigate the social consequences of an asymmetric distribution of economic and political power. Not only is the asymmetrical distribution mitigated, but the very nature of democratic institutions offers the possibility that some time in the future—for example, an election—it could become even more mitigated. Stated another way, "juridical democracy" and "political democracy" are the mechanisms by which the objective interests of various classes are organized, articulated, and proposed to other groups.

These three components of democracy—the juridical, political, and social—are not of equal value; rather, they fall into a hierarchy of dependency. The juridical component depends on the maintenance of the political, and the political in turn depends upon the maintenance of a social compromise. Consequently, the collapse of the juridical form (in this case, the military intervention of 28 May 1926) followed the disaggregation of the political organization, which in turn reflected an already broken (or unrealizable) social compromise. It is unlikely that the collapse of the three components of democracy would be simultaneous. Rather, the political dimension can survive for some time after the social compromise dissolves; likewise, the juridical structure will outlast the disintegrated political organization. Just as a social pact needs corresponding institutions to work out the compromise and to enforce it, so too a simple set of institutions cannot survive without an underlying social compromise. In short, the trifaceted notion of democracy is accompanied by a hierarchy of necessary conditions.

This is the contextualization of the literature on political processes. Many of the theories mentioned in chapter 1 often left unspecified why actors were so contentious or unable to compromise. Because factors of conflict are external to these theories, bad judgments or values are often invoked. Often such theories either assume or impute, when necessary, elements from the social compromise. Although never explicitly recognized, such factors enter the allegedly autonomous political arena in the form of a pregiven "crisis" or "conflict."

Having identified the origins of such conflicts in semiperipheral societies, it is relevant to study the political realm where the dynamics of political institutions take over. The refusals to compromise, to join cabinets for the purpose of problem solving—those unexplained uncooperative activities identified in political process theories—are in fact the political manifestation of a failed social compromise.

The breakdown in the material basis of consent at the economic level is expressed in a shift in the link between interests and their leaders, who during normal times are simultaneously their representatives in the democratic institutions. In reference to the vertical pact, Przeworski argues:

> At this moment the road bifurcates and the leaders-representatives face a sharply defined choice. Either they adopt a strategy of participating in democratic institutions to transform the capitalist system of production or the relation of representation breaks down. . . . Under such circumstances participation no longer expresses consent while withdrawal from participation is a threat to the democratic organization of conflicts (1980, 56).

In reference to the horizontal pact, intrabourgeois conflict resulted in political conflict (chapters 6 and 7). We observed what can be described as the actual disaggregation of the state, a notion that captures political processes such as the separation of representatives from their respective interests (Gramsci 1971; Lipset 1963; Linz 1978; and Poulantzas 1974). Representatives were cut off from their interests and interests regrouped without their representatives. This split was manifested not only in the multiplication of democratic parties and in the formation of new nondemocratic parties, but also in the separation of the GNR from the mainstream of the PDP. Did the bourgeoisie have a political plan that was different from that of the principal political currents? The answer can be seen in the process by which the bourgeoisie separated itself from the major democratic institutions. One democratic current came to represent the general interests of the capitalist class but was denied its own class support. Simultaneously, interest groups organized in "disloyal" democratic groups.

At this historical moment, with politicians cut off from their base and capitalists stripped of democratic institutional supports, the military stepped into the political arena, ending the democratic struggle. Perhaps if a unified bourgeoisie could have dominated both the working classes and the army, it could have pursued a path of democratic development and not abdicated to an authoritarian regime. Having divested itself of its armed wing (the GNR), this fraction of the bourgeoisie vacillated between fighting the army with the help of workers or fighting workers with the help of the army. But the PDP had openly expressed hostility toward the workers and could no longer count on the working classes to join it in support of "democracy." Having dismissed both their political representatives and their armed wing, and having cut themselves off from the democratic press, the economic interest groups stood alone.

The withdrawal of legitimacy—which also plays an important role in the literature (Linz 1978; Lipset 1963)—is the link that connects the political breakdown to the final juridical one. Linz describes the process of breakdown in a probabilistic fashion. After the conflict has worked its way into the body politic, things get progressively worse and compromises are increasingly difficult to make. This perspective suggests that even after the social compromise has come undone and political disintegration has occurred, the juridical system might survive as long as legitimacy in the system can be sustained.

Institutional change is precipitated, according to Linz, by actions of disloyal opposition that question the existence (the efficacy, efficiency, and legitimacy) of the regime and aim to change it (1978, 27). This book has been about those who moved to the disloyal opposition and why they moved there. There was also semiloyal opposition—those who justified nonlegitimate actions in terms of certain goals (Linz 1978, 32). From this perspective, one can judge the consequence of the actions of Portuguese democrats who justified the periodic intervention of the armed forces for preserving democratic order. The bourgeoisie revealed its desire to replace the parliamentary democracy by a pseudo-democratic form in which it would be guaranteed political control. Because the democratic constitution did not admit to a corporatist parliament based upon economic classes instead of citizens, the bourgeoisie had to look outside of the constitution for justification. In this context, they turned to the military. The military had intervened more than once in the political process. In most cases, it had displaced the Democratic party from power and turned the government back to the republicans rather than the PDP. Thus, in 1926, the (semiloyal) bourgeoisie again placed hopes with the military to effect a transformation of the state. A corporatist parliament, it thought, could both unify the bourgeoisie and consolidate a pact with the working class.

The bourgeoisie did not anticipate abdicating all its political powers to the military. Rather, it appeared to want to exploit the force of the military to effect the political transition while retaining full political power. This scenario did not come to pass. The military executed the first phase as scripted by the bourgeoisie — it displaced the Democratic party from power. It did not, however, turn the government back to the nondemocratic parties, nor did it allow them to form a corporatist parliament. Rather, it closed the parliament, banished the politicians, and repressed the masses. But why did not the military act out the script that had been written for it and executed by it so many times before? To answer this question, we need to return to the previous step, the disaggregation of the state. Whereas formerly the military had aided the bourgeoisie in its fight against the working classes, now the bourgeoisie was facing a military over which it had little influence. Thus the bourgeoisie itself was forced to abdicate to the military regime.

Linz also describes the role of political violence and the impact of its treatment by the leadership in power (1978, 57). Here, too, we can see how the trials and questions of amnesty that surrounded the periodic insurrections (popular, monarchist, and military) intensified and consolidated the cleavages in Portuguese society. Linz argues that the loss of monopoly of organized political force and the presence of disloyal or semiloyal opposition within the military accounts for the pulling away of the military from the democratic state. The inability to find solutions in the face of disloyal opposition and increasing violence leads to an increased fragmentation of parties, which in turn may lead to the "transfer of authority to ademocratic elements in the constitution" (Linz 1978, 66).

Institutional tenacity or inertia, bureaucratic persistence, the absence of an actor to displace the ruling body, or lack of an alternative governing force are sociological concepts that might serve to explain the longevity of juridical democracy beyond the expiration of the social compromise. The form of the withdrawal of legitimacy may determine the form and velocity of the collapse of the juridical system, but it can never tell us the fundamental reason for the democratic collapse. In other words, the democratic collapse is the political and juridical manifestation of a broken or blocked social compromise.

One analytical lacuna in this book is the role of the military. Various branches of the military moved on and off the republican stage, playing at the end the pivotal role in terminating the juridical democracy. However, the increased prevalence of the military in political life does not mean that the democratic collapse can be considered a purely military struggle for power or a purely political phenomenon. The military action in turn has to be interpreted in terms of socio-economic processes. Military interventions during the First Portuguese Republic were not homogenous events. Although the 1917 military intervention was on behalf of only the landholders, the 1926 intervention represented more diverse interests and thus was more autonomous from any one project. In some cases, the military installed a civilian government; in other cases, it superimposed its own rule over constitutional rule (1918). An analysis of military complicity against the democratic Republic must address how the military got its mandate to intervene in civil society and also how the military acquired the financial resources and sociopolitical support to do so.

Nevertheless, accounts of military politicization and empowerment are not substitutes for an analysis of the fundamental structural conditions and social conflicts that opened the space for military intervention. Thus I do not take the military, a priori, as a free-floating or autonomous group but rather as a social force that is attached to one or several interest groups. The conditions under which the military becomes attached to some groups or projects and cut off from others is an important question to be asked in studying the causes of democratic instability. In describing the Latin American cases, Cardoso writes:

> In general, the current period of military rule is a response to a crisis provoked in the state by political movements and social struggle before the military takeover. . . . Ruling classes have been unable to control the political pressure launched by workers and radicalized sectors of the middle classes. In such circumstances, the dominant classes cannot maintain their power without open military intervention and support. The price to be paid for this "help" depends on the extent of the political disintegration prior to military intervention (1979, 55).

Social compromises are not given; they need to be constructed and require the existence of a hegemonic project. Here we have seen both the structural and conjunctural hindrances to the establishment of a social compromise in Portugal, the disaggregation of the state, and finally, on 28 May 1926, the formal collapse of the democratic Republic.

AJUDICATING AMONG ALTERNATIVE HYPOTHESES

What proof is there that an alternative uninvestigated hypothesis does not do a better job of explaining the political transformation of the state? The answer to this question is constrained by the fact that a case study cannot be used to test hypotheses, and that data have not been collected that would permit assessment of alternative hypotheses such as cultural propensities or personality conflicts (note 4, chapter 2). Authors who have attempted to fit the Portuguese case into the available frameworks can exercise unlimited creativity because of the paucity of information. In this book, I argue implicitly against some theories and explicitly against others. Three of the more explicit ones are considered below.

Working Class Threats and Democratic Collapse

Two major cleavages exist along which the social compromise necessary for democracy can be sundered: the working classes from the bourgeoisie; and fractions of the bourgeoisie from each other. The rise of nondemocratic states often has been seen as a reaction to the increased threat posed by the working classes. The hypothesis that the Portuguese Republic fell because the bourgeoisie was unable to consolidate a compromise with the working classes, due either to working-class militancy or to capitalist excesses, can be deduced from Marxian theory. He argues that the bourgeoisie would always, as the French did, trade away its political power for the consolidation of its economic power. Such a trade-off would be necessitated by the very character of democratic rule, which puts the two major classes—workers and owners—in political confrontation with each other and simultaneously gives the working classes the tools for challenging the existence of the owning classes (Marx 1969a, 67).

The authoritarian regime of 1926 has been interpreted in this light. Kurth argues that Portugal needed the Estado Novo to demobilize organized labor (1979b, 331). Worker militancy was high soon after the declaration of the Republic. Between 1910 and 1914, 257 strikes were recorded (Oliveira 1974, 256). The first general strike took place in 1912 and resulted in Lisbon's being placed in a state of emergency. Thousands were arrested and the union headquarters was closed. Working-class organizations emerged on the national scene in 1917 with the founding of the Portuguese General Confederation of Labor (CGTP) (Medeiros 1978, 10).

In support of the hypothesis that conflict with the working classes brought down the Republic, one could cite the positions of the owners and the business community. They had hoped for stability and, more, for the political annihilation of the working classes. Such hopes led many to endorse the termination of the democratic regime. Two things are clear: There was heightened worker agitation during the democracy, and the Estado Novo under Salazar repressed working-class organizations. The asymmetry in the distribution of economic and political power was the origin of both worker and capitalist discontent, and the Portuguese democracy unleashed that contradiction—that workers and peasants, although constituting a political majority, did not own a majority of the wealth—which Marx considered essential (and destructive) to democratic capitalism. Second, the military dictatorship, and its successor civilian regime, initiated a new era in which the working classes were repressed. Order was a key ideological building block of the Estado Novo. Salazar rejected class struggle, which meant closing workers' organizations and unions, prohibiting public meetings, censuring the press, and arresting the opposition.

Table 8.1. Number of Strikes by Year, 1910–1925

Year	Strikes	Year	Strikes
1910	85	1918	11
1911	162	1919	21
1912	35	1920	39
1913	19	1921	10
1914	10	1922	22
1915	15	1923	21
1916	7	1924	25
1917	26	1925	10

Source: A. H. de Oliveira Marques, *A primeira república portuguesa* (Lisbon: Livros Horizonte, 1970), 161.

These elements could be taken as prima facie evidence for the working-class threat hypothesis, but other evidence makes such an interpretation too facile. Evidence suggests that the working classes, although always considered a source of capitalist disruption, were not the main threat. Despite their apparent militancy, the workers were on the defensive. Many workers' associations were losing, not gaining, ground on the economic battlefield. Although strike activity was not trivial during the five years preceding the coup (table 8.1), labor confrontations were on the decrease from the postwar high.

One might challenge strike data, arguing that workers were strong enough to achieve their demands without striking. If the purchasing power of workers indicates anything at all about the relative strength of the working classes vis-à-vis the bourgeoisie, one would have to conclude that the industrial workers seemed to be the most successful in keeping pace with the rising cost of living. They were followed by the lower-level civil servants and then by the mid-level civil servants (table 8.2). These figures could either represent their strength or the expansion of those ISIs (chapter 4).

On the other hand, evidence also suggests that neither strikes nor cost of living parity means a strong working class. For example, the Marinha Grande glassmakers did not constitute a threat. Although they organized and struck between 1920 and 1924, and although they won salary concessions netting them a 33 percent increase, by 1925 this workers' association had accepted a 10 percent rollback on wages because of the crisis of overproduction (Monica 1981, 517).

Factory workers, like cork workers, also seemed to be in retreat. The cork workers struck for higher wages in May 1924 during a crisis period in the cork industry (due to protectionist measures that other countries had raised against finished cork products). After a thirty-seven-day strike, the industrialists were forced to offer a 20 percent salary increase instead of the 10 percent already offered (AIP 1924–1925, 44). However, by September 1925, with the intensification of the

Table 8.2. Ratio of Purchasing Power for Some Occupational Categories by Year, 1914–1926 (1914 = 100)

Year	Farm Laborers	Factory Laborers	Mid-level Civil Servants	Low-level Civil Servants
1915	79.9	125.6	89.6	89.7
1916	70.8	131.3	72.9	72.9
1917	74.2	138.6	61.6	61.6
1918	59.0	92.2	36.8	39.2
1919	72.0	100.0	34.0	36.2
1920	22.0	72.5	25.6	43.5
1921	12.0	91.8	32.6	54.2
1922	7.7	79.8	50.8	72.3
1923	5.5	95.9	61.7	83.0
1924	4.1	84.5	47.3	63.8
1925	6.6	101.9	54.9	74.0
1926	7.2	95.8	—	—

Note: This index was obtained by dividing the respective index of salaries for each occupational grouping by the general index of the cost of living. The ratio does not reflect absolute standards of living; rather, it shows how groups did vis-à-vis the cost of living. This is particularly important to remember in the case of farm laborers, whose daily wage was supplemental to subsistence farming.

Source: A. H. de Oliveira Marques, *História da la república portuguesa* (Lisbon: Iniciativas Editoriais, 1980), 319, 367, 405, 406.

crisis in the cork industry, the manufacturers had resolved to lower their prices and to secure a corresponding reduction in the salary increase that had been awarded in June the year before. They asked for a 50 percent reduction of the salary increase in September, with a reduction of the other half coming after the first week in November. Again the cork workers struck, but this time the workers accepted the salary reductions proposed by the industry owners (AIP 1924–1925, 54).

Politically, there was little to fear from radical worker parties. In the November 1925 elections, the Portuguese Socialist party (PSP) won 2 of the 156 deputy seats and no senate seats. Despite constant complaints from business organizations, capitalists still had measurable power and were able to acquire concessions from workers within the democratic framework. This fact argues for some caution in using the "working-class offensive" explanation for the fall of the democratic regime.

A second problem arises with attributing the transition in the form of state to a conscious defense of the bourgeoisie against the working classes: the outcome of the coup. The bourgeoisie had hoped for a controlled working class, and in Estado Novo it did see the workers' political annihilation. However, in the Estado Novo certain bourgeois activities and organizations also were suppressed. The Masonry, for example, received extremely unfavorable treatment under the new regime, even though it was essentially an upper-class organization. In 1927 the National Congress of the Mason was prohibited (Carvalho 1976, 101). In 1928 Mason members were persecuted, imprisoned, and deported (Carvalho 1976, 106). In 1929 the Masonry was criticized as a state within a state (Carvalho 1976, 113), and by 1932, official harassment had driven it underground. In a May 1935 law, it was banned along with all "secret societies" (Carvalho 1976, 123).

Many other business associations were integrated into the Estado Novo corporate structure and had labor-management issues removed from their control and mandated from above. We are faced with the dilemma of why the bourgeoisie would renounce its political vehicle, the political party, for nonrepresentation and political ignominy. Was not some risk involved in giving up political privileges (particularly for the industrial bourgeoisie, which had gained only recently through the Republic a political existence previously denied by the monarchy)? In fact, would not there be even more indeterminacy for the bourgeoisie under the military dictatorship than there had been under the parliamentary democracy? Perhaps the bourgeoisie overestimated the working-class threat, or perhaps it misjudged what its fate would be under the new organization of the state. Such questions are raised by the consideration of the "repress the working classes" hypothesis but certainly not answered by it.

My analysis has not ignored the working classes; rather, I have conceptualized the workers in the vertical pact. The question is, Was the inability to create a vertical pact due to worker militancy more destructive to the democratic state than the unconsummated horizontal one? It is difficult to determine precisely the contributions to the demise of the social compromise, but the interpretation here has been that the contribution of the intrabourgeois conflict far outweighed that of the bourgeois-worker conflict.

Developmental Dictatorship

Portugal's industrial development lagged far behind that of other Western European nations. Was the Estado Novo a developmental dictatorship installed to ameliorate that condition? Although industrial development did follow the installation of the authoritarian regime, it had also taken a leap forward after the protectionist legislation of 1892 and during World War I. World War I created a de facto protectionism that surpassed the most extreme dreams of domestic producers. AIP admitted that the intensification and improvement of national production as well as the establishment of new industries was due to that de facto protection. Consumer durables, consumer nondurables, a few raw materials, and capital goods (tool and machine industry) all saw increased production (AIP

1916, 145). Wartime protectionism was accompanied by government distribution of crucial materials such as coal and sheet metal to major industrial users, thus contributing to the growth of larger companies. With a reduced British penetration of the Portuguese economy, Portugal had the opportunity to make that quantum leap of conquering more of its own domestic market.

However, as we have seen, industrialists were not free to expand in an unfettered fashion. They had to contend with an agrarian bloc that still held political power. So, the argument might go, only the authoritarian regime could resolve these difficulties. Here, too, one must exercise caution because historical evidence shows that capitalists were able under the monarchy as well as the Republic to effect some economic growth. Further, the Estado Novo is not normally considered a progressive regime, but rather a conservative one that benefited landholders.

The world-system variant of this thesis would make the bourgeoisie of a developing sector the carrier of desires for an authoritarian state and would see the Estado Novo as the way to improve Portugal's position in the world economy. For this interpretation of the rise of authoritarianism to be true, one must show first that there was a global (or core) downturn and that the transition from a democratic to an interventionist state resulted from the attempts (if not the successes) of industry to conquer more of the domestic market, a conquest that was not possible under democracy.

The turn of the century saw a general world-system crisis, one that was particularly acute for Britain. It was not just an epiphenomenal crisis; rather, it reflected a major shift in the world political order. Britain was losing its economic dominance to competitor states. For example, the British lead in steel production was challenged by both Germany and the United States. This loss occurred in part because Britain had not engaged in the cartel movement to the same extent as Germany and the United States, thereby rendering it less capable of making the transition from family-based entrepreneurial capitalism to the corporations of monopoly capitalism (Bergesen 1983, 262). Such inflexibility contributed to Britain's loss of economic dominance. There is a general agreement that both Britain and the world economy were in a period of downturn, but it is difficult to partition the contribution of the world downturn from that of World War I. Which contributed more to Portuguese growth? It is difficult to substantiate the association between a core downturn and semiperipheral growth and in turn to link that association with the emergence of an authoritarian state.

If the regime cannot be attributed to conflict with the working classes, and if it was not the outcome of a developmental dictator, does that mean that we have come back around to Moore? Was the authoritarian regime a reassertion of the power monopoly of the landed aristocracy, which had been lost with the collapse of the monarchy? The revolutionary potential of the Portuguese peasantry was modest, and that of the working classes was not yet crystallized; an industrial bourgeoisie was unable to secure political power equal to its recently gained economic power; and the large landowning classes demonstrated a political tenacity greater than their economic power. My dissatisfaction with this explanation, with its emphasis on the agrarian aspect of a society, is its assumption of an underdeveloped industrial class. The theory asks us to suppress precisely those characteristics that distinguish the more developed countries from the less developed ones, that is, the semiperipheral countries from the peripheral ones. This reasoning is certainly erroneous in the Portuguese case to the extent that it was the industrial classes that provided the impetus for the revolution against the monarchy in 1910. If one interprets their sociopolitical or economic development as weak in 1926, then it becomes difficult to understand their contribution sixteen years earlier. Portugal cannot be grouped with underdeveloped countries. Semiperipheral states are different from peripheral ones: The disarticulation is more intense, and the role of the industrial sectors is more integral.

Although such theories (working-class threat, landed aristocracy, and developmental dictator) have some plausibility, each represents only one piece of the explanatory puzzle — they offer justification for why particular groups might have preferred an authoritarian solution. Each is thus a constitutive element, for none alone constitutes the total. Alone, each theory fails to attend to how the preferences of each group were translated into a transformation of the state. Could the resolution of the emergent industrialists in itself produce actions resulting in the democratic collapse and in its substitution by an authoritarian regime? If so, why was the regime not overthrown earlier? Finally, why could they not achieve their desired goals within the political apparatus of the democratic regime? These questions are left unanswered by such explanatory approaches.

NATIONAL DISINTEGRATION

Nations disintegrate through civil wars, regime transformations from above, and revolutions from below. Those concerned with national disintegrations point to a variety of origins. Intense sectoral conflicts threatening national disintegration have been located in ethnic conflicts (Canada), religious conflicts (India-Pakistan), and economic conflicts (American Civil War). Modern societies are economically heterogeneous and may also be ethnically or religiously heterogeneous.[1] Because most societies have farm and industrial sectors, does it mean that democratic instability is endemic to modern industrial or capitalist societies? It is unequivocable that economic heterogeneity does not always result in political instability. To understand the connection between heterogeneity and political instability, it is important to emphasize that economic heterogeneity is *not* synonymous with economic disarticulation.

Articulated heterogeneity is commonly found in the developed world (the core), and conversely, disarticulated heterogeneity in the less developed world (the semiperiphery). Both of these cases are distinguishable from peripheral countries in which economic homogeneity is more common or, when heterogeneity does appear, it is in the form of an enclave. In plantation societies, there are petty commodity producers as well as areas isolated from the plantation economy: "These do not constitute separate modes of production, however, but spheres of social activity maintained for the purpose of ensuring and subsidizing the reproduction of the slave work force, which made up the overwhelming majority of direct producers" (Thomas 1984, 10). Thus economies can be classified in terms of heterogeneity (articulated and disarticulated) and homogeneity.

Whether or not exchanges occur among the various sectors of a national economy has implications for the interests of the respective economic sectors; thus the class conflicts (vertical and horizontal) of articulated societies would look different from class conflicts of disarticulated societies. In articulated heterogeneous economies, exchange among the sectors may be equal or unequal, but exchange exists. In cases approximating equal exchange, sectors will dispute their access to resources through taxes, loans, credit, and the like. In cases of unequal exchange among sectors where one sector clearly dominates, conflicts will be attenuated. The unequal exchange among sectors suggests that subordinate sectors are politically incapable of contesting or altering that unequal exchange. The political manifestation of the first case could be political pacts, compromises, and trade-offs. In the second case, it would be compliance or acquiescence. The incentive and payoff for social pacts, compromises, and acquiescence diminish as the economy becomes disarticulated. In both cases, a horizontal pact is facilitated by the articulation that exists in the economy.

Whether or not exchanges occur among the various sectors of a national economy also has implications for the vertical pact. The reliance on external markets for profits and capital accumulation converts workers' wages into costs. What ISIs require for raising consumption levels and therefore profits will be seen as costs to the agro-export and export-led industries. This is detrimental to the vertical social pact to the extent that "social disarticulation creates an objective basis for the exercise of subjective forces that are unfavorable to workers' economic gains and that justify regressive and repressive labor policies" (De Janvry 1981, 35).

In disarticulated economies, the political conflict emerges from the fundamental incompatibility and irreconcilability of the interests in question. This lack of compatibility and reconcilability stems from the fact that the various economic sectors are more integrated with the world economy than they are with other sectors of the domestic economy. The political effects of economic disarticulation can be posited as the explanation for the Civil War in the United States. The political effects of economic articulation can equally be posited as the explanation for India's relative political stability despite economic conflict.

The pre–Civil War United States economy was composed of several sectors (or economies) that were unintegrated (the economy was both heterogeneous and disarticulated). This condition was a legacy of the colonial era in which the northern colonies imported finished goods from Britain, and sugar (and its derivatives) from the British and foreign West Indies rather than from the South. The northern industrial core and the southern agrarian periphery had different orientations toward the world economy. The core area of the United States functioned as a gateway between the national and world economies by dominance over private investment and its concentration in urbanized areas of higher forms of economic activities. Its industrial activities could be described as ISI.

The agricultural South was integrated into the world-system as a peripheral country — it produced and exported raw materials (Bensel 1984, 51). It continued the pattern established during colonial history: It "traded directly and mainly with Europe, the only exceptions being that a minor share of their [the South's] exports and imports was handled by New England merchants via the ports of New England, and that a part of the plantation supplies was furnished by the farmers and fishermen of the middle and northern colonies" (Johnson 1915, 1:88). Cotton history followed international demand. "When the world market was good, as during the 1830s and 1850s, profits soared, and growth proceeded apace" (Fox-Genovese and Genovese 1983, 46).

Transportation systems reflected this world-system orientation. In the earlier part of the nineteenth century, the economics of transport favored external over internal trade (in the 1790s the cost of 3,000 water miles equaled 30 inland miles) (Wallerstein 1989, 247). Later this export orientation was reflected in railroad construction that bound export-producing districts to the ports rather than facilitating national or regional commodity exchange (Fox-Genovese and Genovese 1983, 50).

The peripheral areas also had been net importers of domestic private capital. During the colonial period, Maryland and Virginia planters produced with foreign credit (Wallerstein 1989, 199). Because this system was perpetuated by the shortage of American capital, it was not altered by the war of independence. Merchants traded with the British, whose supply of capital enabled them to extend the necessary credit to American traders (Johnson 1915, 126). The integration of the North American economy into the world economy is captured in numerous exchanges: Pennsylvania exported crude iron and imported wrought iron and steel (Johnson 1915, 49); by 1807 the United States was supplying 60.6 percent of the cotton imported into Great Britain (Wallerstein 1989, 248), whereas the North imported many raw materials from outside the American colonies. The United States earned a large portion of its income in foreign trade.

Because the United States, a continental nation, re-created on a national scale the core-periphery division of labor that typifies the modern world-system, core-peripheral political conflicts also were re-created. "Political conflict between the core and periphery is and has been inevitable because the economic imperatives of the two polar regions are in almost total conflict" (Bensel 1984, 51). The core had dominated the national political economy through control of the state apparatus. This was due to a number of factors: the comparative wealth of the core; its ability to co-opt political representatives; its control of cultural life; and the recruitment of a disproportionate number of higher level civil servants from its own core region (Bensel 1984, 52). This cursory review suggests that one can reasonably hypothesize that economic disarticulation contributed to a political instability that culminated in a civil war.

This division, which was well defined during the nineteenth century, began to erode as a result of the Civil War and new developments in transportation and communication. "Following the civil war, northern financiers invested heavily in the southern economy and came to control the industrial development and transportation system of the peripheral south and west. Thus the post–Civil War economy became more articulated in a number of ways: northern financial interests moved into southern agriculture; profits from agriculture moved into finance; cotton from the south was sold to the north" (Bensel 1984, 51). The economy became more articulated, and this increased articulation could explain why the sectional stresses that continued after the Civil War did not result in national disintegration.

In his study of India, Bardhan presents a picture of a nation divided by economic conflicts. He argues that the power of the landed aristocracy prevents the state from delivering power to the industrialists, thus hindering the economic development of India. The evidence for the dominance of one sector over another is mixed: Some shows negative terms of trade for the agricultural sector, and some shows transfers from private capital and governmental accounts to agriculture (Bardhan 1984, 56). Why did this situation not result in national disintegration? Bardhan identifies historically incomplete capitalist development as the cause of Indian economic heterogeneity. In turn, this heterogeneity is manifested in fights over taxes, loans, credit, and particularly public investment (Bardhan 1984, 56). Bardhan mentions several social forces that contribute to democratic stability in India. First, ethnic and regional differences prevent potential economic cleavages from becoming organized political ones. Second, the state disorganizes groups by granting special petitions and waivers as well as giving payoffs to certain coalition members. Bardhan sees India as a *ménage à trois* of interests (rather than a marriage of iron and rye) that include the rural aristocracy, industrialists, and bureaucrats (1984, 66). This coalition resulted from the inability of the industrialists to completely displace the landed aristocracy from hegemony (Bardhan 1984, 60). On the other hand, India was a relatively closed economy with a rather small trade contribution to the national income. Heterogeneous it was; disarticulated it was not. The Indian economy appears to be one of articulated heterogeneity. There may well be exploitation of one sector by another, as inferred from references to the intersectoral terms of trade, but the fact of exploitation does not make it disarticulated.

Civil wars and authoritarian regimes are hardly similar alternatives to democratic stability, but they do share, I would argue, a common origin—namely, they occur in systems with propensities for democratic instability. Whether instability is "resolved" in a civil war, authoritarian regime, or renewed instability would be determined by factors not considered in this book. Two factors, however, might be mentioned. The first is the level of geographic separation among the contending sectors. Bensel has this in mind when he defines "sectional stress": "Dividing a nation into two or more cohesive regions with incompatible political goals, sectional stress carries with it the possibility of secession" (1984, 3). The chances of civil war would also be increased with the armed parity among contending forces. Armed parity and geographic divisions among the contending sectors also seem to have been present in the two Chilean civil wars analyzed by Zeitlin (1984). These two factors, which appear to be present in both the North-South division of the industrial-plantation conflict and in the Chilean cases, are not present in the Portuguese case.

This comparative discussion suggests the necessity to determine not only the existence of conflicting sectors within an economy but also the extent to which there are exchanges among these sectors. Articulated heterogeneity, even unequal exchange, presents a socioeconomic panorama quite different from disarticulated heterogeneity.

What we see in these comparative cases are the alternative forms of the state as it moves from democratic stability: either toward the strengthening of the executive or toward Balkanization. Rueschemeyer and Evans regard increased autonomy as more likely, although they add: "Which of these contradictory outcomes is more likely depends on the internal relations of control and coordination within the state and the interest structure of society that have not been considered here" (Evans et al. 1985, 64). Translated into the language of this book, it is not adequate to refer to "division within the dominant class." We must know more about the origins of that division. In this case, we see that the disarticulated economy was the condition under which the state first became more Balkanized and only after the democratic collapse more autonomous.

Portuguese national disintegration was firmly anchored in the incapacity of the bourgeoisie to unite around its common denominator of economic production. It thus disintegrated into individual corporate groups. Left without the possibility of reaching a social compromise—which would have been the operationalization of its common denominator—the bourgeoisie was also left without a coherent political form (party, press, or cabinet coalition).

In explaining the failure of bourgeois unity, I have placed heavy emphasis on the structural factors that handicapped the making of democracy, or democratic stability. These factors were beyond the control of immediate interest groups and politicians. In that inherited world, they participated in an economy that was structured by virtue of Portugal's placement in the world economy. As political actors (some as direct representatives of projects, others as independent advocates), they pursued versions of different economic projects.

Portuguese democratic stability cannot be reduced to literacy, the spirit of cooperation on the part of well-meaning politicians, or world crises. The question of democratic stability is one of the social structure of Portugal and its class struggles where both the structure and struggles are influenced by Portugal's location in the world economy. More generally, the question of democratic stability is a question of the role of the democratic state in capitalism. The democratic state in Portugal has to be taken seriously, not treated as a political aberration that preceded the authoritarian regime. Fractions of the bourgeoisie may always fight among themselves, but there are historical cases in which they disagreed without the overthrow of an agrarian, aristocratic regime by industrialists. There are other cases in which they disagreed yet remained within the democratic state. Perhaps semiperipheral countries count less among them.

APPENDIX A. Defining the Semiperiphery

How do we define the semiperiphery? Aymard argues that "the concept of semi-periphery remains a prisoner of the ambiguity of its usage" (in Arrighi 1985, 40). A review of world-system literature suggests at least three different conceptual locations of the semiperiphery: the hiatus between the ideal types of core and periphery and the observed cases; the transition from periphery to core (or vice versa); and a phenomenon sui generis. These approaches are all of an economic variety and exclude political dimensions such as strength of the state that are sometimes included in semiperipheral definitions. It is crucial that the operationalization be restricted in this manner, not only because the association of state types and world-system location is not empirically verifiable (Skocpol 1979) but also because it incorporates into the definition precisely what is to be explained, namely, the form of the state.

In the first conceptual approach semiperipheral countries are those that fall outside the two ideally defined poles of periphery and core. Whether in terms of attributes or processes, numerous countries do not follow the dynamics identified with either the core or the periphery. The working definition of Gereffi and Evans is of this type.

> They [Brazil and Mexico] bear little resemblance to the classic model of a "peripheral" country: they are too industrialized . . . exports are too diversified . . . unusually strong states. . . . But neither do Brazil and Mexico possess the characteristics commonly associated with "developed" or "core" nations. . . . The position . . . between the core and the periphery on a series of dimensions makes them members of the periphery (1981, 31).

Thus this residual category comes to be called the semiperiphery.

In the second conceptual approach, the semiperiphery is found in the fluidity of the world-system. Here the semiperiphery is a transitional category, a way station through which countries pass, and it is populated by countries that are on their way from the periphery to the core or from the core to the periphery. In this transition, semiperiphery countries find themselves with wage, capitalization, and production levels somewhere between those of the core and the periphery. Because they have a combination of attributes from different points on a global continuum, Goldfrank says that semiperipheral states "best condense the system as a whole" (1981, 300).

A number of variations exist on this theme, and I think a majority of the semiperipheral cases owe their appellation to this second approach. Caporaso (1981), for example, in his work on the semiperiphery, rotates among a series of surrogate definitions of the semiperiphery, such as capitalized semiperiphery, newly industrialized countries, peripheral industrialization, growth in export-oriented industries, and less developed countries (LDCs) with dramatic growth in the last two decades. Thus Caporaso writes that a "small but significant group of less developed countries has grown dramatically in the last two decades at least in economic terms." He also points to a trinity of measures: increases in the gross national product (GNP), increases in industrial growth, and increases in the industrial share of the GNP. These countries specialize in labor-intensive industries where the technologies are relatively standardized. Caporaso's definition is a clear example of the semiperiphery as a transitional case.

The semiperiphery can be conceptualized in still another way that is more sui generis: Semiperipheral countries are those that occupy a contradictory place in the global division of labor, a contradictory place that has resulted from two prominent sets of economic relations—a set of independent relations and a set of dependent ones. Alternatively, one could say that a semiperiphery behaves like a metropole in some of its exchanges and like a colony in others. It is akin to Lenin's notion of "semi-colonial" states (1939, 8) where economic relations are bifurcated.

In describing the particular role that semiperipheral states play in the capitalist world-system, Wallerstein (1979, 97) writes that there have always been a series of countries that concretely fall between high-profit, high-technology, high-wage, diversified production and low-profit, low-technology, low-wage, less-diversified production. They act in part as a peripheral zone for core countries and in part as core countries for some peripheral areas. Semiperipheral countries contain a "double antinomy of class (bourgeois-proletarian) and function in the division of labor (core-periphery)" (Wallerstein 1979, 96).

Although Frank in his article on Eastern bloc countries does not use the word semiperipheral, he says that these countries are in "an intermediate position in the international division of labor" (1977, 101). Their economic organization and insertion into the world economy make them unequivocally semiperipheral. Frank describes the trade dimension of this relationship as follows: "As trading partners, the socialist countries are to the developed capitalist ones as the capitalist underdeveloped ones are to them—or vice versa!" (1977, 99). Thus two types of trade relations are embedded in these semiperipheral relationships. First, there is multilateral trading within the world economy—the core produces for semiperipheral consumption and the semiperiphery produces for peripheral consumption. Second, there is what Frank calls switch trading (for example, the USSR resale on the European market of raw-material purchases to which it was committed but finds itself not needing). This is analogous to the process of re-exporting goods from the metropole to the colonies (or to the neocolonies). Re-exportation goes both ways: from the core to the periphery through the semi-periphery and vice versa.

The third conceptual approach is more consistent with Wallerstein's notion that the world-system is not organized along national boundaries but along commodity chains that intersect states. Thus the semiperiphery, in terms of this methodological rule, is one with a certain concentration of commodity chain linkages (or "an overall fairly even mix") (Wallerstein in Arrighi 1985, 34).

What about the difficult problem posed by Aymard of a "neutral measuring stick"? Any measure that reveals the degree of mix within an economy could be used as an indicator because the issue is the level of mix. Research still relies on continuous scales with arbitrary cut-off points for assigning countries to zones. Assigning zones on the basis of national income or income per capita has continued since it was proposed by Evans. He claims that this "scale is a crude stand-in . . . [and] the classification [of countries that it produces] . . . fits quite nicely with intuitive notions of center, periphery and semiperiphery" (1979, 292).

The ideal measure would be one that would allow the cross-country comparison of detailed commodity production profiles. Evans has done this for Brazil, Mexico, and Nigeria (1979, 298). The final choice of a measure, it seems, requires a trade-off between conceptualization and operationalization. The GNP operationalizes most easily but is far from the original conceptualization of zones in the world-system.

The proposed measure maps countries onto structural positions in the world economy based on patterns of commodity trade. I believe the trade composition index (TCI) is a good analytical tool for mapping the major zones and assigning countries. This TCI, which was popularized by Galtung (1971), provides a net assessment of activities typically associated with advanced countries (importing raw materials and exporting processed goods) and underdeveloped ones (exporting raw materials and importing finished goods); the balance of advanced countries versus underdeveloped ones is summarized. The formula for this statistic is

$$TCI = \frac{(A + D) - (B + C)}{(A + D) + (B + C)}$$

where A = raw materials imported; B = raw materials exported; C = processed goods imported; and D = processed goods exported.

It has certain methodological advantages — it is simple to calculate and has greater fidelity to the conceptualization of functions characteristic of zones. Although the TCI is a continuous scale running from −1 to +1, pluses, minuses, and zeros

Figure A.1.

Trade Composition Index (TCI) for Portugal 1875-1936

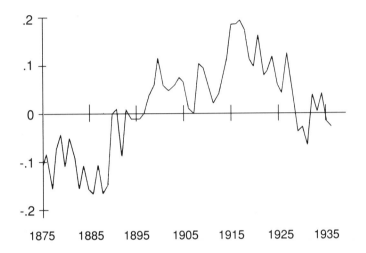

are conceptually distinct. Further, the TCI has the advantage of not building "direct dependency" into the measure, which allows for the possibility of empirically determining the relationship between foreign investment and the trade profile. In short, it allows us to assess the trade composition results of direct foreign investment and the like. It has the advantage (which the GNP lacks) of describing a nation's links with the world economy. It also reveals the nature of a nation's external commodity ties.

The TCI scores for Portugal (figure A.1) are more or less within the + .2 to − .2 range. This adherence to the zero-line could be characteristic of the sui generis aspect of semiperipherality. Despite the overall similarities, the Portuguese TCI is significantly different across the three political regimes — monarchy (data from 1875 to 1910), Republic (1910 to 1926), and Estado Novo (1927 to 1945) (Schwartzman 1988, 168–69).

APPENDIX B. Prime Ministers and Presidents, 1910–1926

PRIME MINISTERS (Presidentes do Ministério)

1.	Teófilo Braga	5 October 1910–3 September 1911
2.	João Chagas	3 September 1911–12 November 1911
3.	Augusto de Vasconcelos	12 November 1911–16 June 1912
4.	Duarte Leite	16 June 1912–9 January 1913
5.	Afonso Costa	9 January 1913–9 February 1914
6.	Bernardino Machado	9 February 1914–23 June 1914
7.	Bernardino Machado	23 June 1914–12 December 1914
8.	Vítor Hugo de Azevedo Coutinho	12 December 1914–25 January 1915
9.	Joaquim Pimenta de Castro	25 January 1915–14 May 1915
10.	José de Castro	17 May 1915–18 June 1915
11.	José de Castro	18 June 1915–29 November 1915
12.	Afonso Costa	29 November 1915–15 March 1916
13.	António José de Almeida	15 March 1916–25 April 1917
14.	Afonso Costa	25 April 1917–8 December 1917
15.	Sidónio Pais	11 December 1917–14 December 1918
16.	João do Canto e Castro	14 December 1918–23 December 1918
17.	João Tamagnini Barbosa	23 December 1918–7 January 1919
18.	João Tamagnini Barbosa	7 January 1919–27 January 1919
19.	José Relvas	27 January 1919–30 March 1919
20.	Domingos Pereira	30 March 1919–29 June 1919
21.	Alfredo Sá Cardoso	29 June 1919–21 January 1920
22.	Domingos Pereira	21 January 1920–8 March 1920
23.	António Maria Baptista	8 March 1920–6 June 1920
24.	José Ramos Preto	6 June 1920–26 June 1920
25.	António Maria da Silva	26 June 1920–19 July 1920
26.	António Granjo	19 July 1920–20 November 1920
27.	Alvaro de Castro	20 November 1920–29 November 1920
28.	Liberato Pinto	29 November 1920–2 March 1921
29.	Bernardino Machado	2 March 1921–23 May 1921
30.	Tomé de Barros Queirós	23 May 1921–30 August 1921
31.	António Granjo	30 August 1921–19 October 1921
32.	Manuel Maria Coelho	19 October 1921–5 November 1921

33. Carlos Maia Pinto   5 November 1921–16 December 1921
34. Francisco Cunha Leal   16 December 1921–6 February 1922
35. António Maria da Silva   6 February 1922–30 November 1922
36. António Maria da Silva   30 November 1922–7 December 1922
37. António Maria da Silva   7 December 1922–15 November 1923
38. António Ginestal Machado   15 November 1923–18 December 1923
39. Alvaro de Castro   18 December 1923–6 July 1924
40. Alfredo Rodrigues Gaspar   6 July 1924–22 November 1924
41. José Domingues dos Santos   22 November 1924–15 February 1925
42. Vitorino Guimarães   15 February 1925–1 July 1925
43. António Maria da Silva   1 July 1925–1 August 1925
44. Domingos Pereira   1 August 1925–17 December 1925
45. António Maria da Silva   17 December 1925–30 May 1926

PRESIDENTS (Chefes do Estado)

Teófilo Braga (president of
   provisional government)   5 October 1910–24 August 1911
1. Manuel de Arriaga   24 August 1911–29 May 1915
2. Teófilo Braga   29 May 1915–5 October 1915
3. Bernardino Machado   5 October 1915–11 December 1917
   Sidónio Pais (prime
   minister)   11 December 1917–9 May 1918
4. Sidónio Pais   9 May 1918–14 December 1918
   João do Canto e Castro
   (prime minister)   14 December 1918–16 December 1918
5. João do Canto e Castro   16 December 1918–5 October 1919
6. António José de Almeida   5 October 1919–5 October 1923
7. Manuel Teixeira Gomes   5 October 1923–11 December 1925
8. Bernardino Machado   11 December 1925–31 May 1926

NOTES

CHAPTER ONE. THE RISE AND FALL OF STATES:
BAD LEADERS OR BAD CYCLES?

1. I give a more detailed historical summary of the events preceding the democratic regime at the beginning of chapter 2.

2. It is clearly impossible to test the theories with one case, but periodically I refer to the ways in which the alternative theories are not adequate to explain the Portuguese case or to the ways in which the Portuguese case contradicts these theories.

3. Poulantzas criticizes historical studies that focus on personalities, party conflicts, and political instability as overpoliticization of the voluntarist kind (1973, 39).

4. Poulantzas insists that this is a dismemberment, not a disintegration, of the state apparatus: "In the sense that the pieces no longer work in the same way as in state form 'preceding' fascism, . . . [i]nternal contradictions and frictions among the state apparatuses increase, as a result of the political disorganization of the power alliance. This often takes the form of splits between the top ranks and the lower levels of a branch or apparatus" (1974, 334).

5. This move from farming to industrialization is the most noted, but much work also addresses other transformations, including transitions from light industry to heavy industry (O'Donnell 1978), and even from domestic market production to export market production.

6. The literature on authoritarian regimes — or bureaucratic-authoritarian regimes, as they are called — in Latin America explains the emergence of these regimes in terms of the characteristics that Latin American societies share, namely, delayed development and dependent development. For countries that are economically dependent and are embarking upon a path of delayed development, Schmitter writes, "this content greatly enhances the likelihood of a stalemated, impotent, nonhegemonic structure of class relations" (1973, 188), which in turn enhances the emergence of authoritarian rule. The elements to which Schmitter refers form the basis of a now vast literature on Latin American authoritarian regimes. In summary [combining elements of O'Donnell (1978) and others], these theories suggest that the initial phase of import-substitution industrialization (ISI) could have and did occur under democratic regimes. When ISI growth became asymptotic, the viable economic options included deepening of the economy or export diversification. These growth projects required not only the mobilization of capital, in a way analogous to that of the Gerschenkron late developers, but, in addition, containment of populist pressures that had evolved prior to and during the initial ISI states. The bureaucratic-authoritarian regime was seen as the vehicle that could mobilize capital (domestic or foreign) and demobilize the already organized citizenry.

7. World-system conceptualization is sufficiently generic to include Poulantzas. Following Lenin, he (1974, 23) assumes a hierarchy of countries along the dimension of imperialism and refers to their location in terms of "strong or weak" links in the imperialist chain. As in world-system analysis, states exist in relation to other states—"they are rela-

tively weaker or stronger" (Poulantzas 1974, 23). The link in the imperialist chain, combined with the stage of economic development, provides the backdrop for the analysis of class struggle and transformations in the form of state. In the case of Germany, Poulantzas identifies the consequences of being a "latecomer" to industrialization, which include a fast concentration of capital, a spectacular growth in capital exports, a net importer of capital, and difficulty in finding external markets. Because the landowners retained political control, the bourgeoisie was indebted to the state whose economic role was indispensable to it (Poulantzas 1974, 28). Italy had a similar place in the imperialist chain (1974, 29), although its later arrival to industrialization placed it in a slightly weaker link in the chain than Germany. Italy had an earlier creation of finance capital, penetration of foreign capital, and unevenness between industrial development and the rural sector. Because it coincided with regions, this unevenness of development contributed to the disunity of Italy.

Poulantzas's *Fascism and Dictatorship* (1974) offers an interpretation of state transformations that combines stages of capitalist development with conjunctural crisis. For Poulantzas, exceptional states accompany a political crisis in the historical period of capitalist formation, in particular the transition toward the dominance of monopoly capital (1974, 53), but this transition appears in states that are weaker links (not the weakest) in the imperialist chain.

8. Evans (1979) on Brazil is a clear exception to these criticisms. In his analysis, the agent of development is an alliance among the state, local bourgeoisie, and multinationalists.

9. Logan (in Arrighi 1985) argues precisely this—that Portuguese democracy was a challenge by the urban middle classes to the landed aristocracy that failed. This failure accounts for its short life and the institutionalized authoritarian rule that followed. Logan's interpretation is consistent with the claim that it was a "blip" and therefore need not be taken seriously (1985, 152).

10. To a certain extent, I strive to push the extremes of economic reductionism. Mouzelis (1980) judges forms of reductionism as deviations from Marx's initial holistic orientation because they consistently neglect the specific and relatively autonomous dynamics of political and cultural phenomena.

11. This concept is taken from Leontief (1966), who argues that when various branches and industries of the nation are woven together by the flow of trade, they cumulate into economic development (15). Disarticulation represents an absence of domestic economic exchanges. It is impossible to measure the actual degree of Portuguese economic integration because it requires data that is unavailable for the period under consideration, yet the model is particularly apt.

12. Most historians use the number forty-five. There were other nominated cabinets that were so short-lived that they never took power, such as the one-day episode of Francisco Costa. Although the argument to include such cabinets might have some merit, to do so would produce a list of cabinets that would deviate from conventional usage and would not be compatible with that already published by Marques (1980).

CHAPTER TWO. AN UNSTABLE AND NONLEGITIMATE DEMOCRACY

1. This historical summary selects aspects of Portuguese history that offer background information as well as highlighting issues of political economy relevant to the focus of this book. Marques's extensive history of Portugal has been translated into English (*History of Portugal*, 1972). Opello, in the introduction to his book *Portugal's Political Development*, provides an abridged history that focuses on aspects of political development since the foundation of the Portuguese monarchy in 1143.

2. In this section, Wallerstein explains why capitalism emerged from the feudal states of the Western Hemisphere instead of the empires of the East.

3. In 1891 wool was still the most important article that the British exported to Portugal (*TE* 23 May 1891: 668).

4. A certain affinity exists between methodologies chosen and conclusions attained. If one consults diaries, memoirs, and daily journal accounts, one sees the opinions, passions, secret hatreds, and frothing of human beings in daily life. Historians who consult such sources to explain the collapse of the Republic cannot help but conclude that the regime's downfall was the result of excessive personality conflicts. Inversely, social processes, which are hidden from daily accounts, are unlikely to emerge as explanations. A second common explanation argues that economic crises caused the collapse. Such conclusions are derived from research that studies crises, and they often argue that the Republic fell because of problems with balance of payments, exchange rates, cost of living, population shifts, and the like. Here methodological determinism would predict crises as the cause of the republican collapse. A third explanation expands this list to include political and social crises, but the principle is identical: search for crises, list them, and infer their explanatory power. In the last two, because of the sources tapped, personality conflicts are unlikely to emerge as the explanation. This comment applies to my own analysis. Although I offer evidence to refute alternative structural explanations (such as the role of the working classes), I have not collected information on personality conflicts. Personality interpretations are not so much refuted as they are precluded by my deductive approach, which assumes a deeper order explanation of observable socioeconomic and sociopolitical patterns.

CHAPTER THREE. THE DEATH OF A PROJECT

1. In 1891 woolen goods still constituted the most important article of export from Britain to Portugal (*TE* 23 May 1891: 668).

2. However myopic, it differed little from the pattern of early modern economic history as described in works by Hobsbawm (1962) and Pirenne (1966). It typified precapitalist economic activities wherein returns on investments were often not reinvested.

3. Pereira writes that port wine experienced a decline in 1860, silk in 1874, oranges and olive oil in 1884, livestock in 1885, and table wines in 1889 (1979, 27). Reis (1979, 769) cites data from one landholder that he thinks are not totally inconsistent with the national situation recorded by the Ministry of Public Works. Those data show a general agricultural crisis as reflected by a drop in income from numerous farm products from 1880 to 1890. Olive oil dropped 30 percent, cattle and wool 25 percent, and pork 20 percent.

4. Although the English threat to favor its own colonial wines over those of the "favored nations" never materialized (ACL 1919, 30), the Norwegian temperance threat did. A plebiscite voted not to sell wines of alcoholic content greater than 24 proof, whereas in Goa in 1922, the duties on wines were increased (ACL 1922, 49). Norway prohibited the import of Port wines except for medicinal uses (ACP 1921, 37), and the Dutch likewise expressed a desire to limit wine consumption in their country. In 1925 Denmark added a supplemental tax to wines higher than 26 proof (ACP 1925, 21), and the Belgium government in 1926 expressed interest in prohibiting the sale of Port wines of more than 36 proof.

5. To create this index for Portuguese trade, I combined live animals, raw materials, and beverages and foodstuffs for the primary products category, and finished goods, including machinery and utensils, for the other category.

6. The correlation of the TCI with partner concentration is − .57, significant at the .0005 level. The correlation of TCI with product concentration is − .58, significant at the .0001 level. The correlation between product concentration and partner concentration is .45, significant at the .005 level.

7. The total volume of wine exports increased continuously (with the exception of the war years). Although the increases are not radical, they are more or less continuous: 1880 − 593,217 hectoliters; 1890 − 913,841; 1900 − 828,660; 1910 − 1,155,537; and 1920 − 1,028,679.

CHAPTER FOUR. PORTUGAL: A DISARTICULATED ECONOMY

1. This colonial empire included Angola, Cabo Verde, Guiné, São Tomé, Príncipe, and Mozambique in Africa; Diu and Goa in India; Macau in China; and Timor in Indonesia.

2. The Spearman rank order correlation (for all districts) of the average-size farm unit and the land area dedicated to agro-export production is significantly negative (r = − .5625, significant at the .05 level). This association is, of course, based on an eco- logical correlation that treats the district as the unit of analysis.

3. According to Marques (1980, 202), there were approximately 37,000 textile work- ers, who accounted for about 26 percent of the industrial workers in 1907. From 1910 to 1926, textiles accounted for about 45 percent of the exported industrial products.

4. Today one can still find small subsistence farming throughout Portugal. In an ethnographic monograph about a small northern village in the 1970s, O'Neill (1987) paints a detailed picture of an essentially subsistence village scarcely integrated into the national monetary economy.

CHAPTER FIVE. ALTERNATIVE ECONOMIC PROJECTS

1. Although the projects described here are expressions of different fractions of the Portuguese bourgeoisie, from time to time they coincided with foreign interests. Britain, for example, had a preference within the range of alternative projects that Portugal, on the one hand, constitute a market for British finished products, machinery, and raw mate- rials and, on the other hand, be a garden that produced foodstuffs and wine for British consumption. This sentiment persisted into the twentieth century. "That a country so close to our shores and able to supply us with so many of the goods that we need in the shape of raw metals, timber, fruit etc., should possess only one export that stands out preeminent as does Portugal's export of wine can surely be remedied to our mutual advantage" (*TE* 1 January 1921: 8).

Although the British preference coincided with a Portuguese project described as "trad- ers and emporiums," the project was the product of a local bourgeoisie and can in no way be reduced to a British "conspiracy."

2. The textile industry and particularly cloth sacks were success stories following on the heels of protectionism. Cloth bags were used extensively in the colonial export busi- ness, and the continental industry employed about 2,000 workers. In general, the textile industry was sensitive to protectionist legislation.

3. The total energy generated at the turn of the century in Portugal was 111,000 Hsp, whereas Belgium generated 720,000 Hsp (Castro 1971, 37).

4. Although I have argued that domestic wheat could "replace" imported wheat, the debate was far from resolved. It had raged since the eighteenth century and still maintained

advocates on both sides. Supporters of domestic wheat argued that during the protected years, even the rocks yielded wheat. The import advocates argued that Portugal never had adequate wheat production even with protectionism (Fortes 1923, 8). In fact, Portugal had the lowest yield per hectare in Europe, and, for most of its history, it has had to import wheat to supplement local production.

CHAPTER SIX. POLITICAL COALITIONS IN STRUCTURAL CRISIS

1. Owners questioned whether machine cleaning would be included in the eighthour minimum. They protested the need for hiring three eight-hour shifts instead of two twelve-hour ones. They also protested the 1915 stipulation that factories that exceeded fifty employees had to provide a lunchroom. AIp insisted that it was a disadvantage to workers to have to publicly show (and possibly share) their food (AIp 1915, 47). Throughout 1916, no regulations or instructions were published on the 1915 law (AIP 1916, 139).

2. The Decree of 1914, Articles 3 and 4, states that only wine sailing from Oporto and Leixoes (north of Oporto) can be called "finimisso" (very fine) and "velho" (aged), and sweet wines sailing from other ports had to be clearly labeled as wine processed in south and central Portugal.

3. The democrats literally begged Britain to request Portugal's formal intervention. Thus the PDP considered Britain's request a "great diplomatic victory" (Seara Nova Antologia 1971, 2:173) that probably saved the colonies from occupation not only by Germany but most likely by Britain too.

4. To deal with such cases, a coding-up rule has been applied. Reasons are ranked from administrative (resignation, dismissal, and no confidence) to active and sometimes violent (military *golpes* and popular uprisings). In practice, the reasons that appear higher on the list are assigned to particular cabinets. Because resignation normally follows other factors, termination by resignation is coded as such only when no other factor is present. Likewise when a presidential dismissal was a response to a popular uprising, it was the uprising that was coded. Such a scheme gives more analytical weight to non-constitutional or nonpredictable factors. There are many data sources. Data have been accumulated from sources that include governmental documents, memoirs, historical documents and accounts, and contemporary histories of the Republic. The data have been analyzed in ways that render it classifiable within the framework devised.

5. When members of the cabinet belonged to one political party (or all but one who was independent), the cabinet was classified as a party cabinet. In many cases, the classification system disregards the disclaimers of cabinet members that they were not representing their party in any official capacity or that they would not make party politics. When all or most of the cabinet members were part of the military, the cabinet was classified as such; when all were independent, it was classified as independent. Two or more parties forming a cabinet constituted a cabinet of coalition unless it included elements of all the political parties represented in parliament, in which case, it was considered a cabinet of concentration.

6. Cabinets were classified according to their constellation of policies and ministerial statements. Lists of decrees, policies, and statements were compiled for each cabinet. As this compilation was done from secondary literature, it does not contain all of the decrees and utterances of each cabinet. The cabinets described in this analysis are those that seemed to fit the projects or combination of projects previously described. Some cabinets were not particularly active or lacked a clear policy profile (based on the classification scheme) and were therefore excluded. The characterization may well be at variance with the attitudes or intentions of individual cabinet participants but, one hopes, not with

a characterization that would have been derived had I had access to the total population of policies.

7. ACL made numerous accusations against the government that had a tone more or less like the following: "Somebody who is not fit to direct a commercial house is not fit to direct the Portuguese government" (ACL 1920–1921, 354). "The state will not benefit with the bankruptcy of commerce" (ACL 1922, 105). The ACL "propaganda against the constituted powers of the government" were noted in the senate (Senado 15 June 1924, 3).

CHAPTER SEVEN. POLITICAL COALITIONS
IN CONJUNCTURAL CRISIS

1. Some of the ministerial declarations were taken from the *Diário das sessões do senado*. The cabinet number is followed by the date and page number: 6: 10 February 1914, 14; 7: 23 June 1914, 25; 8: 14 December 1914, 110; 11: 25 June 1915, 5; 13: 16 March 1916, 6; 19: 3 February 1919; 25: 30 June 1920, 6; 26: 26 July 1920, 4; 29: 14 March 1921, 3; 30: 2 August 1921, 6; 42: 3 March 1925, 9. Other declarations are taken from the *Diário da câmara dos deputados*: 14: 26 April 1917, 820; 18: 8 January 1919, 9; 21: 30 June 1919, 10; 22: 22 January 1920, 11; 23: 9 March 1920, 4; 28: 2 December 1920; 31: 31 August 1921, 16; 38: 19 November 1923, 7; 40: 9 July 1924, 6; 41: 27 November 1924, 12; 43: 6 July 1925, 10; 44: 5 August 1925.

2. In his chapter on the decline of the mark in 1921–1922, he essentially predicted that the reparation payments forced on Germany would provoke the collapse of the Republic. It was a conjunctural crisis because of the unique conjugation of events. Keynes argued that forced reparations would lead to a crisis in the exchange value of the mark, which would completely disorganize business. Because Germany lacked resources to make its payments, reparations produced a decline in the value of the mark. One consequence was an insufficient money supply, which left business at a standstill (Keynes 1978, 27). Another consequence of the devaluation was the hardship put upon industrialists who needed to import raw materials. This new difficulty in importing production factors led capitalists to reduce the operating capacity of their factories, which, Keynes argued, would in turn lead to unemployment (1978, 27). A third consequence of the devaluation was the inability of fixed charges to keep pace with the exchange. This was particularly damaging to state receipts and would contribute to an increased state deficit (Keynes 1978, 28). The banks suffered cash shortages with the rapid inflation and were unable to cash their customers' checks for payment of weekly wages (Keynes 1978, 29). Then, in 1922, weather damaged the harvest.

Keynes predicted that if the quantity of currency could be controlled, sooner or later its value would stabilize: "This simple truth still holds good. The quantity of a currency can be controlled unless the government is in financial difficulties" (1978, 71). This was a problem in the Portuguese case: How can the state deficit be paid without increasing monetary circulation?

3. According to W. Arthur Lewis (Meier 1976, 256), an economic growth in LDCs of 4 percent per annum requires that one quarter of the national output be withheld from personal consumption. In his formulation, one half of that withheld should be devoted to infrastructure (further divided into 3 percent on education, 2 percent on health, 3 percent on infrastructure, and 4 percent on general administration and welfare), with the other half devoted to capital formation.

4. In some cases, the motivation may not originate in a desire for growth but rather in the necessity to reequilibrate a negative balance of payments. Assuming near capacity

productivity, the principal solution left to decrease expenditures was to switch the patterns of expenditures. Although this discussion addresses a problem conceptualized as industrial growth, it applies equally to the problem of readjusting the balance of payments.

5. The salary increases caused dissension within the cabinet, and the minister of finance, Portugal Durão, resigned in disappointment.

CHAPTER EIGHT. SOURCES OF NATIONAL DISINTEGRATION

1. In a review of Bardhan's analysis of India in which he attributes decelerated economic growth to the heterogeneity of the dominant classes, Kohli asks: "Are the dominant classes of high growth developing countries relatively homogeneous" (1987, 241)? He argues that Bardhan has left the variable of heterogeneity ambiguous and impressionistic.

SELECTED BIBLIOGRAPHY

Abreu, Paulo Cancella de. 1922. *Os transportes marítimos do estado*. Lisbon: Edição das Juventudes Monarchicas Conservadoras.

Almeida, A. Duarte. [1936]. *Regímen republicano*. Lisbon: Romano Torres & Co.

Almeida, António Ramos de. 1974. *O pensamento activo de Bernardino Machado*. Oporto: Brasília Editora.

Alves, Raymundo. 1914. *O parlamento: 1911–1914*. Lisbon: By author.

Amaro, Rogério Roque. 1982. "O salazarismo na lógica do capitalismo em Portugal." *Análise social* 18, nos. 72–74: 995–1011.

Amin, Samir. 1976. *Unequal Development*. Translated by Brian Pearce. New York: Monthly Review Press.

Andrade, Anselmo de. 1918. *Portugal económico. Theorias e factos*. Coimbra, Port.: F. França Amado.

Antunes, José Freire. 1978. *A desgraça da república na ponta das baionetas*. Lisbon: Livraria Bertrand.

Apter, David E. 1965. *The Politics of Modernization*. Chicago: University of Chicago Press.

Arriaga, José de. 1911. *Os ultimos 60 anos da monarchia*. Lisbon: Livraria Editora.

Arriaga, Manuel d'. 1916. *Na primeira presidência da republica portugueza*. Lisbon: Livraria Classica Editora.

Arrighi, Giovanni. 1985. *Semiperipheral Development: The Politics of Southern Europe in the Twentieth Century*. London: Sage Publications.

Arrighi, Giovanni, and Jessica Drangel. 1986. "The Stratification of the World-Economy: An Exploration of the Semiperipheral Zone" (unpublished manuscript). Binghamton, N.Y.

Associação Central da Agricultura Portuguesa. 1899–1930. *Relatórios das gerências*. Lisbon.

Associação Comercial de Lisboa. 1908–1929. *Relatório da direcção*. Lisbon.

Associação Comercial de Lojistas de Lisboa. 1908–1926. *Boletim*. Lisbon.

Associação Comercial de Pôrto. 1910–1926. *Relatório*. Oporto.

Associação Industrial Portuense. 1910–1928. *O trabalho nacional*. Oporto.

———. 1923. *1ª Congresso de Trabalho Nacional*. Oporto.

Associação Industrial Portuguesa. *Relatório da direcção da Associação Industrial Portuguesa*. Lisbon: Imprensa Limitada.

Baptista, Henrique. [1916]. *Presidencialismo e parlamentarismo*. Oporto: Livraria Magalhães & Moniz.

Baptista, Jacinto. 1964. *O cinco de outubro*. Lisbon: Arcadia Limitada.

Barbosa, José. 1922. *O problema económico e financeiro*. Lisbon: Portugal-Brasil Limitada.

Bardhan, Pranab. 1984. *The Political Economy of Development in India*. New York: Basil Blackwell.

Barros, Henrique de. 1941. *O problema do trigo*. Lisbon: Cosmos.

Bensel, Richard F. 1984. *Sectionalism and American Political Development 1880–1980*. Madison: University of Wisconsin Press.

Bergesen, Albert. 1983. "1914 Again? Another Cycle of Interstate Competition and War."

In *Foreign Policy and the Modern World System,* ed. Charles Kegley and Pat Mc-Gowan. Beverly Hills, Calif.: Sage Publications.

———. 1985. "Cycles of War in the Reproduction of the World Economy." In *Rhythms in Politics and Economics,* ed. Paul Johnson and William R. Thompson. New York: Praeger.

Bragança-Cunha, V. de. 1911. *Eight Centuries of Portuguese Monarchy.* London: Stephen Swift.

———. 1937. *Revolutionary Portugal.* London: J. Clark & Co.

Brazil. Ministério da Fazenda. 1911. *Comércio exterior do Brasil.* Rio de Janeiro.

Brenner, Robert. 1977. "The Origins of Capitalist Development: A Critique of Neo-Smithian Marxism." *New Left Review* no. 104 (July-August): 25–92.

British Chamber of Commerce in Portugal (BCCP). 1919, 1924, 1925. *Annual Report.* Lisbon.

Bukharin, Nikolai Ivanovich. 1967. *Imperialism and the World Economy.* New York: H. Fertig.

Cabral, Alexandre. 1973. *Os crimes da monarquia.* Lisbon: Seara Nova.

Cabral, Manuel Villaverde. 1977. *O desenvolvimento do capitalismo em Portugal no século XIX.* Lisbon: A Regra do Jogo.

———. 1979. *Portugal na alvorada do século XX.* Lisbon: A Regra do Jogo.

Cabreira, Thomaz. 1916. *O problema tributario portuguez.* Lisbon: Imprensa Libanio da Silva.

———. 1917. *A defeza económica de Portugal.* Lisbon: Imprensa Libanio da Silva.

Cabreira, Tomás António. 1914. *A questão corticeira.* Lisbon: Papelaria e Tipografia a Tentadora.

Campos, Ezequiel de. 1924. *Política.* Oporto: Edição de Maranus.

A Capital. 1914, 1915. Lisbon.

Caporaso, James A. 1981. "Industrialization in the Periphery." *International Studies Quarterly* 25, no. 3: 347–84.

Cardoso, António Lopes. 1976. *Luta pela reforma agrária.* Lisbon: Diabril.

Cardoso, Fernando Henrique. 1979. "On the Characterization of Authoritarian Regimes in Latin America." In *The New Authoritarianism in Latin America,* ed. David Collier. Princeton, N.J.: Princeton University Press.

Carqueja, Bento. 1908. *O capitalismo moderno e as suas origems em Portugal.* Oporto: Livraria Chardron.

———. 1916. *O povo portuguez.* Oporto: Livraria Chardron.

———. 1920. *O futuro de Portugal.* Oporto: Livraria Chardron.

Carr, Edward Hallett. 1964. *The Twenty Years' Crisis, 1919–1939.* New York: Harper Torchbooks.

Carvalho, António Carlos. 1976. *Para a história da maçonaria em Portugal.* Lisbon: Editorial Vega.

Castro, Alvaro de. 1925. *A acção financeira do governo Alvaro de Castro.* Lisbon: Lumen.

Castro, Armando. 1971. *A revolução industrial em Portugal no século XIX.* Oporto: Limiar.

———. 1973. *A economia portuguesa do século XX.* Lisbon: Edições 70.

———. 1978. *História económica de Portugal.* Lisbon: Editorial Caminho.

———. 1978. *O sistema colonial português em Africa.* Lisbon: Editorial Caminho.

Castro, Joaquim Pimenta de. 1915. *O dictador e a affrontosa dictadura.* N.p.: Weimar.

Cavalheiro, Rodrigues. 1966. *Por que se fez o 28 de maio.* Lisbon: n.p.

Chagas, João. 1915. *A ultima crise.* Oporto: by author.

Chase-Dunn, Christopher. 1975. "The Effects of International Economic Dependence on Development and Inequality." *ASR* 40, no. 6 (December): 720–38.

————. 1981. "Interstate System and Capitalist World-Economy." *International Studies Quarterly* 25, no. 1 (March): 347–84.

Chirot, Daniel. 1977. *Social Change in the Twentieth Century*. New York: Harcourt Brace Jovanovich, Inc.

Clarence-Smith, Gervase. 1985. *The Third Portuguese Empire 1825–1975*. Manchester, Eng.: Manchester University Press.

Cody, John, Helen Hughes, and David Wall, eds. 1980. *Policies for Industrial Progress in Developing Countries*. New York: Oxford University Press.

Companhia União Fabril (CUF). 1910–1921. *Relatório do Conselho d'administração*. Lisbon: n.p.

Congresso das Associações Comérciais e Industriais de Portugal. 1923. *Teses e actas*. Lisbon: n.p.

Correira, Velhinho. 1916. *Problemas económicos e colóniais*. Lisbon: Ferreira Ltd. Editores.

Costa, Constâncio Roque da. 1916. *Questões económicas, financeiras, sociaes e colóniaes*. Lisbon: Aillaud e Bertrand.

Costa, Ramiro da. 1975. *O desenvolvimento do capitalismo em Portugal*. Lisbon: Assirio e Alvim.

————. 1979. *Elements para a história do movimento operário em Portugal*. Lisbon: Assirio e Alvim.

Cunhal, Alvaro. 1976. *Contribuição para o estudo da questão agrária*. Lisbon: Edições Avante.

Cutileiro, José. 1971. *A Portuguese Rural Society*. Oxford: Clarendon Press.

Dahrendorf, Ralf. 1967. *Society and Democracy in Germany*. Garden City, N.J.: Anchor Books.

De Janvry, Alain. 1981. *The Agrarian Question*. Baltimore: Johns Hopkins University Press.

Delzell, Charles F. 1971. *Mediterranean Fascism*. New York: Walker and Company.

Dogan, Mattei, and Dominique Pelassy. 1984. *How to Compare Nations*. Chatham, N.J.: Chatham House Publishers, Inc.

A dominação ingleza. 1883. Lisbon: João António Rodrigues Fernandes.

The Economist (TE). 18 January 1890–24 March 1928. London.

Eley, Geoff. 1983. "What Produces Fascism: Preindustrial Traditions or a Crisis of a Capitalist State?" *Politics and Society* 12, no. 1: 1–52.

Eschenburg, Theodor, Ernst Fraenkel et al. 1966. *The Path to Dictatorship 1918–1933*. New York: Praeger.

O Estado Novo princípios e realizações. 1940. Lisbon: SPN Edições.

Evans, Peter. 1979. *Dependent Development*. Princeton, N.J.: Princeton University Press.

Evans, Peter, Dietrich Rueschemeyer, and Theda Skocpol. 1985. *Bringing the State Back In*. New York: Cambridge University Press.

Ferrão, Carlos. 1963. *Em defesa da república*. Lisbon: Inquerito.

Ferreira, Alfredo. 1923. "A liberdade do comércio." Lisbon: Primeiro Congresso das Associações Comérciais e Indústriais de Portugal.

Ferreira, David. 1973–1981. *História política da primeira república portuguesa*. 2 vols. Lisbon: Livros Horizonte.

Figueiredo, António de. 1975. *Portugal: Fifty Years of Dictatorship*. Middlesex, Eng.: Penguin Books Ltd.

Fortes, Mário. 1923. *A questão cerealifera portuguesa*. Oporto: Companhia Portuguesa Editora.

Fox-Genovese, Elizabeth, and Eugene D. Genovese. 1983. *Fruits of Merchant Capital*. Oxford: Oxford University Press.

Frank, André Gunder. 1977. "Long Live Transideological Enterprise! The Socialist Economies in the Capitalist International Division of Labor." *Review* 1, no. 1 (Summer): 91–140.

———. 1981. *Crisis: In the Third World.* New York: Holmes & Meier Publishers.

Galtung, Johan. 1971. "A Structural Theory of Imperialism." *Journal of Peace Research* 18, no. 2: 81–117.

Gereffi, Gary, and Peter Evans. 1981. "Transnational Corporations, Dependent Development, and State Policy in the Semiperiphery." *Latin American Research Review* 16, no. 3: 31–64.

Gerschenkron, Alexander. 1962. *Economic Backwardness in Historical Perspective.* Cambridge, Mass.: Harvard University Press.

Godinho, Vitor Magalhaes. 1971. *A estrutura da antiga sociedade portuguesa.* Lisbon: Editora Arcadia.

Goldfrank, Walter L. 1981. "Silk and Steel: Italy and Japan between the Two World Wars." *Comparative Social Research* 4: 297–315.

Gomes, Carlos. 1919. *Portugal comercial.* Coimbra, Port.: n.p.

Graca, Silva, ed. 1920. *O século traidor.* Lisbon: O Tempo.

Gramsci, Antonio. 1971. *Selections from the Prison Notebooks of Antonio Gramsci.* New York: International Publishers.

———. 1977. *Selections from Political Writings: 1910–1920.* London: Lawrence and Wishart.

Gregor, James A. 1979. *Italian Fascism and Developmental Dictatorship.* Princeton, N.J.: Princeton University Press.

Harrison, Lawrence E. 1985. *Underdevelopment Is a State of Mind.* Boston: University Press of America.

Helferding, Rudolf. [1910] 1981. *Finance Capital.* Reprint. London: Routledge & Kegan Paul.

Hobsbawm, Eric. 1962. *The Age of Revolution 1789–1848.* New York: New American Library.

Jessop, Bob. 1982. *The Capitalist State.* New York: New York University Press.

Johnson, E. R. 1915. *History of Domestic and Foreign Commerce of the United States.* 2 vols. Washington, D.C.: Carnegie Institution of Washington.

Jornal de comércio e das colónias (JCC). 1910–1926. Lisbon.

Kay, Geoffrey. 1975. *Development and Underdevelopment.* London: Macmillan Press Ltd.

Key, V. O. 1949. *Southern Politics in State and Nation.* New York: Alfred A. Knopf.

Keynes, J. M. 1978. "Activities 1922–1923: The End of Reparations." In *The Collected Writings of John Maynard Keynes,* ed. Elizabeth Johnson. London: Macmillan Press Ltd.

Kiernan, V. G. 1974. "The Old Alliance: England and Portugal." In *The Socialist Register 1973,* ed. John Saville Miliband. London: Merlin Press.

Kohli, Atul. 1987. "The Political Economy of Developmental Strategies." *Comparative Politics* 19, no. 2 (January):233–46.

Kurth, James R. 1979a. "The Political Consequences of the Product Cycle: Industrial History and Political Outcomes." *International Organization* 33 (Winter): 1–34.

———. 1979b. "Industrial Change and Political Change: A European Perspective." In *The New Authoritarianism in Latin America,* ed. David Collier. Princeton, N.J.: Princeton University Press.

Leal, Cunha. [1926]. *Eu, os políticos e a nação.* Lisbon: Arthur Brandão e C.

———. 1966. *As minhas memórias.* 3 vols. Lisbon: By author.

Lenin, V. I. 1969. *Imperialism: The Highest Stage of Capitalism.* New York: International Publishers.

Leontief, W. W. 1966. *Input-Output Economics.* New York: Oxford University Press.

Lima, A. A. Lisboa de. 1925. *As colónias portuguesas e a crise económica e financeira de Angola*. Lisbon: Sociedade de Geografia de Lisboa.

Linz, Juan, and Alfred Stepan, eds. 1978. *The Breakdown of Democratic Regimes*. Baltimore: Johns Hopkins University Press.

Lipset, Seymour. 1963. *Political Man*. Garden City, N.J.: Anchor Books.

Logan, John. 1985. "Democracy from Above." In *Semiperipheral Development*, ed. Giovanni Arrighi. Beverly Hills, Calif.: Sage Publications.

Luke, Timothy W. 1985. "Reason and Rationality in Rational Choice Theory." *Social Research* 52, no. 1 (Spring): 65–98.

Mahler, Vincent A. 1980. *Dependency Approaches to International Political Economy*. New York: Columbia University Press.

Maier, Charles S. 1975. *Recasting Bourgeois Europe*. Princeton, N.J.: Princeton University Press.

Marini, Rui M. 1973. *Dialéctica de la dependencia*. Mexico City: Nueva Era.

Marques, A. H. de Oliveira. 1970. *A primeira república portuguesa*. Lisbon: Livros Horizonte.

————. 1972. *History of Portugal*. 2 vols. New York: Columbia University Press.

————. 1976. *Afonso Costa discursos parlamentares 1911–1914*. Lisbon: Livraria Bertrand.

————. 1977. *Afonso Costa discursos parlamentares 1914–1926*. Lisbon: Livraria Bertrand.

————. 1980. *História da 1a república portuguesa*. Lisbon: Iniciativas Editoriais.

Martins, António Viana. 1976. *Da 1a república ao Estado Novo*. Lisbon: Iniciativas Editoriais.

Martins, José Soares, ed. N.d. *Subsidios para a história da CUF*. Oporto: Afrontamento.

Martins, Rocha. 1921. *Memorias sobre Sidónio Paes*. Lisbon:Sociedade Editorial A B C.

Marx, Karl. 1969a. *Class Struggles in France 1848–1850*. New York: International Publishers.

————. 1969b. *The 18th Brumaire of Louis Bonaparte*. New York: International Publishers.

Medeiros, Fernando. 1978. *A sociedade e a economia portuguesas nas origems do salazarismo*. Lisbon: A Regra do Jogo.

Meier, Gerald M. 1976. *Leading Issues in Economic Development*. New York: Oxford University Press.

Mendes, J. M. Amado. 1979. "Sobre as relações entre a indústria portuguesa e a estrangeira no século XIX." In GIS *O Século XIX em Portugal*, ed. Jaime Reis, Maria Filomena Monica, and Maria dos Santos. Lisbon: Editorial Presença.

Mitchell, Brian R., ed. 1980. *European Historical Statistics*. Cambridge, Mass.: Macmillan.

Da monarquia a república. 1915. Lisbon: Imprensa Nacional de Lisboa.

Monica, Maria Filomena. 1979. "Uma aristocracia operária: os chapeleiros (1870–1914)." *Análise social* 60, no. 4: 859–945.

————. 1981. "Poder e saber: os vidreiros da Marinha Grande." *Análise social* 67–69, no. 3–5: 505–72.

Moniz, Egas. 1919. *Un ano de política*. Lisbon: Portugal-Brasil Limitada.

Moore, Barrington, Jr. 1966. *The Social Origins of Dictatorship and Democracy*. Boston: Beacon Press.

Mouzelis, Nicos. 1980. "Reductionism in Marxist Theory." *Telos* 28, no. 1 (January): 173–85.

————. 1986. "On the Rise of Postwar Military Dictatorships: Argentina, Chile, Greece." *Comparative Studies in Society and History* 28, no. 1 (January): 55–80.

Muller, Edward N. "Democracy, American Power, and Inequality." Unpublished manuscript, n.d.

Nemeth, Roger J., and David A. Smith. 1985. "International Trade and World-System Structure: A Multiple Network Analysis." *Review* 8, no. 4: 517–60.

Neumann, Franz. 1944. *Behemoth: The Structure and Practice of National Socialism*. New York: Oxford University Press.

Neves, Hermano. 1910. *Como triumphou a república*. Lisbon: Empreza Liberdade.

Nogueira, Franco. 1977. *Salazar*. Coimbra, Port.: Atlantida Editora.

O'Donnell, Guillermo. 1978. "Reflections on the Patterns of Change in the Bureaucratic Authoritarian State." *Latin American Research Review* 13, no. 1: 3–38.

———. 1979. *Modernization and Bureaucratic-Authoritarianism*. Berkeley: University of California Press.

Oliveira, César. 1974. *O operariado e a república*. Lisbon: Seara Nova.

O'Neill, Juan. 1987. *Social Inequality in a Portuguese Hamlet*. New York: Cambridge University Press.

Opello, Walter. 1985. *Portugal's Political Development*. Boulder, Colo.: Westview Press, Inc.

Organski, A. F. K. 1965. *The Stages of Political Development*. New York: Alfred A. Knopf.

Paixão, Braga. 1964. *Cem anos do Banco Nacional Ultramarino na vida portuguesa: 1864–1964*. 4 vols. Lisbon: BNU.

Paxeco, Oscar. 1937. *Os que arrancaram em 28 de maio*. Lisbon: Editorial Império.

Payne, Stanley. 1973. *Spain and Portugal*. 2 vols. Madison: University of Wisconsin Press.

———. 1980. *Fascism: Comparison and Definition*. Madison: University of Wisconsin Press.

Pereira, João. 1915. *Portugal: Diccionario Histórico*. Lisbon: n.p.

Pereira, José de Campos. 1915. *A propriedade rustica em Portugal*. Lisbon: Imprensa Nacional.

Pereira, Miriam Halpern. 1972. "O papel da classe dirigente oitocentista e a formação do capitalismo na agricultura." *Económia/sociologia*, 492–96.

———. 1979. *Política e economia (Portugal nos séculos XIX e XX)*. Lisbon: Livros Horizonte.

Peres, Damião. 1954. *História de Portugal, suplemento*. Oporto: Portucalense Editora SARL.

Pintado, Xavier. 1964. *Structure and Growth of the Portuguese Economy*. Geneva: European Free Trade Association.

Pirenne, Henri. 1966. "Stages in the Social History of Capitalism." In *Class, Status and Power*, ed. Reinhard Bendix and Seymour Martin Lipset. New York: Free Press.

Portugal. 1924. *Constituição política da república portuguesa*. Lisbon: Imprensa Nacional.

———. 1925. *Código eleitoral*. Lisbon: Imprensa Nacional.

———. Congresso. *Diário da câmara dos deputados*.

———. Direcção Geral da Estatística. 1914. *Resumos estatísticos/estatística agricola*. Lisbon: Imprensa Nacional.

———. Instituto Nacional de Estatística. 1941. *Estatística das sociedades 1939*. Lisbon: Imprensa Nacional.

———. Ministério das Finanças. 1872–1920. *Comércio e navegação*. Lisbon: Imprensa Nacional.

———. Ministério das Finanças. 1909–1928. *Anuário estatístico de Portugal*. Lisbon: Imprensa Nacional.

———. Ministério das Finanças. 1913. Direcção Geral da Estatística. *Censo da população de Portugal: no 1 de dezembro de 1911*. Lisbon: Imprensa Nacional.

———. Ministério das Finanças. 1921–1940. *Estatística comercial*. Lisbon: Imprensa Nacional.

———. Ministério do Trabalho. 1926. *Estatística industrial ano de 1917. Boletim do trabalho industrial*. Lisbon: Imprensa Nacional.

———. Ministério das Finanças. 1916. Direcção Geral da Estatística. *Censo eleitoral da metrópole*. Lisbon: Imprensa Nacional.

———. Secretariado da Propaganda Nacional. 1940. *O Estado Novo princípios e realizações*. Lisbon: Edições SPN.

———. Senado. 1911–1926. *Diário das Sessões do Senado*. Lisbon: Imprensa Nacional.

Poulantzas, Nicos. 1973. *Political Power and Social Classes*. London: NLB and S & W.

————. 1974. *Fascism and Dictatorship*. London: NLB.
————. 1976. *The Crisis of the Dictatorships*. London: NLB.
Proenca, Raul. 1972. *Obra política de Raul Proenca*. 4 vols. Lisbon: Seara Nova.
Przeworski, Adam. 1980. "Material Bases of Consent: Economics and Politics in a Hegemonic System." *Political Power and Social Theory* 1: 21–66.
————. 1986. "Some Problems in the Study of the Transition to Democracy." In *Transitions from Authoritarian Rule: Comparative Perspectives*, ed. Guillermo O'Donnell, Philippe C. Schmitter, and Laurence Whitehead. Baltimore: Johns Hopkins University Press.
O que e a democracia dos partidos. [1974]. N.p.
O que eles fizeram o que nos fizemos. 1945. Lisbon: Edições S.N.I.
Quintela, João G. P. 1976. *Para a história do movimento comunista em Portugal*. Oporto: Afrontamento.
Ránki, Gyorgy. 1985. "Problems of Southern European Economic Development (1918–1938)." In *Semiperipheral Development*, ed. Giovanni Arrighi. Beverly Hills, Calif.: Sage Publications.
Reis, Jaime. 1979. "A 'lei da fome': As origens do proteccionismo cerealífero (1889–1914)." *Análise social* 60, no. 4: 745–93.
————. 1982. "Latifúndario e progresso técnico: a difusão de debulha mecânica no Alentejo—1860–1930." *Análise social* 71, no. 1: 371–433.
————. 1983. "Portuguese Economic Backwardness in Historical Perspective, 1860–1913." Paper presented at 14th Conference of SSPHS, Boston, 22 April.
Relvas, José. 1977–1978. *Memórias Políticas*. 2 vols. Lisbon: Terra Livre.
Rey, Pierre-Phillippe. 1982. "Class Alliances." *International Journal of Sociology* 12, no. 2 (Summer): 2.
Reynolds, Lloyd. 1983. "The Spread of Economic Growth to the Third World: 1850–1980." *Journal of Economic Literature* 21 (September): 941–80.
Rostow, W. W. 1960. *The Stages of Economic Growth*. London: Cambridge University Press.
Ruíz, Joaquin del Moral. 1980. "A independência brasileira e a sua repercussão no Portugal da epoca (1810–1834)." *Análise social* 64: 779–95.
Santos, Machado. 1916. *A ordem pública e o 14 de maio*. Lisbon: Lamas & Franklin.
Schmitter, Philippe. 1973. "The Portugalization of Brazil." In *Authoritarian Brazil*, ed. Alfred Stepan. New Haven, Conn.: Yale University Press.
————. 1978. "The Impact and Meaning of Non-competitive, Non-free, and Insignificant Elections in Authoritarian Portugal: 1933–1974." In *Elections without Choice*, ed. G. Hermet, R. Rose, and A. Rouquie. London: Macmillan.
Schoenbaum, David. 1966. *Hitler's Social Revolution*. New York: Anchor Books.
Schwartzman, Kathleen. 1988. "Portugal at the Neocolonial Fringe of the British Empire." In *Rethinking the 19th Century: Contradictions and Movements*, ed. Francisco Ramirez. Westport, Conn.: Greenwood Press, Inc.
Seara Nova Antologia (Sottomayor Cardia Comp.). 1971–1972. *Pela reforma da república*. 2 vols. Lisbon: Seara Nova.
Serrão, Joel, ed. 1971. *Dicionário de história de Portugal*. 4 vols. Lisbon: Iniciativas Editoriais.
————. 1976. *Pequeno dicionário de história de Portugal*. Lisbon: Iniciativas Editoriais.
Sideri, S. 1970. *Trade and Power*. Rotterdam, Neth.: Rotterdam University Press.
Silva, António Maria da. 1982. *O meu depoimento*. Lisbon: Publicações Europa-America.
Silva, Fernando Emygdio da. 1919. *Cousas de Portugal*. Coimbra, Port.: Franca & Armenio.
————. 1920. *O problema financeiro português*. Lisbon: By author.
————. 1924. *A crise financeira e a revisão das despezas públicas*. Lisbon: Associação Comercial de Lisboa.
Silva, José da. 1958. *Anastácio Ramos*. Oporto: By author.
Silva, Manuel Duarte Guimarães Pestana da. 1924. *A desordem financeira do estado*. Oporto: By author.

Skocpol, Theda. 1973. "A Critical Review of Barrington Moore's Social Origins of Dictatorship and Democracy." *Politics and Society* (Fall): 1–34.

———. 1977. "Wallerstein's World Capitalist System: A Theoretical and Historical Critique." *American Journal of Sociology* 82, no. 5 (March): 1075–1090.

———. 1979. *States and Social Revolutions.* London: Cambridge University Press.

Smith, Adam. 1957. *The Wealth of Nations, Vol. 1.* 2 vols. London: J. M. Dent and Sons Ltd.

Sociedade de Geografia de Lisboa. 1919. *Questões Colónias e Económicas.* Lisbon: Sociedade de Geografia.

Stein, Stanley, and Barbara Stein. 1970. *The Colonial Heritage of Latin America.* New York: Oxford University Press.

Stinchcombe, Arthur L. 1978. *Theoretical Methods in Social History.* New York: Academic Press.

Szymanski, Albert. 1981. *The Logic of Imperialism.* New York: Praeger.

Teles, Basilio. [1905] 1968. *Do ultimatum as 31 de janeiro.* Lisbon: Portugalia Editora.

Telo, José. 1977. *O sidonismo e o movimento operário portugues.* Lisbon: Ulmeiro.

———. 1980. *Decadência e queda da 1a república portuguesa.* Lisbon: A Regra do Jogo Edições.

Thomas, Clive Y. 1984. *The Rise of the Authoritarian State in Peripheral Societies.* New York: Monthly Review Press.

Turner, Henry A., ed. 1975. *Reappraisals of Fascism.* New York: New Viewpoints.

United States Bureau of Foreign and Domestic Commerce. 1927. *Trade Information Bulletin*, no. 455. Washington, D.C.: Government Printing Office.

United States Department of Commerce and Labor. 1911. *Cotton Goods in Spain and Portugal.* Special Agents Series no. 46. Washington, D.C.: Government Printing Office.

Veiga, Caetano Beirão da. 1923. *O papel das actividades económicas na redução das despesas públicas.* Lisbon: By author.

Ventura, António. 1976. *Subsídios para a história do movimento sindical rural no Alto Alentejo.* Lisbon: Seara Nova.

———. 1977. *O sindicalismo no Alentejo.* Lisbon: Seara Nova.

Vieira, Anselmo. 1926. *A crise nacional.* Lisbon: By author.

Wallerstein, Immanuel. 1974. *The Modern World System.* New York: Academic Press.

———. 1979. *The Capitalist World-Economy.* New York: Cambridge University Press.

———. 1981. "Dependence in an Interdependent World: The Limited Possibilities of Transformation within the Capitalist World Economy." In *From Dependency to Development*, ed. Heraldo Muñoz. Boulder, Colo.: Westview Press, Inc.

———. 1982. "Dependence in an Interdependent World." In *From Dependency to Development*, ed. Heraldo Muñoz. Boulder, Colo.: Westview Press, Inc.

———. 1984. *The Politics of the World Economy.* Cambridge, Mass.: Cambridge University Press.

———. 1989. *The Modern World-System III.* San Diego: Academic Press.

Wheeler, Douglas L. 1978. *Republican Portugal.* Madison: University of Wisconsin Press.

Wiarda, Howard J. 1977. *Corporatism and Development: The Portuguese Experience.* Amherst: University of Massachusetts Press.

Woolf, Stuart J. 1968. *European Fascism.* London: Weidenfeld Nicolson.

Zeitlin, Maurice. 1984. *The Civil Wars in Chile.* Princeton, N.J.: Princeton University Press.

INDEX

Abreu, Paulo Cancella de, 168
Absolutists, 30
ACAP. *See* Central Association of Portuguese Farmers
ACI, 145
ACL. *See* Commercial Association of Lisbon
ACLL. *See* Commercial Association of Lisbon Retailers
Açores, 2
ACP. *See* Commercial Association of Oporto
Afonso V (king of Portugal), 28
Africa, 16, 109. *See also* Portugal, African colonies of
Agrarian capitalism, 81
Agrarian reform, 101, 104, 135-36. *See also* Land reform
Agrarian sector, 12, 13, 102-3, 185. *See also* Portugal, agriculture of
Agricultural domestic production, 91, 92(table), 102, 103, 118, 160(table), 161, 162
policies, 127
Agricultural Union (UA), 148
Agriculture, Ministry of (1918), 102, 135
Agriculture for export, 76, 80. *See also* Portugal, as agro-exporter
AIp. *See* Industrial Association of Oporto
AIP. *See* Industrial Association of Portugal
Almeida, José de, 147
Almonds, 80
Alvito, 85
Amin, Samir, 63, 81
Amnesty, 34
Anarchists, 33, 34
Anarcho-syndicalists, 136
Andrade, Anselmo de, 105
Anglo-Portuguese telephone company, 81
Angola, 31, 49, 58, 77, 107, 108, 109, 110, 116, 165, 166, 202(n1)
Anticlericalism, 38, 142, 143
Arabian regions, 28, 55
Arriaga, Manuel de, 130
Association of Commerce and Industry (ACI), 145
Association of metallurgical workers, 62
Atlantic islands, 2, 28

Austria, 32, 98, 131
Authoritarianism, 2-3, 6, 12
Authoritarian regimes, 1, 2, 3, 6, 7, 13, 21, 189
and international influences, 15, 16
and parliament, 20
social origin of, 11, 12, 14, 19
and traditional forces, 12
and world system, 16, 17, 18
See also Estado Novo, authoritarianism of
Autonomy of the state, 173-74, 175, 190
Aveiro, 85, 86(table)
Aymard, Maurice, 18, 193, 195

Bachoffen, Henry, and Co., 94
Balance of payments, 62, 114
Balance of power, 75
Balance of trade, 63(table), 118, 155, 157, 166, 174
Balkanization of the state, 21, 174, 190
Bank of Portugal, 32, 106, 166
Bardhan, Pranab, 189
Barker, Ernst, 10
Basto, Lima, 46
Batalha, O (socialist newspaper), 172
Beans, 95
Beer, 109
Beja, 84
Belgium, 69, 166
Bensel, Richard F., 190
Bergesen, Albert, 4
Black death (1348), 27
Bolsheviks, 40, 45, 167
Bombings, 47, 48
Bonaparte, Louis Napoleon, 7, 20
Bourgeois democracy, 105
Bourgeoisie, 12, 13, 15, 23, 36, 46, 53, 81, 99, 110, 120, 125, 136, 138, 152, 172, 175, 179, 181, 182, 183-84, 185
fractions, 153-54, 159, 166, 174, 175, 181, 184, 191
unity, 127, 128-30, 131, 141-45, 146, 147, 150, 154, 174, 177-78, 190
Braga, Teófilo, 35(table note)
Braga, 1, 85, 86(table)
Bragança-Cunha, V. de, 123

215